The Making

of the

LAST PROPHET

The Making

of the

LAST PROPHET

A Reconstruction of the Earliest Biography of Muhammad

by
Gordon Darnell Newby

University of South Carolina Press

152619

Published in Columbia, South Carolina, by the
University of South Carolina Press

Manufactured in the United States of America

Library of Congress Cataloging-in-Publication Data

Ibn Isḥāq, Muḥammad, d. ca. 768.
   [Kitāb al-Mubtadaʾ. English]
   The making of the last prophet : a reconstruction of the earliest
biography of Muhammad / [reconstructed] by Gordon Darnell Newby. —
1st ed.
     p.   cm.
   Bibliography: p.
   Includes index.
   Translation of first section of Ibn Isḥāq's Sīrat Rasūl Allāh.
   ISBN 0–87249–552–3. — ISBN 0–87249–623–6 (pbk.)
   1. Prophets, Pre-Islamic. 2. Muḥammad, Prophet, d. 632.
3. Bible—Islamic interpretations. 4. Legends, Islamic. I. Newby,
Gordon Darnell, 1939–   . II. Title.
BP137.I2413   1989
297'.63—dc19
[B]   88–36818
                                             CIP

To My Parents

CONTENTS

Contents

viii

Preface

My interest in the biography of Muhammad was originally sparked by the inquiries of a group of unusually talented and curious students who read Arabic with me when I was a member of the faculty of the now defunct Department of Mediterranean Studies at Brandeis University. Only a few of those students had a primary interest in Arabic and Islamic studies, but all were interested in how Islamic literature related to older Near Eastern religious texts with which they were more familiar.

It had long been claimed that individual themes and motifs had been "borrowed" from Jewish and Christian sources, but my investigations into the matter showed that there was a more organic relationship between Islamic religious and historical literature and its Near Eastern and Jewish antecedents. Themes and anecdotes had not been "borrowed" here and there to fill in the lacunae in the Quranic narrative, as was commonly asserted in the older scholarship. Early Muslims' Quran commentary and the biographies of Muhammad and his prophetic predecessors were a result of a hagiographic and hermeneutic process in Islam that continued the living traditions of Midrashic and Haggadic studies found in the Jewish communities encountered by Muslim scholars. The stories, anecdotes, tales, and legends in the *Sîrah* are the crystallized remains of an intellectual process among early Muslim scholars who were continuing the traditions of their Jewish counterparts. When early Muslims incorporated salient aspects of the Jewish and Christian methods of treating holy persons and texts, the details, the anecdotes, and the themes naturally followed.

In order to gain a more complete understanding of the first Islamic century, the period in which this process developed, I felt that it would be important to be able to look at one of the most influential narratives of the era, the *Sîrat Rasûl Allâh* (hereafter *Sîrah*) of Muhammad b. Ishaq, the earliest complete biography of Muhammad. The *Sîrah* existed only in an epitomized form in the edition of Ibn Hisham. The remaining portion was no longer extant in any manuscript that I could locate. Quite a number of quotations existed in the works of Quran commentators and historians, and, encouraged by F. Sezgin's belief that the text was recoverable, I set about reconstructing the Arabic text. From the reconstruction I prepared a translation and wrote an introduction and notes.

When I came to North Carolina State University, I was encouraged by the members of my department and by colleagues at Duke and Chapel Hill to continue investigating the process by which early Islamic literature developed in relationship to Jewish and Christian literary traditions. Professor David Halperin of the Department of Religious Studies at Chapel Hill and Professor Bruce Lawrence of the Department of Religion at Duke University have been most helpful to me. Our frequent discussions and their constant support have helped me through some difficult spots in the preparation of this book.

I owe a debt of gratitude to Professor Marilyn Waldman of Ohio State University. Her gentle challenge to my frequent wrongheadedness has always been encouraging, instructive, and helpful. She has been a good guide for my recent intellectual *Rihlah*.

The result of my labors and my friends' encouragement is this volume, *The Making of the Last Prophet*. For the first time in the modern era it is possible to view all of Ibn Ishaq's original biography of Muhammad. When my reconstruction is added to A. Guillaume's reconstruction and translation of the last portion of the *Sîrah*, his *Life of Muhammad*, we see Ibn Ishaq's work to be of enormous scope and rich color. It is a well-developed literary piece that culminates Umayyad scholarship. It also became the basis for Abbasid Quran commentary, history, and prophetic hagiography. It is my hope that Islamicists, students of religion, and particularly scholars interested in comparative religious literature will find the text of my reconstruction a source of information about the literary and religious interactions between Islam, Judaism, and Christianity in the early Islamic period.

Some mention should be made at this point about the translation of the Arabic text. Like all translations, this one is a compromise. On the face of it, the Arabic text of the *Sîrah* seems simple. It has the feel of an oral transmission or performance of a traditional story, occasionally embellished by the narrator. When we examine the text more closely, we see that the vocabulary is replete with references and overtones which evoke the antecedent and underlying literary heritage. Often this is not apparent unless one is conversant with the related rabbinic and hagiographic texts. An ideal translation would provide notes, discussions, and references for each of the words used in the text. I intended to provide such an extensive apparatus, but it soon became apparent that even a minimal attempt would extend the length of the work into several large volumes. Instead, I chose to reflect my understandings of the text in a style of translation designed for persons who will not generally be able to consult the Arabic text.

I have reworked most idioms into their English equivalent except when the color and texture of the original conveys some religious or aesthetic idea which I regarded as important to the text. The style of *Hadîth* reports tolerates a high level of indefinite pronoun reference. When this is coupled with the general rules of Arabic, which do not always require pronouns to agree in number and gender with their antecedents, a literal rendering of a sentence or paragraph will often produce a mass of confusing pronouns. In the Arabic the brevity of the narrative and, one must assume, the inflection of the narrator minimized any ambiguity; but for the sake of clarity for the English reader I have often restated the antecedent of the pronoun. For the same reasons I have reordered the sentences to follow more closely the expectations of one who is reading only in English. The short notes at the beginning of each section should provide enough context to get through the passages. Most readers will benefit, however, from having a copy of the Quran and a copy of L. Ginzberg's *Legends of the Jews* close at hand.

Addendum to Preface:

Finally, I wish to thank W. R. Levin who kept faith in me and this project through trying and difficult times.

The Making

of the

LAST PROPHET

Introduction

The Making of the Last Prophet is a reconstruction of the missing first portion of Ibn Ishaq's *Sîrah*, the earliest full biography of Muhammad. It is also a study of Ibn Ishaq's vision of Islam as the universal religion, the Quran as God's word, and Muhammad as the ultimate prophet. By means of the reconstructed text we can examine an early attempt to shape Muslim self-perceptions and understandings.

When Ibn Ishaq wrote the *Sîrah*, sometime before 767 C.E., the Prophet and founder of Islam had been dead for over a century and a quarter.[1] During that first Islamic century Muslim conquerors and settlers had established themselves from southern France and the Iberian peninsula in the west to the Indus valley in the east. They captured the empire of the Persian Sassanids and took over the major eastern territories of the Byzantine empire. The conquering forces from Arabia became the rulers of Alexandria, Antioch, Ctesiphon, Damascus, Jerusalem, and similar major centers of religion and power. But Muslim political control did not mean that the population instantly converted to Islam. The population in the newly acquired Islamic lands changed religions only very slowly, even though they acknowledged the Muslims as masters. It is estimated that by the middle of the eighth century C.E. only about 8 percent of the population of Iran had become Muslim.[2] Similar rates of conversion can be assumed for the other areas conquered by Muslim forces. Ibn Ishaq lived and wrote in a world where Christians, Jews, and Zoroastrians vastly outnumbered Muslims.

The dynamic first century of Muslim political expansion was also a period of contention and conflict about the nature of the new religion of Islam and the nature of Islamicate society.[3] When Muslims began writing histories of the beginnings of Islam, most of which date no earlier than the end of the second Islamic century, members of the Islamic community were depicted as agreeing on some fundamental assumptions about their past; for example, that Muhammad had founded a new religion called Islam, that God had spoken to the world through Muhammad, that the record of God's message was the Quran, that the Quran was complete in Muhammad's lifetime, and that Islam was the natural and proper heir to the prophetic traditions of Judaism and Christianity. But the development of foundation stories in Islam covered over political and doctrinal disputes in ways similar to the role played by foundation stories in Christianity or Judaism. The myth of an original orthodoxy from which later challengers fall away as heretics is most always the retrospective assertion of a politically dominant group whose aim is to establish their supremacy by appeal to divine sanction.

Two of the most important topics of discussion in the first Islamic centuries were the nature of the Quranic canon and the source of authority in Islam. A close examination of the historical record shows that there was very little agreement about these fundamental areas of religious discourse.[4] Indeed, the first centuries of Islam are marked by a proliferation of rival groups, each with a religious and political message. Civil wars, the rise of the Kharijites, the beginnings of the Shi'ites, and dynastic revolutions are all part of the social and intellectual scene. Is in this context that Ibn Ishaq composed his biography of Muhammad, not as a neutral, dispassionate piece of scholarship but as an active voice in the polemical debate. As John Wansbrough has shown about the *Sîrah*, "Informing the narrative is a polemical concern to depict the emergence of a religious polity (*umma*) out of more or less traditionally articulated theophany (*wahy*)."[5] The purpose was to write "salvation history," the aim of which is kerygma, the preaching of the religious message.[6] In the *Sîrah*, Ibn Ishaq helped form an image of Muhammad that accounted for the rise of Islam, explained the course of the history of the world, established the primacy of the Quranic text as scripture, and installed Muhammad as the central religious authority for Muslims. The effect of the *Sîrah* was the making of the image of the last prophet.

Ibn Ishaq set an ambitious plan for his biography of Muhammad, a plan that went well beyond the events of Muhammad's life and political career. The *Sîrah* began with creation, described the lives of all the prophets mentioned in the Quran—and some who were not mentioned—and ended with Muhammad. The form was universal history; the content was a mixture of Jewish Haggadah, Arab legend, and Christian martyrology; and the effect was hagiography and prophetology. Characteristic features associated with earlier prophets were also attached to the description of Muhammad. Adam founded God's worship in Mecca, Abraham restored both the worship and the shrine, and Muhammad, by cleansing the Ka'bah and restoring God's worship, became the new Adam and the new Abraham. Islam, by extension, was cast as the new dispensation, a theological parallel to growing Muslim hegemony over Jews and Christians in the conquered territories.

There are three sections of the *Sîrah*: the *Kitâb al-Mubtada'*, the *Kitâb al-Mab'ath*, and the *Kitâb al-Maghâzî*. Each of these sections is distinguished by subject and, to some extent, by source material. The *Kitâb al-Mubtada'*, the first section, covers the period from Creation up to the beginning of Arabian pre-Islamic history. It includes the Arabian prophets Hud and Salih as well as the Arabian interests of Adam, Abraham, Solomon, and Bilqis, but its primary focus is on the ancient history of God's revelations to the world.

Introduction

3

The title, *Kitâb al-Mubtada*², can be translated as "The Book of Beginnings" or "The Book of Genesis."

The *Kitâb al-Mabᶜath* starts with Arabian events that lead directly to the stories of the birth and early life of Muhammad. The scope is first all Arabia, but as the chronological presentation comes closer to Muhammad's birth, the focus is on the Hijaz, and finally on Mecca. There are tales of Jews, Christians, and pagans foretelling the coming of Muhammad and his prophetic mission. The *Kitâb al-Mabᶜath* is "The Book of the Sending Forth" or "The Book of the Advent."

The *Kitâb al-Maghâzî* covers Muhammad's career as a prophet, community leader, and military commander. This is the section of the *Sîrah* that is most biographical in the modern, Western sense of the term. This "Book of Military Campaigns" is the political and military history of the formation of the community of Islam up to Muhammad's death in 632 C.E.

Ibn Ishaq includes or refers to passages from the Quran in all three sections of the *Sîrah*, although it cannot be considered a Quran commentary primarily. Each of the stories assumes a knowledge of the Quran. Short references usually suffice to tie the passage to a particular verse in Scripture, and only occasionally is the Quran cited *in extenso*. But there is some question about the state and completeness of the canon of the Quran at the time that Ibn Ishaq was writing.[7] Both the image of Muhammad and the nature of the Quran appear to have been in flux. Insofar as the *Sîrah* supplies material that locates the occasion of the revelation of a Quranic passage within the history of Muhammad's career or supplies auxiliary material for understanding the meaning of a particular passage, Ibn Ishaq helped form a view of the Quran that became part of the community's understanding of the canon.

Ibn Ishaq had a catholic view of what sources could be used to set the life of Muhammad in a world history context. He drew on a wide variety of material available to him: Arab legends, oral reports from converts to Islam, recollections by older women, and assorted books and inscriptions. Among the materials which Ibn Ishaq used in the *Sîrah* was a body of stories called in Arabic *Isra²iliyat* [Judaica]. These were stories about and usually derived from Jews and Christians. *Isra²iliyat* are used most extensively in the first part of the biography, the *Kitâb al-Mubtada*² and the *Kitâb al-Mabᶜath*, although they are scattered throughout the *Sîrah*. In their Jewish or Christian contexts the literary sources for *Isra²iliyat* are haggadic and midrashic treatises which explicated Scripture. One effect of Ibn Ishaq's use of *Isra²iliyat* is to link the *Sîrah* and the Quran to previous Scripture through these stories. The *Sîrah*, particularly the *Kitâb al-Mubtada*², is a commentary on the Bible as well as a commentary on the Quran. It fosters the Muslim claim that Islam is the heir to Judaism and Christianity.

The Making of the Last Prophet

4

Ibn Ishaq started collecting information for the *Sîrah* in Arabia, in his native city of Medina. He was the grandson of a Persian war captive who had converted to Islam, and he was educated by his father and his uncle, who were collectors of stories about Muhammad. He made at least one trip to Egypt to research the biography among the few Companions of Muhammad still alive and their descendants who had moved there, but there are good reasons to believe that only the *Kitâb al-Maghâzî*, the political and military history of the community, was composed at this period of his life. With the rise of the Abbasids around 750 C.E., Ibn Ishaq left Medina and journeyed to the Abbasid center of power in Iraq, where he became attached to the court of the caliph al-Mansur (754–775) at his palace in the new city of Baghdad. Ibn Ishaq was the court tutor for al-Mansur's heir, Muhammad b. ʿAbdullah al-Mahdi (775–785). Although we know little of his duties, the *Sîrah* appears to have been part of the instructional material for the future caliph.

In the generation after Ibn Ishaq the use of extra-Islamic sources fell into disrepute. Use of *Israʾiliyat* was frowned upon by many Muslims and banned by the most scrupulous scholars. In that climate an epitomized version of the *Sîrah* was made by the Egyptian scholar Ibn Hisham (834 C.E.). His shortened version disposed of most of the *Israʾiliyat*. The epitome eliminated almost all of the *Kitâb al-Mubtadaʾ* and some portions of the *Kitâb al-Mabʿath* as well. The new version of the *Sîrah* started with a genealogy that linked Muhammad to the biblical past, but concentrated on his mission and the history of the founding of the Islamic community. Ibn Ishaq's world history perspective and catholic methodology was excised. Ibn Hisham's version of the *Sîrah* became the popular one, as the number of extant manuscripts and editions can testify.[8]

Nevertheless, the material of Ibn Ishaq's *Kitâb al-Mubtadaʾ* did receive wide and favorable circulation among Quran commentators, purveyors of stories of the prophets, and historians. In particular, the famous historian Muhammad b. Jarir at-Tabari (839–923 C.E.) quoted Ibn Ishaq's *Sîrah* extensively in his monumental history, *Kitâb Taʾrîkh ar Rusul wa-l-Mulûk*, and his Quran commentary, *Jâmiʿ al-Bayân ʿan Taʾwîl al-Quran*. Ibn Ishaq's world history vision set the pattern for at-Tabari's scholarship and for scholars after him. But the *Kitâb al-Mubtadaʾ* was not copied widely enough to survive on its own, and as far as we can tell, no complete manuscript of the original *Sîrah* survives.

This volume, *The Making of the Last Prophet*, is a recovery and reconstruction of the *Kitâb al-Mubtadaʾ* from the extant quotes. It is also a brief examination of role and function of each of the biographies of the pre-Islamic prophets. Much of what is in this volume makes reference to the Quran and to the rest of the *Sîrah*. The reader would benefit from having a copy of the Quran and a copy of Ibn Hisham's *Sîrah* available while reading, although every effort has been made within the confines of space to make the *Kitâb al-Mubtadaʾ* understandable.[9]

Introduction

5

The Author

Muhammad b. Ishaq b. Yasar al-Muttalabi al-Madanî Abu ʿAbdullah, known as Ibn Ishaq, was born in the Arabian city of Medina around the year A.H. 85.[10] Yasar, his grandfather, had been brought as a prisoner from ʿAyn at-Tamr near Kufah in southern Iraq when the town was captured in A.H. 12 by Khalid b. Al-Walîd. It is reported that he was the first prisoner brought from Iraq, and the caliph, Abu Bakr, gave him as a slave to Qays b. Makhramah b. al-Muttalib b. ʿAbd Manaf.[11] When he accepted Islam, he was manumitted and became a client of Qays' family, taking the tribal name al-Muttalabi. Yasar had three sons, Ishaq, Musa, and ʿAbd ar-Rahman. Ishaq was born around the year A.H. 50. When Ishaq was a young man, he campaigned in Syria with the army of Maslamah b. ʿAbd al-Malik, and he and his brother Musa became well-known collectors and transmitters of *Hadith*, gathering information from their fellow soldiers about the early period of Islam, about Muhammad, and about the Quran.

Ibn Ishaq was born in an era when non-Arab Muslims were achieving greater social prominence in Islamic society through their participation in intellectual pursuits. They had been virtually excluded from the economic and social mainstream of Arab society and relegated to the second-class position of clients [Arabic *Mawla*, pl. *Mawali*]. The second caliph, ʿUmar, had established a method of distributing the spoils of the expanding empire in a rank order determined by how early one's family joined Islam during the life of Muhammad. Non-Arabs had to join Arab tribes in client status as part of being accepted into Islam, and were thus at the bottom of the distribution lists. The restrictions placed on the non-Arab Muslims would ultimately prove onerous to them and contribute to the Abbasid revolution in 750 C.E., but the limited opportunities meant that non-Arab Muslims participated where they were least discriminated against: as transmitters of *Hadith*, grammarians, and clerks. They used their literacy and the educational traditions of their families to gain greater social prominence in an Islamicate society that was rapidly becoming dependent on the developing bureaucracy.

Little is known of Ibn Ishaq's early training. He probably began early to collect and study *Hadith* reports about Muhammad and the Companions. It is possible that he collected reports from his father and his father's companions which could have formed the nucleus of the *Kitâb al-Futûh* [The Book of Conquests] ascribed to him, as well as the *Kitâb al-Maghâzî*.[12] Since the *Kitâb al-Futûh* is no longer extant, it is difficult to do more than speculate about it, but in any event both his father and his uncles appear in the *Sanads* of the *Sîrah*.[13] He studied with the second generation of traditionists, such as az-Zuhri, ʿAsim b. ʿUmar b. Qatadah, Muhammad b. Salih b. Dinar, and Muhammad b. Kaʿb b. Sulaym al-Qurazi, all men whose names are featured prominently in early Islamic *Hadith* reports. At the age of thirty Ibn Ishaq made a scholarly journey [Arabic *rihlah*] to Alexandria, Egypt, to attend the lectures of Yazid b. Abu Habib.[14] He must have made a good impression, for the teacher with whom he went to study collected traditions from him and cites him as an authority.[15] After completing his Egyptian sojourn, Ibn Ishaq returned to his home city of Medina and continued his scholarly pursuits.[16]

Ibn Ishaq's fame grew as a collector of *Hadith* reports during his career in Medina. He was best known as an expert in the life of Muhammad. Az-Zuhri, from whom Ibn Ishaq quotes numerous *Hadith* reports, praised him by saying that knowledge [Arabic *ʿilm*] would not disappear from Medina as long as Ibn Ishaq was there.[17] During this period he was primarily engaged in collecting his corpus of *Hadith* reports about the conquests and possibly working on the now lost juridical compendium, his *Sunan*.[18] While he may have conceived the plan for the whole of the biography of Muhammad at this time, studies tend to show that only the *Kitâb al-Maghâzî*, the portion that deals with Muhammad's life after the Hijrah in 622 C.E., was collected in any way near a final form.[19]

Ibn Ishaq seems to have been an assiduous and ardent collector of scholarly information, and he seems to have employed every means at his disposal to ferret out the information. He used the accepted means of oral transmission, in which he personally heard *Hadith* reports recited from a transmitter. He was also a devotee of the shops of the *warraqs*, the paper makers and book publishers, who were plying a profitable trade purveying editions of Qurans, Scriptures from Jews and Christians, and various works represented as Scripture but which were, in reality, such things as commentaries on Scripture and apocrypha.[20] A story is told that Ibn Ishaq as a young man was compelled to change his usual seat in the mosque because he would sit in the back, near the women, and pester them for *Hadith* reports and stories.[21]

Two professional controversies eventually drove Ibn Ishaq from his native city. The first involved a younger contemporary, Malik b. Anas, the famous legist. We have few details of the actual reasons for the bad feelings between the two scholars, but Ibn Ishaq is reported to have said that he would act as a veterinary surgeon for Malik's corpus of *Hadith* reports. This prompted Malik to remark to a third party that he counted Ibn Ishaq among the Antichrists.[22] As this dispute is later reported, there seems to have been a mixture of personal animus and disagreement over methodology. Ibn Ishaq was criticized for using Jewish converts as sources for Muhammad's biography.[23] Shortly after the incident with Malik, Ibn Ishaq was accused of being a Qadarite or a Shiʿite.[24]

The second incident revolved around Ibn Ishaq's having included Fatimah, the wife of Hisham b. ʿUrwah, in his *Sanads*. Hisham claimed that it was not possible for his wife to have reported anything to Ibn Ishaq because she, as a proper wife, would not have talked with anyone outside the family without his permission and knowledge.[25] The fact that the woman was at least forty years Ibn Ishaq's senior and could have transmitted information to him in any number of socially acceptable ways, including in the mosque, is not mentioned by his critics. Whether Hisham was scrupulously defending the reputation of his wife or whether he was merely jealous of the fact that *Hadith* reports which might properly have been regarded as belonging to himself and his family were being cited by Ibn Ishaq, his defamation of character contributed to the general slandering of the scholar's reputation.

Whether these two incidents were the main cause of Ibn Ishaq's departure from Medina we shall never know. It is possible that he felt the need to make another scholarly journey, especially since his reputation had been so enhanced by his first one. It is also possible that the troubles associated with the rise of the Abbasids made life difficult for him as a non-Arab Muslim. His professional antagonist, Malik, seems to have harbored no long-lasting ill will toward Ibn Ishaq. In all fairness, the quarrel seems to have been based on the passions of two ambitious and competing scholars. When Ibn Ishaq departed from Medina, Malik gave him a gift of fifty dinars and half his crop of dates, and later he acknowledged Ibn Ishaq as an expert in genealogy and *maghazi*.[26]

Ibn Ishaq's second journey took him east, first to Kufah, then to al-Jazirah, then to Rayy, and finally to the newly built Baghdad, where he attached himself to the court of the caliph al-Mansur. While in the caliphal service he seems to have completed his plan for the *Sîrah*, which would begin with Creation and continue through the life of the Prophet, Muhammad. The *Sîrah* would be followed by a history of the caliphs, taking the plan up to al-Mansur's own time. This ambitious scheme was evidently sponsored by the caliph, partly as an educational sourcebook for Prince al-Mahdi, for whom Ibn Ishaq was engaged as a tutor to provide a liberal education.[27] Another reason for the patronage of the *Sîrah* would have been its universalist message about Islam. By including all the world's history the work demonstrated that time's course led to Islam, which embraced the prophets and holy men of Judaism and Christianity, and finally produced the regime of the Abbasids, whose empire embraced Muslims, Christians, and Jews.

The *Sîrah* was conceived as a whole made up of two basic sections, the second section divided into two units. The first section the *Kitâb al-Mubtada⁾*, started with Creation and included all the Jewish, Christian, and Arabian prophets mentioned in the Quran and some who are not. This portion set the stage for the advent of Muhammad and Islam, and explained the history of the world and God's purpose for it. The second section dealt with the life of Muhammad. Muhammad's life was divided into two distinct periods: the time from his birth in 570 C.E. to age forty, covered in the *Kitâb al-Mabʿath*, and the time from age forty, when he became the Messenger of Allah and the Prophet of Islam, until his death in 632 C.E., found in the *Kitâb al-Maghâzî*.

This ambitious work proved too much as a textbook for the prince, who was no scholar, and Ibn Ishaq was compelled to give him an abbreviated version of the masterpiece. According to some reports, however, the full version was prepared for the caliph and added to the caliphal library.[28]

Throughout a career marked by great fame and considerable controversy, Ibn Ishaq attracted a relatively large following of students who were to become important in the transmission of traditional history. We know of at least eighteen students who can be credited with a complete or nearly complete version of the *Sîrah*.[29] With the exception of Ibrahim b. Sa'd, who was a pupil from Ibn Ishaq's days in Medina, all of the students were from the eastern part of the empire, which leads us to assume that the *Sîrah* was completed while Ibn Ishaq was attached to the Abbasid court. There were many other students who transmitted a few *Hadith* reports from Ibn Ishaq, but their surviving corpora from him are too sparse to include them in a list of major pupils. Of all the students Salamah b. al-Fadl al-Abrash is to be counted as the chief pupil. He heard all of his master's material and was able to have his notes checked for accuracy.[30] More important for us, he received an autograph copy of Ibn Ishaq's lecture materials, probably toward the end of the master's career.[31] From him we have the most reliable transmission of the original *Sîrah*.

We know next to nothing about Ibn Ishaq's personal life; the sources are remarkably silent about anything but his generation's assessment of his scholarly achievements. He was not always regarded favorably, even at the height of his fame, and certainly not after his death in Baghdad around the year 767. Yet his scholarship was sound enough and his vision broad enough that he influenced Muslim historians for many generations.

Historical Setting

As far as we know, no manuscript of the entire *Sîrah* survives. What does survive is an epitome of it composed by Abu Muhammad 'Abd al-Malik b. Hisham, known as Ibn Hisham, an Egyptian scholar who died around 833 C.E., a little more than half a century after Ibn Ishaq. This is the work that is known in the Muslim world as the *Sîrah*. In it most of the *Kitâb al-Mubtada'* and some of the *Kitâb al-Mab'ath* were eliminated. Ibn Ishaq represented the end of an era of open scholarly inquiry into Jewish and Christian knowledge, and Ibn Hisham's epitome marks a closing of the doors of such open investigation. The closing of those doors coincided with and was part of the formation of a new Islamic self-image. Ironically, Ibn Ishaq's *Sîrah*, notwithstanding its wide vision, was one of the instruments that crafted a more self-contained Islamic self-image. By concentrating on Muhammad and raising Muhammad above the other prophets, Ibn Ishaq helped make Islamic scholarship independent of Jewish and Christian sources.

The reasons for Ibn Hisham's abridgment of the biography and the subsequent loss of manuscript transmission of one of its portions are relevant to discovering how biblical material was received and used in the early Islamicate world. In the introduction to his epitome of the *Sîrah*, Ibn Hisham offers the following criticism of Ibn Isḥâq:

> God willing I shall begin this book with Ismaʿîl and mention those of his offspring who were the ancestors of God's apostle one by one with what is known about them, taking no account of Ismaʿîl's other children, for the sake of brevity, confining myself to the prophet's biography and omitting some of the things which Ibn Isḥâq has recorded in this book in which there is no mention of the apostle and about which the Quran says nothing and which are not relevant to anything in this book or an explanation of it or evidence for it; poems which he quotes that no authority on poetry whom I have met knows of; things which it is disgraceful to discuss; matters which would distress certain people; and such reports as al-Bakkâʾî told me he could not accept as trustworthy—all these things I have omitted. But God willing I shall give a full account of everything else so far as it is known and trustworthy tradition is available.[32]

Actually, this means that Ibn Hisham eliminated the entire contents of the *Kitâb al-Mubtadaʾ* from the *Sîrah*. On the basis that the biographical material pertaining directly to Muhammad was composed first and the other material added later, it has been argued that the biography was divisible.[33] But in Ibn Isḥâq's scheme the initial material, the "biblical" portion, formed an introduction to the events of Muhammad's life and an explanation for them. Muhammad was the fulfillment of prophecy; Isaiah had foretold his coming.[34] His life was the replica of the prophets and the patriarchs, just as Islam was the restoration of the true monotheistic worship of God. Ibn Isḥâq's vision was to place Muhammad in the context of the history of the salvation of the world.[35]

The most damaging charges leveled by Ibn Hisham, and the ones requiring some explanation, are those which refer to the disgraceful matters, those matters which would distress certain people, and the reports based on untrustworthy accounts. The thrust of Ibn Hisham's criticism cannot be simply that Ibn Isḥâq was faulty in method and therefore produced corrupt recitations. Ibn Hisham himself would have been subject to the same criticism in his *Kitâb at-Tîjân*, in which he quotes material from Ibn Isḥâq.[36] The answer to these charges seems, rather, to be in the change in social and intellectual climate which was developing during Ibn Isḥâq's lifetime and reached fruition shortly after his death.[37]

As Islam spread after the death of Muhammad, Muslims encountered and conquered the oldest portions of the Judeo-Christian world, along with a population well schooled by long centuries of sectarian conflict to meet the challenge of Muslim missionaries. When Muhammad had encountered the Jews of Medina, he had used scriptural arguments against them. Some of those arguments were recorded in the Quran and the *Sîrah*. The Quran, however, was not a complete guide for understanding Jewish and Christian Scriptures, and one of the goals of early Muslim scholars was to make adequate sense of the "biblical" references in the Quran through the use of Jewish and Christian Scriptures and other literature derived from the People of Scripture.[38]

Many of the Companions of Muhammad were ardent seekers after traditions from the Jews and Christians. Abu Hurayrah, although illiterate, had extensive knowledge of the Torah, and the biblical interests of ʿAli, Salman al-Farisi, and Ibn ʿAbbas are well known.[39] Abu Dharr, who was a monotheist in the pre-Islamic period, was influenced by Jewish thought, and Muhammad, Abu Bakr, and ʿUmar made visits to the Bet Midrash in Medina.[40] Zayd b. Thabit, who was so instrumental in producing the recension of the Quran, is reported to have learned *Yahudiyyah*, an early Judeo-Arabic, in a Bet Midrash in order to read Jewish material to Muhammad.[41] Converted Jews, such as ʾUbayy b. Kaʿb (642 C.E.), transmitted much information originally derived from rabbinic traditions found in the Talmud and Midrashim.[42] The same can be said of Kaʿb al-Ahbar, the Yemenite Jew who converted under the caliphate of Abu Bakr and was the author of numerous works on biblical matters. But the primary credit for assimilating biblical traditions into Islam must go to Ibn ʿAbbas, who is the ultimate authority for many of the *Hadith* reports found in the *Kitâb al-Mubtadaʾ*. Ibn ʿAbbas was so important for the development of Quran commentary, particularly the type called *Israʾiliyat,* that subsequent generations, confronted with the necessity of assigning attribution and authority to already accepted anonymously derived *Hadith* reports, chose his name as the one figure who would not be controverted.

The generation after Muhammad, the Followers continued the practice of seeking extra-Islamic material for Quran commentary, biography of prophets, and for personal devotion. For example, Abu Jald of Basrah was accustomed to reading both the Quran and the Torah in his devotionals, claiming that divine mercy derived from reading both of them.[43] Wahb b. Munabbih was another source for the introduction of Judeo-Christian material into the Islamic mainstream, for, as can be seen from a perusal of the *Sanads* of the *Kitâb al-Mubtadaʾ*, much of the detailed material derived from rabbinic sources can be traced no earlier than Wahb, even though there was general knowledge of the material prior to his time.[44] As Marshall Hodgson has observed, "It is clear that a significant part of the population that accepted Islam in its formative centuries was composed of Jews, whose narrative traditions, called *Isrâ*-*îlîyât,* dominated the popular legendry of early Islam. It would appear that much of the spirit that formed Muslim expectations of what a religion should be was inspired by Jewish example."[45] Ibn Isḥâq was not alone in his pursuit of *Israiliyat.*

The attitudes of the Islamic community toward this form of scholarship began to change with the beginning of the Abbasid empire or a little before. In many respects the community of those whom Hodgson terms "Piety-Minded," those concerned with implementing a version of Islam which held that each individual Muslim's life should be under the direct governance of God's laws, began to devalue and finally reject Jewish and Christian materials as a basis for their religious and social vision. As Nabia Abbott observed,

> The early Muslims' preoccupation with non-Islamic thought and literature was reflected in the subsequent negative approach to such questions as whether it was possible for Muslims to read such books and to transmit *akhbâr* and *hadîth* from the "people of the Book" and, conversely and logically enough, whether Islamic literature, particularly the Quran, should be taught or even exposed to the "people of the Book." The comparatively tolerant attitude that characterized the first century yielded—for all but a few liberals—first to caution, then to avoidance, and finally, about the middle of the second century, to all but complete prohibition of all three practices.[46]

The period of time to which Abbott referred is the time of the consolidation of Abbasid power, the emergence of the major early schools of Islamic law, the heyday of the Muʿtazilites, and a period of anti-Muslim revolts. It was a time of major social change. Some of the social change is a result of patterns of conversion within the Islamicate society. Richard Bulliet sees competition between early and later converts to Islam manifesting as "different orthodoxies that would be mutually acceptable insofar as they did not deem each other to be heterodox but that might otherwise be violently antagonistic. This situation occurred in the fields of law, theology, and personal religious behavior."[47] The struggle for defining acceptable and correct behavior resulted in competing schools of law and conflicting theological doctrines, all remaining within Islamic society. There were enough shared texts, religious leaders, and ideas among the competing groups that each group responded to the other's accusations of heterodoxy, and it is only by the end of the fourth Islamic century that personal behaviors designed to prove one's centrality within the community begin to decline.[48] With the total Muslim population only around 8 percent in the middle of the second Islamic century, and with increasing internal division within the community, it is understandable that reliance on the texts and scholarship of those in the religious majority would be rejected. No longer was it possible to tolerate what al-Bukhari records as current in Muhammad's time, that the "Jews used to read the Torah in Hebrew and interpret [Arabic *fassara*] it to the people of Islam in Arabic."[49] The doctrine developed that former Scriptures were corrupt and not to be relied on.[50] While a compromise ultimately developed in which it was possible to make restricted use of *Hadith* reports from the People of Scripture, such *Hadith* reports never again enjoyed the enthusiastic currency that they did in the first century of Islam.

Several factors contributed to the changed attitudes toward *Isra'iliyat* and the subsequent abridgement of the *Sîrah*: the development of Islamic religious law, *Shari'ah;* the competition among various groups in the Islamic community for supremacy; the inability of the caliphs to impose absolute authority over the religious community; and the elevation of Muhammad to a privileged position as personal exemplar for the pious Muslim. The *Sîrah* was written at the beginning of the period of increased veneration of Muhammad and was epitomized as that veneration became institutionalized in the *Shari'ah*.

The implementation of the vision of society held by the Piety-Minded Muslims resulted in the codification of practice deemed correct by the Muslim community into *Shari'ah*.[51] It also resulted in the elevation of the status of certain individuals who had specialized knowledge of *Hadith* reports and Quran. These were called *'ulama'* [sing. *'alim*], those who possessed knowledge [*'ilm*]. They were not priests and possessed no special rights other than their knowledge and their ability to offer convincing and locally acceptable judgments about piety and practice. *'Ulama'* in various metropolitan centers had formed schools of law which reflected local practice, but there was no central authority to unify these groups.[52] While these groups generally remained local, pious scholars would travel from area to area to study with a respected *'alim*. This cross-fertilization meant that the speculations of theorists often had wide acceptance and influence.

One of the earliest theorists of the new *Shari'ah* was Malik b. Anas [796 C.E.]. He was a younger contemporary of Ibn Isḥâq in Medina and a sometime antagonist of his. The *Muwaṭṭa'*, his famous treatise on legal questions, raised the status of *Sunnah*, customary practice based on the record of Muhammad's actions, and reduced the importance of *ra'y*, judicial ratiocination. Muhammad was still *primus inter pares* in Malik's system, but Muhammad's actions could be ignored in favor of another *Sunnah*, particularly the customary practice of the inhabitants of Medina during Muhammad's lifetime.[53] Malik was particularly noted for his rigorous criticism of *Hadith* reports, which may be part of the basis for his fights with Ibn Isḥâq.

In the next generation after Ibn Isḥâq, Islamic law underwent a thoroughgoing theoretical reform, primarily due to the efforts of Muhammad b. Idris ash-

Shafi^{c}i [820 C.E.].[54] Prior to ash-Shafi^{c}i's composition of his major work, the *Risâlah*, the various schools of Islamic law, while exercising rigorous methodology within the confines of their own jurisdictions, had developed extensive rivalries among themselves. There was no unifying element or theoretical foundation accepted by all the schools. Ash-Shafi^{c}i proposed that there were four major roots to Islamic law. The primary root was God's revealed word, the Quran. This had been the position of the Quran among the jurists prior to ash-Shafi^{c}i, but he argued that the Quran not only provided positive and negative precepts but also sanctioned the means by which its regulatory commandments could be interpreted and supplemented. The Quran was often too terse or entirely silent about issues of primary importance to the community.[55]

For ash-Shafi^{c}i, the solution to the problem was found in the Quranic command "He who obeys Allah and His Messenger and fears Allah and keeps duty, such are the victorious" (Q 24:52). By stressing this command, ash-Shafi^{c}i placed the Quran in a privileged and protected position in *Shari^{c}ah*. Verses from the Quran could not be rejected in favor of other customary practice, as had been done by some. He also raised Muhammad to a new level above all other men, including all previous prophets. *Sunnah* now came to refer specifically to the practices of Muhammad as recorded in the *Hadith* reports. Muhammad's actions became almost equal to the Quran and were the means through which the Quran was understood.

The developments in Islamicate society which privileged Muhammad and made an idealized image of him central in the *Shari^{c}ah* arose in a climate of theological and political conflict. At the end of the Umayyad period there had been a revolt against Muslim rule by a sect of Jews called the ^{c}Isawiyya. They held that Muhammad was indeed a prophet, but only for the Arabs.[56] The popularity of the ^{c}Isawiyya movement threatened one of the cornerstone beliefs of the Piety-Minded: that Islam was a universal religion.

Revolts by non-Muslims continued against Muslim rule after the Abbasids came to power, as did revolts by Shi^{c}ites disappointed that the Abbasids had failed to implement their Imami vision of Islam.[57] For the caliphs, the rising importance of Muhammad and his *Sunnah* threatened their authority as interpreters of Islam. When the caliph al-Mansur said, "I am simply the authority of God on his earth," he was continuing the view that had been held by the Umayyad caliphs before him.[58] This fit the Abbasid claim of privilege because they were descended from Muhammad's family.[59] The Shi^{c}ites claimed the same privilege for their imams and for similar reasons, although they restricted the acceptable genealogy to the direct descendants of Muhammad through Ali. The conflict between Abbasid assertions of religious authority and the resistance of the Piety-Minded continued until the caliph al-Mutawakkil abolished the inquisitional *Mihna* in 848 C.E. and bowed to the notion that the caliph was only equal to any other Muslim in the sight of God.[60]

The elevation of Muhammad and his *Sunnah* also provided a means to resolve religious differences among the Piety-Minded proponents of *Shariʿah*. They had a notion of social responsibility that allowed for a certain degree of accommodation to differences and variations within the community.[61] Appeal to Muhammad's authority obviated the differences among the various schools of law, all of which subscribed to the same notions of authority.[62]

The elevation of Muhammad and the *Sunnah* to a position of privilege had an impact on Ibn Isḥâq's *Sîrah*. In the *Shariʿah* construct biographical details about Muhammad had the force of law. *Hadith* reports were subject to close scrutiny for authenticity and rejected if the sources proved inadequate. Ibn Hisham, in the preparation of the epitome, appears to have applied the more strict jurisprudential standard of his time because the subject was Muhammad. He eliminated from the *Hadith* reports in the biography much material that was derived, on the face of it, from Jews, Christians, heretics, schismatics, political misfits, and anyone ruled by the community as unworthy to participate in the development and transmission of *Hadith* reports legally binding on the Muslim community. Ibn Isḥâq's wider scholarly vision was relegated to nonjuridical areas: tales of the prophets, histories, and nonlegal Quran explication. In effect, two types of biography of Muhammad developed. The one used by the jurists was the atomistic *Hadith* reports that constituted Muhammad's *Sunnah*. It had no sustained narrative and concentrated only on those aspects of Muhammad's life from which legal precedent could be derived. The other biography of Muhammad was the *Sîrah*.[63] It was narrative, popular, and provided Muslims, whether scholars or not, with a vivid picture of their Prophet.[64] The lives of the prophets before Muhammad, the subject of the excised *Kitâb al-Mubtadaʾ*, were enjoyed as tales told by popular preachers or used piecemeal by scholars to comment on the Quran.

We can detect the beginnings of the split between the two types of biographical reports about Muhammad soon after Muhammad's death. The faithful Muslims collected Muhammad's sayings and reports of his deeds for personal edification, but they also collected and expanded miraculous stories that "proved" Muhammad's prophethood.[65] They were more careful about the reliability of *Hadith* reports that would be used as guides for personal behavior than they were about the miracle stories, and as a result fabulous tales abounded. One of the earliest *Sîrah* works, the *Sîrah* of Wahb b. Munabbih, who was an older contemporary of Ibn Isḥâq and one of his sources, included much legendary and entertaining material.[66] But most collections of biographical reports were not organized so as to cover all of Muhammad's life. Most, in fact, concentrated on Muhammad's military and political exploits, the *maghazî*.[67] Ibn Ishâq had much material from which to select, but the working out of the vision of Muhammad's place in the history of the world belongs to him.

Introduction

15

The Reconstruction

At some point the manuscript tradition for the *Kitâb al-Mubtada'*, the portion excised by Ibn Hisham, became lost. We do not know when, but it must have been some time after Ibn Hisham, for a number of later authors quote portions of it. Because it dealt with the lives of the past prophets and other biblical matters, it was of interest to those who were commenting on the Quran and writing stories of the prophets (*Qisas al-'Anbiya'*).

The chief of those whose scholarly vision embraced the disfavored material was Abu Ja'far Muhammad b. Jarir at-Tabari (A.H. 310).[68] At-Tabari's major works, his *Ta'rîkh* and his *Tafsîr*, of which only portions survive, contain significant portions of Ibn Ishaq's writings through the transmission of Salamah b. al-Fadl al-Abrash through Muhammad b. Humayd b. Hayan at-Tamimi ar-Razi. This is the preferred source for my reconstruction for the same reasons that it seemed to be the preferred source for at-Tabari. Salamah was Ibn Ishaq's closest pupil. He heard all of the material from his master, had his notes checked, and received his master's lecture notes. At-Tabari uses the *Sanad* Ibn Humayd–Salamah b. al-Fadl–Ibn Ishaq almost to the exclusion of all others when he quotes the *Kitâb al-Mubtada'*. He also uses *Sanads* from other students of Ibn Ishaq, but with far less frequency.

Another fruitful source for the reconstruction of the *Kitâb al-Mubtada'* is Abu Ishaq Ahmad b. Muhammad b. Ibrahim ath-Tha'labi [427 C.E.], *Qisas al-'Anbiyâ'*. Because of his tendency to combine individual traditions into a continuous narrative, sometimes with and sometimes without attribution to the original sources, ath-Tha'labi is less useful for the reconstruction than at-Tabari. He appears to be a reliable source, however, and sometimes provides material not available elsewhere.

The *'Akhbâr Makkah* of Abu al-Walid Muhammad b. 'Abdullah al-'Azarqî provides a number of traditions from Ibn Ishaq, but the content is limited to those traditions which have particular reference to Mecca. He transmits from his grandfather from Sa'îd b. Salim al-Qaddah (second half of the second century A.H.][69] from Ibn Ishaq's pupil 'Uthmân b. Saj.[70]

The *Kitâb al-Bad' wa-t-Ta'rîkh*, ascribed by Clement Huart to al-Balkhi but written by al-Mutahhar b. Tahir al-Maqdisi (A.H. 355),[71] contains material from Ibn Ishaq without full attribution. The author seems to have had knowledge of the *Kitâb al-Mubtada'*, which he describes as "the first book done on the beginning of Creation."[72] A few additional quotations can be found in the *Lubâb at-Ta'wîl* of 'Ali b. Muhammad b. Ibrahim al-Khazin al-Baghdadi, the *al-Mu'ammarun wa-l-Wasaya* of Abu Hatim as-Sijistani, and the *Kitâb at-Tîjân* if Ibn Hisham. Sources such as Yaqut's *Mu'jam al-Buldân* and al-Kisa'i's *Qisas al-'Anbiyâ'* contain stories obviously derived from Ibn Ishaq, but since these versions are without attribution, they have been used only for general reference in the reconstruction. The fragments of the *Kitâb al-Mubtada*ᵓ identified by Nabia Abbott do not seem to correspond to any portion of the work I have been able to reconstruct, but this may be due to a lacuna in the reconstruction.[73]

Fuat Sezgin suggests that the material to be found in the *Kitâb al-Aghânî* and the anonymous *Kitâb Bakr wa-Taghlib* belongs to the *Kitâb al-Mubtada*ᵓ.[74] At this point, I am inclined to think that this comes from a separate work, ancillary to but independent of, the *Sîrah*. From my examination of the structure of the *Kitâb al-Mubtada*ᵓ it is difficult to find a place where the material would fit. It should probably rank with Ibn Ishaq's *Akhbâr Kulaib wa-Jassâs* and his *Taᵓrîkh al-Khulafâ*ᵓ.

In determining the order of the traditions that make up the reconstructed text, I have chosen to follow the order found in at-Tabari when that order is not in conflict with the order of the narratives of the Quran, which is to be preferred. In those instances where neither at-Tabari nor the Quran proves to be sufficient guide, biblical or historical order was used, and when all else failed, the material was arranged in an attempt to present a coherent whole. I feel justified in preferring at-Tabari not only because at-Tabari seems to have had access to the best copy of the original material but also because he followed it somewhat slavishly. According to Yaqut, he "erected" his universal history on the foundations laid by Ibn Ishaq.[75]

Structure and Content of the *Kitâb al-Mubtada*ᵓ

When we add the *Kitâb al-Mubtada*ᵓ to the rest of the *Sîrah*, Ibn Ishaq's plan for a history of the world becomes clear.[76] We can read his original version of what we call the biography of Muhammad, which starts with creation and the first prophet, Adam. It includes descriptions of the lives of all the prophets mentioned in the Quran and some who have no Quranic mention. After the pre-Islamic prophets are enumerated, the *Sîrah* focuses on the prehistory of Arabia, and culminates with a detailed description of the life of the last prophet, Muhammad. It is arranged chronologically and has the outward form of a world history.

The *Sîrah* is that form of biography that we call a "sacred biography." Sacred biographies "both recount the process through which a new religious ideal is established and, at the same time, participate in the process." This dual role for the writer of sacred biography, historian and devotee, complicates our understanding of the biography and the process of its composition: "The central issue here is the relation of biographical fact to the emerging mythical ideal. Given that the mythical ideal remains somewhat fluid at the time the sacred biography is written or compiled, the selection of biographical material is an extremely vexing problem. A single reported episode may have a constitutive effect on the resulting mythical ideal."[77]

Sometimes Ibn Ishaq gives an indication of his awareness of the process of selecting the materials to be included in the *Sîrah*. This is the case with the report of the battle of Uhud, often characterized as Muhammad's first defeat. Ibn Ishaq lists the learned *Hadith* reporters who are responsible for the narrative and then gives a running account of the battle.[78] This is one of the few times that we get a statement of his methodology. More often we have only the results of his choices. Ibn Ishaq's end product is a combination of what some have called myth and history, resulting in "mythomorphism."[79] By mythomorphism I mean that the biographer describes the subject in terms of already existing ideal types. Some of those types in the *Sîrah* are Muhammad as Prophet, Muhammad as Community Leader, Muhammad as Ideal Man, and Muhammad as Spiritual Guide.[80] The ideal mythomorphic types operate as a sort of paradigm on which the sacred biography is patterned. They are ahistoric, and in the case of relationships between Muhammad and the other prophets recognized by Islam, we can observe that the telling about Muhammad affects the telling about the other prophets as well as the reverse.

The story of Muhammad's mother's pregnancy illustrates mythomorphism. When Muhammad's father, 'Abdullah, was going to marry Muhammad's mother,[81] the sister of a man who predicted Muhammad's birth propositioned 'Abdullah because, as she later explained, there was a "white blaze" between his eyes, and she had hoped to be the bearer of his child because she knew of her brother's prophecy. When the marriage between 'Abdullah and Muhammad's mother, Aminah, was consummated, the blaze passed to Aminah's womb, and she heard a voice say to her, "You are pregnant with the lord of this people, and when he is born say, 'I put him in the care of the One from the evil of every envier'; then call him Muhammad." This is evocative of the annunciation reported in both Luke 1:31 and Matthew 1:21. The blaze is the traditional nimbus, the mark of a holy person, which was bright enough, according to one report, to shine from inside Aminah's womb far enough to light up the castles in Syria![82]

The previous example could be construed as hagiographic hyperbole, the biographer drawing with words what an artist in an iconographic tradition would have done with paint and color. But in another version Muhammad is represented as participating himself in the mythomorphic process. In the story of Muhammad's early childhood, Ibn Ishaq quotes, "The Apostle of God used to say, 'There is no prophet but has shepherded a flock.' When they said 'You, too, Apostle of God?', he said, 'Yes.' " And, "The Apostle of God used to say to his companions, 'I am the most Arab of you all. I am of the Quraysh, and I was suckled among the Banu Sa'd b. Bakr.' "[83] Here Muhammad is depicted as a pagan Arab pastoral hero—a model much like our American cowboy and with as much reality—and also portrayed as the model of the religious leader as pastor.

Not only is Muhammad defined by the mythomorphic process, but so are the members of his family, and here the problem becomes even more complex. The *Sîrah* portrays Muhammad as the last in a line of prophets selected by God. Prophethood is an office. Prophets receive a commission from God sometimes portrayed as a heavy mantle.[84] Prophets are bound by the commission to act in a manner predetermined by the office. Since their actions affect those around them, it is not surprising to find elements of the mythic shape of the prophets interacting with all the figures of the biography. So we see Muhammad's grandfather, ʿAbdu-l-Muttalib, and Muhammad's father, ʿAbdullah, represented as mythomorphs of Abraham and Isaac. ʿAbdu-l-Muttalib, in preparation for the restoration of the Meccan well of Zamzam, slept one night in the Hijr, the area near the Kaʿbah containing the graves of Hagar and Ishmael.[85] While in the holy area, ʿAbdu-l-Muttalib received a vision which commanded him to dig the well. In the midst of the digging, he decided to sacrifice his son, ʿAbdullah, Muhammad's father.[86] As in the biblical and rabbinic stories, God intervenes and accepts alternative sacrifice.

The sacrifice motif in the *Sîrah* lies within a larger frame which is designed to make Mecca the new Jerusalem and the Kaʿbah the new Temple.[87] In rabbinic legend it had been long understood that the Temple was the location for the binding of Isaac, so ʿAbdu-l-Muttalib's intended sacrifice can be understood to be evocative of the earlier Abrahamic intention.[88] A consequence of the equation of Muhammad's grandfather with Abraham is that Muhammad can be understood as Jacob. By the time of Ibn Ishaq, a body of literature had developed around the first verse of *Surah* 17, which represented Muhammad as having made a heavenly ascension from the Temple Mount in Jerusalem. The point of departure was the rock that had come to be identified as Jacob's Pillow.[89] This trip to heaven is called *Miʿraj* in Arabic, meaning "ladder," and refers to Jacob's vision of a heavenly ladder. Of course, following the bias of the hagiography, Muhammad does Jacob one better by actually ascending to heaven.

The relationship between Muhammad and the other prophets in the *Sîrah* is not a simple one of antecedent–consequent influence, where Muhammad's behaviors are predetermined by others' past actions. All prophets share a common experience as a consequence of having been chosen for the role. Adam is said to have founded proper worship of God in Mecca at the Kaʿbah. Abraham restored the Kaʿbah, building the shrine on Adam's foundations. Then Abraham [re-]instituted the rite of Pilgrimage. He included not only the circumambulation of the Kaʿbah, but also the veneration of the stations of as-Safa, al-Marwah, Minah, Muzdalifah, and ʿArafah. He stoned the Devil and pronounced the formula "Labayka, at your service, O God." When Muhammad instituted the rites of the Pilgrimage, he performed the same actions and included the same places.[90] In addition, Muhammad and Abraham are equated in looks as well as function. After returning from his visit to heaven, Muhammad is reported as saying. "I have never seen a man more like myself than Abraham."[91]

The representational similarity of one prophet to another raises the issue of the relationship between the *Sîrah* and other versions of the lives of the prophets. For those who privilege the biblical story of Abraham, the story in the *Sîrah* can appear as derivative from the biblical version.[92] The story is "borrowed," to use common parlance, and the features which make Abraham the same as Muhammad are understood as additions. But Muslims privilege the Quran and regard the story in the Bible as having been corrupted.[93] However, Ibn Ishaq has used material derived from Jews and Christians to build the images of both Muhammad and Abraham even though he was a Muslim who privileged the Quranic accounts. Here we see Ibn Ishaq in the dual role as believer and as sacred biographer. We can begin to understand his methods by examining the choices he makes when he uses material derived from Jews and Christians.[94]

We can see some of the ways Ibn Ishaq uses Jewish and Christian material to write the *Sîrah* and to comment on the Quran when we examine the story of Solomon. The story of Solomon is found in seven different *Surahs* of the Quran, and no single *Surah* contains the complete account. *Surah* 2 [2:101–102] contains an allusion to the practice, evidently Jewish, of regarding Solomon as a magician. *Surah* 4 [4:163] includes Solomon in a list of prophets starting with Noah: Noah, Abraham, Ishmael, Isaac, Jacob and the tribes, Jesus, Job, Jonah, Aaron, Solomon, and David. *Surah* 6 [6:85–86] also places Solomon in a list of prophets, but in a different order: Isaac, Jacob, Noah, David, Solomon, Job, Joseph, Moses, Aaron, Zachariah, John, Jesus, and Elias. *Surah* 21 [21:78–82] alludes to a story concerning a judgment made by David and Solomon, credits Solomon with the discovery of protective clothing for warfare, and asserts that God gave him power over the wind and certain diving devils.

Surah 27 [27:15–44] is the longest of the Solomon stories. It contains the story of Solomon and the ant and Solomon and the Queen of Sheba. But, as we will see, there seems to be an underlying presumption that there is a larger narrative context to which this is an allusion. *Surah* 34 [34:12–20] alludes to the story of Sheba, to the submission of nature to Solomon, and mentions his remarkable death. Finally, *Surah* 38 [38:31–41] tells of Solomon's sin, the loss of his throne, his repentance and restoration to kingship, and the submission of nature to him.

When we try to arrange these elements of the story in some order—for example, chronologically according to the sequence of revelation—we are unable to find a satisfactory key to producing an integrated text from the various pieces. In the first place, we would have to choose criteria of order, as a number of Muslim and non-Muslim scholars have done. In the order proposed by Noeldeke, *Surah* 27 would come before *Surah* 34, but if one were to choose either of the orders proposed by Grimme or Hirschfeld, we would have the allusion to the story of the Queen of Sheba precede the fullest explication of Sheba's story in the Quran.[95] That is, we would have a situation in which the earliest Quranic citation would be the version with the fewest details and descriptions but which refers to more. *Surah* 34 explicates a situation in which the inhabitants of Sheba rejected God's blessings and were punished by a flood and a scattering, while *Surah* 27 speaks of the submission of Bilqis, the Queen of Sheba, and her conversion to true Islam. In either order, one version does not seem to be a development from the other. They both seem to assume a larger "Story of Solomon" not found in the Quran but to which the various Quranic passages refer.

Ibn Ishaq has woven a narrative commentary around the Quranic material so that we are able to follow Solomon's life from the time he acquired his father's throne until his death. He uses material from *Surahs* 21, 38, 34, 27, and 2, in that order, but he does not use all the material available to him in the Quran. The story of the slaughter of the horses from *Surah* 38 is entirely missing,[96] but a protracted expansion of verse 34 of the same *Surah*, "We tried Solomon, and we placed on his throne a body; then he repented," contains the famous story of Solomon's forty-day loss of his seal, its miraculous recovery from the belly of a fish, and the sealing of Solomon's evil imposter into a bottle. Our usual perception of the several Solomonic passages I have mentioned is that there is an assumed underlying version which informs all the subsequent versions. This view was shared by early Muslim Quran commentators. But the subsequent versions come into conflict with each other, as *Surahs* 27 and 34 seem to do when they are fleshed out. It is hard to imagine a version of the story which would be abstract enough to embrace them both. Also, we are left to wonder why Ibn Ishaq left out the story of the slaughter of the horses. We are presented with a problem of narrative versions.

If we understand Ibn Ishaq's situation correctly, he was faced with a wide variety of *Hadith* reports and written texts from which he chose those that were consonant with his understanding of the story of Solomon. For him, the Quran was a faithful (but incomplete) representation of the *Umm al-Kitâb* (Q 43:4), the heavenly exemplar that informed all versions. More than that, the Quran was the measure of the correctness of all versions. This means that for Ibn Ishaq and other Muslims the Quran served as a sort of Platonic ideal form, what Barbara Herrnstein Smith describes as a "versionless version." Such a version occupies "a highly privileged ontological realm of pure Being within which it unfolds immutably and eternally. . . . It is clearly unknowable—and, indeed, literally unimaginable—by any mortal being."[97] We can assume that

Ibn Ishaq held the Quranically supported view that there was such an ideal form, the *Umm al-Kitâb,* to which all material could be compared. Such an assumption allows us to understand how he could use material from Jews and Christians even though that material was potentially corrupt through *tahrif.* If the version in question fit the Quranic pattern, even though it went beyond what was explicitly in the Quran, it could then be understood as fitting the heavenly model and thereby be acceptable.

Smith rejects the notion of a versionless version. For her, not only is there not an underlying versionless version which informs all occurrences of a narrative, but such a notion hinders our understanding of the function of narratives. She posits that narratives are acts or social transactions which reflect the varying circumstances between the narrator and the listener. Such a view, she proposes, would move us beyond the "problematic of language" and help resolve some of the difficulties of assuming a correspondence between "language" and the "world." She views utterances

not as strings of discrete signifiers that represent corresponding sets of discrete signifieds but as *verbal responses*—that is, *acts* which, like any acts, are *performed in response to various sets of conditions*. These conditions consist of all those circumstantial and psychological variables of which every utterance is a function. . . . For any narrative, these conditions would consist of (1) such circumstantial variables as the particular context and material setting (cultural and social, as well as strictly "physical") in which the tale is told, the particular listeners or readers addressed, and the nature of the narrator's relationship to them, and (2) such psychological variables as the narrator's motives for telling the tale and all the particular interests, desires, expectations, memories, knowledge, and prior experience that elicited his telling it on that occasion, to that audience, and that shaped the particular way he told it.[98]

The state of our sources does not allow us to discover all of the conditions set forth by Smith, but her call for a contextual examination points us in the right direction for understanding the *Sîrah*.[99] We can, for example, ask for whom the *Sîrah* was intended. We have already seen that Ibn Ishaq wrote the *Sîrah* as a history for the Abbasid court where he was the court tutor. In the *Kitâb al-Mubtada*ʾ we can identify some elements that could be used as didactic pieces for Prince al-Mahdi. In particular, the stories of Solomon and David model proper and improper conduct for rulers.

In addition, the *Sîrah* appears to have had a Jewish and Christian audience in mind. Barakat Ahmad has observed that Ibn Ishaq lived in a time when there were numerous Jewish revolts against both the newly established Abbasid regime and the established Jewish authorities.[100] He speculates that "the

B. Qaynuqâʿ, the B. al-Naḍîr and above all the B. Qurayẓah were not so much a part of the *maghâzî* of the Apostle as much as a warning to the Jews of the Abbasid empire."[101] Although his conclusions about the slaughter of the B. Qurayẓah have been refuted,[102] he correctly contextualizes the *Sîrah*. As the revolts show, the Muslims had not at that point successfully built a state where the Jews and Christians were reduced to *dhimmî* status, to the stable position of protected non-Muslims. There was still competition over political and ideological dominance. And, finally, Ibn Ishaq was writing from a perspective of faith. All these factors contribute to the shape of the stories in the *Sîrah*.

A frequent theme throughout the *Sîrah* is that prophets suffer, their messages are rejected, but a community forms under the prophetic leadership that believes the message and ultimately triumphs over the rejectors. Ibn Ishaq says, "Prophecy is a troublesome burden—only strong, resolute messengers can bear it by God's help and grace, because of the opposition which they meet from men in conveying God's message." Almost all the prophets in the *Kitâb al-Mubtadaʾ* have their messages rejected. The Quranic statement, "If they deny you, messengers before you have been denied, who came with proofs, and the Psalms, and light-giving scripture" (Q 3:184), confirmed that a messenger who suffered was in the tradition of those who had gone before. The truth would necessarily be rejected by many, but the few believers would be saved. When we remember that less than 10 percent of the population had become Muslim when Ibn Ishaq was writing, we can understand his emphasis on the theme of rejection and redemption.[103]

To counter the theme of rejection and to assert Islam's primary position in the cosmological scheme, the whole of the *Sîrah* appears to be an apology for Islamic religious superiority over Judaism and Christianity. To do this, Ibn Ishaq chose an overall structure for his history patterned on a kind of "Old Testament–New Testament" model. The *Kitâb al-Mubtadaʾ* starts with creation and concludes its chronological exposition just prior to the new dispensation, Islam. Muhammad is foretold by Isaiah and foreshadowed by all the prophets. The *Kitâb al-Mabʿath*, the portion of the *Sîrah* that describes the beginnings of Islam and the coming of Muhammad, starts with a double genealogy of Muhammad that relates him not only to the line of all the noble families of Arabia but also through Ishmael and Abraham back to Adam.[104] The structure of the *Sîrah* would have made the apologetic points obvious to a Christian and even a Jewish readership. By this literary device Muhammad and the Arabs are depicted as the heirs to the Abrahamic heritage.

The theme of the passing of the Abrahamic inheritance to the Arabs underlies the version in the *Kitâb al-Mubtadaʾ* of the Binding, where Ishmael and not Isaac is the intended sacrificial victim.[105] Ishmael's depiction as victim is a clear statement that he rather than Isaac was chosen by God. Not only is the binding/election motif associated with Muhammad through his father and grandfather, but Muhammad received some of the same blessings as Ishmael. When the first prayer was taught to Muhammad, Gabriel produced water for Muhammad, as had been produced under his direction for Ishmael.[106] Contesting the Abrahamic inheritance is not new, of course. Christians had long regarded themselves as heirs to Abraham, just as the church had become the new Jerusalem.

Muhammad, as the new bearer of the law, is equated with Moses. Both were precocious infants and both had foster mothers. Both had believing communities to protect, and both were exiled from their lands, Moses first going to Midian and then making his *Hijrah* to God's promised land. Muhammad saved his community through his Exodus to Medina just as Moses saved the Jews through his flight from Egypt with the Jews. Both Moses and Muhammad received revelation, and both saw God. Moses saw God through his apocalyptic vision, Muhammad through his night journey to heaven. Both Moses and Muhammad acted as military leaders of their communities, eventually restoring pure worship of God around the sacred shrine. But Muhammad betters Moses by entering heaven alive in his night journey, a feat accomplished by the other promulgator of the Law, Ezra. And Muhammad bests Ezra by returning to tell the tale.

Muhammad's mythomorphic relation to Jesus is not only made through the structure of the *Sîrah*, placing Muhammad's life in the "New Testament" section, but Muhammad also is depicted as performing miracles. In the Quran, Muhammad is said to by only a man and a messenger (Q 3:144), but the *Sîrah* has him performing several miracles. At the Battle of the Trench, the Muslims working on the fortifications encountered a boulder that was difficult to remove. Muhammad spat on some water, prayed over it, sprinkled the water on the rock, and the rock fell apart like sand.[107] In another instance Muhammad was given a small handful of dates. He threw them on a robe and invited all the inhabitants of Medina to come and eat. The handful fed all the people of Medina, with some left over.[108]

Not only is Muhammad related to other prophets in the *Sîrah*, but the other prophets are given similar biographies. Abraham and Moses have similar birth stories. Both are born during regimes which try to kill them by slaughtering innocent children born at the same time. Both are predicted by astrological seers. Angels and nature, conspire to spare both infants. Both Abraham and Moses confound the greatest black magic by God's "white magic." In another example George and Job endure extreme suffering and torment, and both survive with faith intact. The emphasis on the commonality of the prophetic experience not only supports the claim that Muhammad was himself a prophet, but the commonality also demonstrates that all prophets brought the same message, called Islam by Muslims. When Ibn Ishaq was writing the *Sîrah*, Muslims, Jews, and Christians were working out the problems of melding three competing religions into one Muslim state. Unity of the prophets argued for unity of the community.

The success of Ibn Ishaq's writings brought the complex interrelationship of Quran, *Sîrah*, and *Isra'iliyat* into the forefront of Muslims' understanding of the formation and early history of Islam. By the time at-Tabari used the *Sîrah* to write his history and his Quran commentary, Ibn Ishaq's literary stamp was widely disseminated.[109] This meant that subsequent promulgators of stories of the prophets often accepted and expanded on the themes originally chosen by Ibn Ishaq to the exclusion of other themes in the Quran. For example, Ibn Ishaq concentrated on the magical powers of Solomon and neglected the story of Solomon's repentance of his overinvolvement with material possessions. The eleventh century author Muhammad b. ʿAbdullah al-Kisaʾi expands those themes even more, including motifs of the taming of the king of the demons and the cutting of the stone for the Temple by means of a powerful worm.[110] Solomon's involvement with magic becomes a popular literary theme in spite of the Quranic statement that such a notion was the work of devils (Q 2:101–102).[111]

Ibn Ishaq used a wide range of language and style levels in the *Sîrah*. They range from polished and literary, such as the story of Job, to conversational and casual, such as the interchange between the fish and the eagle in the story of Adam. The level is probably a result of both the sources of the stories and the mode through which they reached Ibn Ishaq. We know that he relied on both oral and written sources. He frequented the shops of the booksellers [Arabic *warraq; warraqun*], which had become common meeting places for scholars and poets. In the shops he had access to Quran commentary, *Hadith* reports, history, and stories from Jews and Christians which were being translated into Arabic by the bookseller/publishers to satisfy a heavy demand for whatever could explicate the Quran. On the other hand, Ibn Ishaq interviewed older women, descendants of Jewish and Christian converts to Islam, and People of Scripture themselves.

Some of the oral sources were informed by the popular storytellers so prominent in early Islamicate society. Many of the storytellers appeared around the time of Umar I and gained great public support. They preached on street corners and in mosques. Some received monetary support from the state. Their popularity reached such heights that the storytellers were often in competition with the judges for legal opinions. For example, the mother of the famous jurist Abu Hanifa went to a storyteller for a legal judgment. The storyteller protested that Abu Hanifa was a better judge, but the mother insisted, so the storyteller gave a judgment in accord with Abu Hanifa's opinion and the mother was happy.[112] The *Sîrah* contains a number of anecdotal stories which reflect an oral venue.[113] Ibn Ishaq was a scholar of catholic interests and tastes, as reflected by the range of material included in the *Sîrah*.

Introduction

25

For Ibn Ishaq and his contemporaries the *Kitâb al-Mubtadaɔ* and the rest of the *Sîrah* explained the history of the world in Quranic and Muslim terms. It put Muhammad into the divine scheme and integrated his actions with actions of the prophets of the past. The Quran promotes such a view of history; the *Sîrah* merely makes it explicit, expands it, and offers more proof than the sparse references in Scripture. The restoration of the *Kitâb al-Mubtadaɔ* and its addition to the *Sîrah* lets up peek at one of Islam's earliest attempts to come to terms with Judaism and Christianity. We see Islam before the development of the great scholastic schools of Greek philosophy. We can hear the echoes of rabbinic lore as it is read into Islamicate literary traditions. To historians and students of religion the collection of reports assembled by the genius of Ibn Ishaq is a trove of insights into the Judaic and Islamic past.

NOTES

1. The various titles and subtitles of Ibn Ishaq's work and their meanings will be discussed below. In modern Arabic it is known as *Sîrat Rasûl Allâh* [*The Biography of the Messenger of God*] or just *Sîrah* [*Biography*].
2. R. W. Bulliet, *Conversion to Islam in the Medieval Period*, 44.
3. The term "Islamicate" means the civilization founded and dominated by Muslims but which includes non-Muslims as well. It is a term coined by M. G. S. Hodgson in his *Venture of Islam*. The term "Islamic" is used to refer to matters pertaining to the religion of Islam.
4. A radical reading of this early period can be found in Patricia Crone and Michael Cook, *Hagarism*. Their reading of both the Muslim and non-Muslim sources leads them to reject nearly all the commonly held views about the origins of Islam. Some of the notions that these authors advance are not new. Ignaz Goldziher, *Muhammedanische Studien*, and J. Schacht, *The Origins of Muhammadan Jurisprudence*, challenged the notions of the beginnings of Islamic law by showing that the development of *Hadith* transmission was a result of sectarian and party disputes in Islam after the death of Muhammad. The thesis of *Hagarism* has been rejected by many reviewers in part on polemical grounds. The value of the thesis is that it underscores the complexity of early Islamic beginnings which are often covered over by the simplicity of the foundation myths.
5. John Wansbrough, *The Sectarian Milieu*, 70.
6. Wansbrough, *Sectarian Milieu*, 1.
7. There are several stories about the canon of the Quran within the Muslim commentaries on the Scripture. In one version it is assumed that what Muhammad received was complete within his lifetime, that it was checked by the angel Gabriel to ensure that it conformed to the heavenly prototype [Arabic *Umm al-Kitâb*, "Mother of the Book"], and that this material was transmitted to the Companions. But in addition there is the story that the Quran was in danger of becoming corrupted or lost, so that the caliph Uthman commissioned a group of scholars headed by Zayd b. Thabit, Muhammad's secretary, to collect and write down an official version. Copies of the Quran in use today are supposed to derive from the Uthmanic recension that was sent out to all the metropolitan centers of Islam with orders to destroy all deviant copies. Notwith-

standing the acceptance of a notion of a single authoritative recension, many Muslims also admit to a series of canonical versions or reading of the text, often reckoned as seven in number.

John Burton, *The Collection of the Qurʾân*, examined the various Muslim traditions about the formation of the Quranic canon and concluded that the Quranic text was essentially complete within Muhammad's lifetime. John Wansbrough, *Quranic Studies*, examining the same traditions, concludes that the process of canonization was tied to the formation of the community and was protracted over a considerable length of time. He would not date the recognition of the canon of the Quran before the beginning of the third/ninth century (p. 52). See below for the implications of these differing views with respect to the Sîrah.

8. Fuat Sezgin, *Geschichte des arabischen Schrifttums* 1:297–99.

9. I recommend Alfred Guillaume, *The Life of Muhammad*, as the best translation of Ibn Hisham's epitome.

10. The chief sources for the biographical details of Ibn Ishaq are: Ibn Saʿd, *Kitâb at-Ṭabaqât al-Kabîr* vii–2:67; Ibn an-Nadim, *Kitâb al-Fihrist*, 92; Yaqut, *Irshâd* vi–1:399–401; al-Khaṭîb Al-Baghdadi, Taʾrîkh Baghdâd 1:214–34; Ibn Hajar, *Tahdhîb at-Tahdhîb* 9:38–46. These are presented in the second volume of Wuestenfeld's edition of the Sîrah. Johannes Fueck's monograph, *Muḥammad b. Isḥâq: literarhistorische Untersuchungen*, is still to be relied on for an analysis of this material, but one should also see Guillaume, introduction, and the discussions in N. Abbott's *Studies in Arabic Literary Papyri,*, vols. 1 and 2. An up-to-date bibliographic discussion of Ibn Ishâq's literary output and his relation to other writers is to be found in Sezgin, *Geschichte*. See also J. M. B. Jones, "Ibn Isḥâk."

11. Yaqut, *Irshâd*, 399.

12. Sezgin, *Geschichte*, 290.

13. A. Fischer, *Biographien, von Gewährsmännern des Ibn Isḥâq*; Guillaume, *Life*. A *Sanad* (also *Isnad*) is a chain of attribution for a tradition much like the rabbinic *shalshelet*. It starts with the reciter and proceeds backward to the ultimate source: I heard from so-and-so, who heard from so-and-so, who heard from so-and-so, etc. Eventually Muslim scholars regard the best *Sanads* as those in which each member is above reproach, lived in the correct place and time to have heard and transmitted the information, and whose words are corroborated by other reliable witnesses. This becomes the standard method of authenticating *Hadith* reports in Islam, and the oral base is preserved even when material is transmitted through written form.

14. Fischer, *Biographien*.

15. Fueck, *Muḥammad b. Isḥâq*, 30.

16. Guillaume, *Life*, xii.

17. Ibn Hisham, *Sîrat*, 2:vii.

18. Guillaume, *Life*, xxxiv.

19. Abbott, *Studies* 1:87ff.

20. Abbott, *Studies* 1:87.

21. Yaqut, *Irshâd* 6:400.

22. Yaqut, *Irshâd*, 6:400. He is reported to have said that Ibn Ishaq was a *dajjal* from among the *dajajil*.

23. Ibn Hajar al-ʿAsqalani, *Tahdhîb at-Tahdhîb* 9:41. This methodology would be regarded as quite reliable today, and is often called oral history. Attitudes toward non-Arab Muslims and converts to Islam in the early periods were often harsh and prejudiced. Those who claimed true Arab descent would often reject traditions from non-Arab Muslims, and the non-Arab would often try to hide his genealogy. The dispute

between Ibn Ishaq and Malik b. Anas may have been a result of Ibn Ishaq's repeating a charge that Malik was of non-Arab stock.

24. Guillaume, *Life*, xl. It is probable that the charges of heterodoxy leveled against Ibn Ishaq do not reflect the opinions of his contemporaries but those of later scholars looking back. If so, then the disagreement between Malik and Ibn Ishaq was based on competition between two powerful scholars.

25. Guillaume, *Life*, xl.

26. Guillaume, *Life*, xl.

27. Abbott, *Studies* 1:89ff. It can be noted that the prince's name was Muhammad b. ʿAbdullah, the same as the Prophet, and that Ibn Ishaq's name was also Muhammad.

28. Abbott, *Studies*, 1:89.

29. Fueck, *Muḥammad b. Isḥâq*, 44; Abbott, *Studies*, 92. The chief students of Ibn Ishaq were (dates where known are according to the Islamic calendar):

ʿAbdah b. Sulaym (187)
ʿAbdullah b. Idris al-Awdi (115–192)
ʿAbdullah b. Numayr (115–199)
Abu Yusuf (113–182)
ʿAli b. Mujahid (100–182)
Harun b. Abu ʾIsa
Husayn b. Hasan al-ʿAwfi (201)
Ibrahim b. al-Mukhtar
Ibrahim b. Saʿd (110–184)
Jarir b. Hazim (85–170)
Muhammad b. Salamah al-Harrani (191)
Muhammad b. Saʿid al-Umawi
Salamah b. al-Fadl al-Abrash (191)
Saʿid b. Baziʿ
ʿUthman b. Saj (ca. 180)
Yahya b. Saʿid al-Umawi (114–194)

30. Abbott, *Studies*, 1:94. This was the approved method of receiving traditions, the combination of *samʿ* (hearing) and *ʿard* (presenting the notes taken during *samʿ* for correction). In large lectures the master would have assistants who would repeat what the master had said and would often check the notes of the students. When the student was able to recite verbatim the words of the master, he was entitled to an *ijaza*, usually written in his notebook, which certified that he was empowered to teach the material to someone else.

31. Abbott, *Studies* 1:94.

32. Ibn Hisham, *as-Sîrah an-Nabawiyya*, vol. 1; English text in Guillaume, *Life*, 691.

33. Abbott, *Studies* 1:88ff.

34. See the section on Isaiah, below, in which the prophet is made to predict the advent of both Jesus and Muhammad.

35. A glance at Sezgin, *Geschichte*, will show that *maghazi* collections existed before Ibn Ishaq and were available to him in more or less final form. We assume that this is also true of some of the sections in the *Kitâb al-Mubtadaʾ*. Ibn Ishaq united independent sources into a thematic whole to produce his innovative world history.

36. In addition, many of his *Sanads* are incomplete or otherwise defective. See Ibn Hisham, *Kitâb at-Tîjân*, passim.

37. The question of the elimination of some of the poetry from the *Sîrah* remains problematic pending a thorough study of it against the poetry, both good and bad, of the ʾUmayyad period. Without a doubt much of it falls short of the expectations of both

medieval and modern critics; see Guillaume, *Life*, xxvff. Only a few lines survive from the corpus of the *Kitâb al-Mubtada*ʾ and probably for reasons advanced in the criticism of the poetry of the other sections. The charge that Ibn Ishaq made up or had his friends make up poetry for the various sections remains unproved and, for the most part, unlikely; see Ibn an-Nadim, *Fihrist*, 92. Ibn Ishaq's attribution of the poetry to known transmitters and his generally careful attribution of sources leads one to believe that he cared less about the quality of the poetry which he found than the fact that it was included in the traditions he was transmitting. It is true that the matter of the preservation of poetry from the people of ʿAd, all of whom were supposed to have been destroyed, strains one's credulity, but no more so than the whole of the story; and it is hard to imagine Ibn Ishaq making up verses in the face of such an obvious anachronism.

38. F. Rosenthal, "Influence of Biblical Tradition on Muslim Historiography," 5. The question of making sense of the "biblical" references in the Quran is complicated by the absence of a fixed canonical text at this early period of Islamic history; see Wansbrough, *Quranic Studies*, 52. The very process of explaining the Quran in terms of Jewish and Christian Scripture necessarily changed what was understood as the Quranic canon. Nevertheless, it appears that the early Muslim exegetes granted authority to antecedent Jewish and Christian texts as long as those texts did not disagree with what, in their opinion, was in the Quran. There was no agreement about the content of the Quran, however.

I have chosen to translate *Ahl al-Kitâb* as People of Scripture rather than People of the Book, as it is usually translated, because God's word, which was what seems to have been meant by *Kitâb*, referred to more than just written scripture bound in a book or scroll. It included oral scripture, as, for example, the oral Torah for Jews.

39. Abbott, *Studies* 2:9.

40. Abbott, *Studies* 2:8.

41. G. D. Newby, "Observations About an Early Judaeo-Arabic," 212–21.

42. His interest in ancient texts was coupled with Quranic studies, and he was one of the four whom Muhammad directed to be community leaders for Quran instruction.

43. Abbott, *Studies* 2:9.

44. This is shown by the readiness with which even the pagan Meccans understood the biblical references in the Quran.

45. Hodgson, *Venture of Islam* 1:317.

46. Abbott, *Studies* 2:9–10.

47. Bulliet, *Conversion to Islam*, 59.

48. As Bulliet observes, it is only by the year 1000 that it became acceptable for a child to have a Persian rather than an Arabic name (*Conversion*, 71). Before that, Arabic and distinctly Islamic names were given as badges of one's centrality in the Islamic community.

49. M. J. Kister, "Ḥaddithû ʿan banî isrâʾîla." This is clear indication that we can assume, at least in oral form, an Arabic "Targum" to account for some of the passages of Scripture found among Islamic commentators on the Quran.

50. This is the doctrine of *tahrif*, in which it is assumed that Jews and Christians "corrupted" their Scriptures to their advantage. This allowed the Quran to hold the preeminent place as the corrective to the mistakes of the past. This doctrine is discussed by many commentators on the Quran; see, e.g., az-Zamakhshârî, *al-Kashshâf*, 1:530 et passim. In modern times the Mormons have held a similar doctrine about the relationship between the Book of Mormon and the Bible.

51. It is difficult to translate *Shari'ah*. The usual definition, Islamic religious law, comes close in most cases, but *Shari'ah* is more like Jewish Halakhah than Christian canon law in its scope and structure. For a thorough explication of the problem, see Hodgson, *Venture of Islam* 1: 315–58, and N. J. Coulson, *A History of Islamic Law*.

52. "School" is the word usually used to translate *madhhab*, "chosen way [of behavior]." The schools are usually named after a founder: Maliki after Malik b. Anas, Hanafi after Abu Hanifa. Sometimes the groups would split when there were rival disciples strong enough to form their own factions. The process in Shi'i Islam is similar to Sunni Islam; the major differences revolve around areas of Shi'i personal piety and loyalty to the imams.

53. For a discussion of the use of an idealized notion of Medina in Malik's legal thinking, see, Hodgson, *Venture of Islam*, 1:320–22.

54. See J. Coulson, *History of Islamic Law*, 53ff.

55. Judaism had faced a similar problem earlier when the Torah alone proved insufficient as a guide for conduct in a complex society. A means had to be found to preserve the integrity of Scripture while allowing for dynamic adaptation. For Judaism, the answer was found in rabbinic commentary in the Talmud.

56. See S. Pines, "Al-'Îsâwiyya," and S. Wasserstrom, "Species of Misbelief: A History of Muslim Heresiography of the Jews," 314–40. The group also held that Jesus was a prophet for the Christians. This accommodationist approach seems aimed at raising the status of Jews, who were losing political power and religious influence.

57. Hodgson, *Venture of Islam*, 1:372–84.

58. Patricia Crone and Martin Hinds, *God's Caliph*, 85.

59. They claimed to be *Ahl al-Bayt* (members of the Prophet's extended family).

60. The Abbasids made use of Mu'tazilite theology in this struggle. The notion that the Quran was created has to be seen as an attempt to prevent its being privileged over caliphal authority in religious matters. Similarly, Mu'tazilite rejection of any allegorical interpretations which could elevate Muhammad above the status of a mere man also contributed to their arguments with those advancing the supremacy of the *Shari'ah*. See Crone and Hinds, *God's Caliph*, 97ff. for a discussion of the results of al-Mutawakkil's abolishing the *Mihna*.

61. An example of this is the preservation of the so-called Constitution of Medina in the *Sîrah*, in which Jews as well as Muslims constitute the *Umma* (community).

62. Shi'ites were not as easily tolerated because they held a drastically different view of authority. The interposition of the imam between the believer and God ran exactly counter to the *Shari'ah* proponents' notion of the equality of Muslims before God.

63. The word *Sirah* originally was synonymous with the word *Sunnah*. *Sirah* meant "course or way," and parallels the Hebrew Halakhah, which also meant "course or way" before becoming the term for Jewish law. After the period of the elevation of *Sunnah*, the word *Sirah* loses its legal meaning and becomes the normal term for biography, particularly the biography of Muhammad.

64. At the popular level of personal pietistic veneration of Muhammad, celebrations of the Prophet's birthday developed which are part of Muslim festivities in many places today. One feature of these is the recitation of the events of Muhammad's life, often in panegyrical verse, but following the events as they are presented in Ibn Ishaq's *Sîrah*.

65. See M. J. Kister, "The *Sîrah* Literature," 356.

66. See R. G. Khoury, *Wahb b. Munabbih*.

67. See Sezgin, *Geschichte*, 275–87.

68. For a discussion of at-Tabari's life and works, see Yaqut, *Irshâd*, and R. Paret, "Al-Tabarî," with bibliography cited there.

69. Sezgin, *Geschichte*, 343.

70. Ibn Hajar, *Tahdhîb*, 7:144–45.

71. Sezgin, *Geschichte*, 337.

72. al-Maqdisi, *Kitâb al-Bad* 1:149.

73. Abbott, *Studies* 1:32ff.

74. Sezgin, *Geschichte*, 289.

75. Yaqut, *Irshâd*, 6:430.

76. The best available English translation of Ibn Hisham's recension of the *Sîrah* is Guillaume, *The Life of Muhammad*. Guillaume has recovered some portions of the biography excised by Ibn Hisham but none of the *Kitâb al-Mubtada*.

77. Frank E. Reynolds and Donald Capps, *The Biographical Process*, 3.

78. Guillaume, *Life*, 370: "I have pieced together the following story about the battle of Uḥud, from what I was told by Muhammad b. Muslim al-Zuhrî and Muhammad b. Yaḥyâ b. Ḥibbân and ʿÂṣim b. ʿUmar b. Qatâda and Al-Ḥuṣayn b. ʿAbduʾl-Raḥmân b. ʿAmr b. Saʿd b. Muʿâdh and other learned traditionists. One or the other, or all of them, is responsible for the following narrative." Compared to the narrative of the battle of Badr, Muhammad's first victory, the flow of the telling is rough and disorganized. One gets the sense that there was still active debate among the descendants of the battle's participants who were trying to vindicate the actions of their fathers or grandfathers.

79. Douglas J. Stewart, "Mythomorphism in Greco-Roman Historiography: The Case of the Royal *Gamos*," 188–89. Explications of "myth and history" can be found in the numerous writings of M. Eliade.

80. These categories are patterned after those given by Earle Waugh, "Following the Beloved: Muhammad as Model in the Ṣûfî Tradition," 63.

81. Aminah bt. Wahb, who, in keeping with hagiographic patterns, was described as the most excellent woman among the Qureysh in birth and position at that time.

82. Guillaume, *Life*, 68.

83. Guillaume, *Life*, 72.

84. See the story of Jonah, who fled from God because the mantle of prophethood was too heavy for him to bear.

85. Zamzam was the well in Mecca dug for Abraham's son Ishmael after he was sent out into the desert.

86. Guillaume, *Life*, 62–68.

87. G. D. Newby, "Abraha and Sennacherib: A Talmudic Parallel to the Tafsir on Surat al-Fil."

88. *Genesis Rabbah* 55.7.

89. The rock is the Foundation Stone [Hebrew *'Eben Shtîyah*]. God is supposed to have stood on this rock when he formed the earth and left his footprint there. In Christian legend Jesus is supposed to have ascended to heaven from this rock, and the footprint is his. In Islamic lore Muhammad stood on the rock on his way to heaven, leaving his footprint. Many Jews believe that the rock supported the Holy of Holies when the Temple stood. The Islamic shrine of the Dome of the Rock now covers this rock. It can be noted that Abraham left his footprint near the Kaʿbah in Mecca when he made his Pilgrimage there, thus equating the two sites.

90. Guillaume, *Life*, 652.

91. Guillaume, *Life*, 183.

92. By "privileging" the Bible, I mean that it is regarded as an "ur-version." Those

who privilege the Bible regard it as earlier than rabbinic literature or the Quran. When a figure such as Abraham occurs in both, then the earlier version is the privileged version and the model against which all subsequent versions are measured. If one assumes with Muslims that the Quran represents the correct version of God's word (or actually God's word), then it is the privileged version despite the appearance of the Quran historically later than the Bible.

93. This is the notion of *tahrif* referred to above.

94. Frequently Ibn Ishaq reports that he derived material from Jews and/or Christians. In addition, his detractors recognized that as part of his methodology.

95. R. Bell, *Introduction to the Qurʾân*, 110–13.

96. Q. 38:33–34 alludes to Solomon's preference for the things of this world, in this case horses, which distracted him from God's worship. Therefore, he slaughtered the horses so that they would not be a temptation for him. They were also intended as a sacrifice to God.

97. Barbara Herrnstein Smith, "Narrative Versions, Narrative Theories," 212. For Muslims, as well as Jews and Christians, there needs to be divine intervention, usually a heavenly messenger, to overcome the barrier between the realm of "pure Being," God's abode, and our earthly realm. For Muslims that messenger was Gabriel, who brought a portion of the heavenly book to Muhammad.

98. Smith, "Narrative Versions," 222.

99. For a discussion of some of the problems of the historiography of the early Islamic period, see G. D. Newby, *A History of the Jews of Arabia*.

100. Barakat Ahmad, *Muhammad and the Jews*, 9–11.

101. Ahamd, *Muhammad and the Jews*, 10.

102. M. J. Kister, "The Massacre of the Banû Qurayẓa: A Re-examination of a Tradition."

103. The theme of redemption through struggle and sacrifice against the rejectors is found early in Islam. The Arabic root **f-d-y* has that sense, and from the root we get the word "Fedayeen" (fidaʾiyun), "freedom fighters," those who are willing to sacrifice themselves to redeem a land, a cause, etc.

104. There is not the question in the two genealogies in the *Sîrah* of linking Muhammad to the Davidic line and the house of Jesse as was the case with the genealogies of Jesus in the Gospels of Matthew and Luke. Ibn Ishaq does not present Muhammad as a claimant to the Jewish messianic position.

105. The story of the binding of Isaac in Genesis 22 has provided powerful symbols for Judaism, Christianity, and Islam. Isaac was understood to be a lamb for slaughter (after Gen. 22:8) who did not protest (Is. 53:7). Jewish sacrificial laws required that the sacrificial victim be without blemish. When Jesus is called the Lamb of God (John 1:29) in a reprise of Isaac's binding (Hebrew *ʿAqêdah*), two claims are made: one, that Jesus is perfect, and two, that Jesus is the new heir to the Abrahamic legacy. In the *Kitâb al-Mubtadaʾ*, Ishmael willingly submits to the sacrificial preparations, thus establishing his place as the unprotesting lamb and the unblemished heir to Abraham's God-given heritage.

106. Guillaume, *Life*, 112.

107. Guillaume, *Life*, 451.

108. Guillaume, *Life*, 452. In a version of this report that follows immediately after, Muhammad is said to have performed the same miracle with lamb and rice pilaff.

109. Sezgin, *Geschichte*, 288–90.

110. W. M. Thackston, *The Tales of the Prophets of al-Kisaʾi*.

111. The popular practice of magic in pre-Islamic West Asia was associated with

Solomon in the *Sefer HaRazim* and the *Testament of Solomon*, two pseudepigraphic works. See James Charlesworth, *The Old Testament Pseudepigrapha*, 1:949n. Solomon also appears within the praxis of magic bowls, inscribed bowls which contained prophylactic incantations designed for maintaining good health. There is only the faintest support in the Bible for the notion that Solomon possessed esoteric wisdom, so it is easy to understand the Quranic objections.

112. See G. D. Newby, "Arabian Jewish History in the Sîrah."

113. See e.g., the story of ʿAmir b. Zarib and his servant, Sukhayla, discussed in G. D. Newby, "The Sîrah as a Source for Early Arabian Jewish History."

Creation, Adam and Eve

The narrative of creation and the stories about Adam and Eve serve two functions. The first function is to fill in the gaps in the Quranic stories. The Quran does not give a complete narrative of the sequence of creation, and what passages are there often seem fragmentary or epigrammatic. The stories that Ibn Ishaq has collected fill in the spaces and expand the Quranic material. In only one place is his inclusion at variance with the Quran; namely, in deciding what was created first, Ibn Ishaq reports that light and darkness were the first creations, after which Allah distinguished between the two of them, making night and day. At-Tabari prefers the traditions derived from Ibn ʿAbbas, which contend that God was seated on his throne above the heavenly waters before creation, and that the first thing he created was the pen. Ibn Ishaq adheres more closely to the biblical account, probably because his sources were the People of the Scripture. The notion, popular among later Muslims, that the pen was the first creation is most likely based on *Surah* 96, but could reflect an extension of the Christian notion that the pen is an extension of the Logos or Word.

In addition to commentary on the Quran, a second important function of this section is to associate Adam with Mecca and the first worship of God. This is part of a larger literary movement that sought to replace Jerusalem with Mecca, often by extensive use and modification of Jewish traditions about Jerusalem. After the expulsion from Paradise, Adam fell to earth in Ceylon (now Sri Lanka) and Eve fell in Arabia at Jiddah. The Arabic text does not explain why they did not fall together, but according to one Jewish tradition Adam and Ever were separated while Eve was pregnant (Ginzberg, *Legends* 1:105ff). After the fall, Adam immediately went to Mecca, where he established proper worship of God. This tradition, too, accords with Jewish legend that has Adam establish the Jewish festivals (see *Midrash Bereshit Rabbah 26.1* and 34.9, where Noah reestablishes worship at Adam's altar, an account that parallels Abraham's reestablishing worship at the Kaʿbah.) Adam's journey to Mecca makes him the first pilgrim. According to Islamic belief, all the major prophets performed the Pilgrimage to the Kaʿbah. Before his death Adam wrote down what had been commanded by God and thus became the first prophet. The tradition of Adam's prophethood is found in Jewish sources (*Seder Olam* 21) but is also paralleled by the Christian notion that Adam is the first of a series of which Jesus is the last. (See Rev. 1:8 et passim, where Jesus is referred to as the Alpha and Omega, which itself is a quote of Isaiah 44:6.)

The stories in this section, like most of the stories in Ibn Ishaq's collection, appear to be based on stories that have already been shaped by rabbinic discussions. For example, the story that the tree from which Adam and Eve ate was called the wheat tree shows the dependence of these traditions on rabbinic exegesis. The word for wheat in Hebrew is a homonym with the word for sin, and the rabbis identify the plant as a wheat tree which grew as tall as the cedars of Lebanon. The version of the story here is merely a translation into Arabic of the rabbinic exegetical pun. This pun is carried through the narrative when we see that Cain offers wheat to God as his sacrifice.

Even when the discussions appear to be from a purely Islamic context, we can often see parallels with earlier Jewish and Christian exegesis. For example, we read that Adam was created in the last hour of the last day of Creation. This is usually taken as a gloss to Quran 76:1, "Has there come upon man any period of time in which he was an unremembered thing?" But in *Sanhedrin* 38a the rabbis also argue that Adam was created last so that the Sadducees could not say that God had a partner in Creation. The etiology for *Yawm al-jum'ah* (the Day of Congregation, or Friday, the day of Muslim congregational prayer) as the last day of Creation because this was the "fullness" [*Ijtima'*] of the creative acts is part of the polemic against the Jews and Christians. Jewish sources contain God's conversation with the angels and their opposition to the creation of Adam because he and his offspring would defile the earth. (See, e.g., *Midrash Bemidbar Rabbah* 19.3, and references cited in Ginzberg, *Legends* 5:69.) The identification of the angel 'Azazil with the Devil is made by Origen (*Contra Celsum* 6.43); in *Pirke R. Eliezer* (46) the identification is with Samael.

Text

In the name of God, the Merciful and the Compassionate

Concerning God's saying, "And He was the One who created the heavens and the earth in six days; and His throne was upon the water" [Q 11:7], Muhammad b. Ishaq said: It was as the Blessed and Most High described Himself: There was nothing but water upon which was the throne, which possessed might, power, and authority. The first thing that God created was light and darkness. Then He separated the two of them, and He made the darkness into night, black and murky. He made the light into day, bright and sight-giving. Then He vaulted the seven heavens out of smoke. Some say that it was out of steam, but God knows best. Thus they stood by themselves. He had not yet set orbits for the stars, and He made night dark in the lowest heaven and doused its light. Night and day coursed through it, but it was still without a sun or a moon or stars. Then He spread out the earth and anchored it with mountains. He assigned nourishment for the earth and put what creatures He pleased on it. And in four days, He completed the earth and the nourishment He had decreed.

Then He turned to the heavens, which were smoke, as was said, and He gave them their courses. He fixed the sun, the moon, and the stars in the lowest heaven, and He imparted rule to each heaven. He completed their creation in two days and finished the creation of the heavens and the earth in six days. On the seventh day He mounted His heavens. He said to the heavens and the earth, "Come, willingly or unwillingly"; do as I wish, and be calmed willingly or unwillingly. Both of them said, "We come willingly" [Q 41:11].

The People of the Torah say that He began the Creation on Sunday and finished it on the Sabbath, and He made it a festival for His servants, making it great, honored, and noble. The People of the Gospels say that the beginning was on Monday and that the end was on Sunday. Muslims say that the beginning of creation was on the Sabbath and the completion was on Friday, for Friday is called the Day of Congregation on account of the coming together of creation on that day.

The People of the Book claim that God created the angels from fire. Fire and light are the same here in the sense of refined light. Ibn Ishaq said on the authority of Khallad b. ʿAtâ, who got it from Taus, who reported from Ibn ʿAbbas: Before Iblis fomented rebellion among the angels, his name was Azazil. He dwelt on earth and was the most diligent and the most knowledgeable of the angels. That is what led to his pride. He was of a race called the Jinn.

Ibn Hamid reported something similar on the authority of Salamah, who got it from Ibn Ishaq reporting from Khallad, who got it from Taus or Mujahid Abu-l-Hajjaj, who got it from Ibn ʿAbbas, only he said: He was an angel whose name was Azazil. He lived on the earth, and among the angels who dwelt on the earth were those called the Jinn.

When God wished to use His power to create Adam as an obedience test of Adam, the angels, and all of creation, He assembled the heavenly and earthly angels and said, "I am going to put a viceroy on earth" [Q 2:30], an inhabitant or dweller who will live in it and populate it with creatures other than you. Having told them about His plan, He said, They will act corruptly on the earth, shed blood, and foment rebellion. Together they said, "Will you put there one who will act corruptly and shed blood while we sing praises to you and sanctify you?" [Q 2:30] We do not disobey nor do we do anything which you hate. He said, "I know what you do not" [Q 2:30]. I have more knowledge than you. There is no other way but for them to be rebellious, corrupt, shedders of blood, and doers on the earth of what I hate, as I stated about the sons of Adam. God said to the angels, " . . . I will create a mortal of clay, and when I have fashioned him and breathed my spirit into him, fall down prostrating to him" [Q 38:72]. The angels heeded His admonition and took the words to heart. All agreed to obey Him except Iblis, the Enemy of God. He kept silent because of the envy, covetousness, and pride in his soul.

God created Adam from earth out of sticky clay which He shaped with His hand, giving him honor and making him great by His command. It is said, and God knows best, that God created Adam and then put him aside for forty days before he breathed the spirit in him so that he became dry clay like pottery untouched by fire. His creation was on Friday at the last hour. That is because of God's words, "Has there come upon man a time when he was a thing not remembered?" [Q 76:1] The People of the Torah give an exegesis that God created Adam in His image when He wished to give Adam dominion over the earth and what is in it. It is said, and God knows best, that when the spirit got into his head, he sneezed and said, Praise be to God, and his Lord said to him, God bless you.

When Adam stood up, the angels fell down prostrating to him, remembering God's admonition, obeying His order. The Enemy of God, Iblis, stood among them, and he did not prostrate himself out of pride, desire, and envy. He said to him, "O Iblis, what prevents you from prostrating to what I created with my hands . . . up to His words . . . I will fill Hell with you and those who follow you" [Q 38:76–86]. When God finished censuring Iblis and he still refused to do anything but rebel, God cast a curse on him and expelled him from the Garden. Then He went to Adam and taught him all names. He said "O Adam, inform them of their names . . . up to His words . . . You are the Knower, the Wise" [Q 2:31-32].

Adam walked upright, and there was no other animal on the earth walking like him. The Eagle came to the sea and said to the Fish, I have seen a creature walking on his hind feet. It has two hands to attack with, and on each hand are five fingers. The Fish said, It is my opinion that you are describing a creature that will not leave you alone in the height of the air nor leave me alone in the depth of the sea.

ʿAbdullah b. al-ʿAbbas reported on the authority of the People of Scripture, the People of the Torah, and other scholars that God cast a sleep over Adam. He took one of his ribs from an opening in his left side and repaired the place with flesh while Adam slept, not waking from his slumber. Then God created Eve from his rib as a mate for him. He made her a woman so that Adam would find her a comfort. When sleep was lifted from him, and he awoke from his slumber, he saw her at his side, and he said, according to what they say, and God knows best, My flesh and my blood and my mate. So he was comforted by her.

Now that God had made a mate for Adam and gave him comfort, He said to him, "Enter, O Adam, you and your mate; dwell in the garden and eat what is pleasant there. But do not come near this tree, for you will be among the sinners" [cf. Q 2:35]

Creation, Adam and Eve

Ibn ʿAbbas used to say on the authority of a scholar who got it from Mujahid that the tree which Adam was forbidden was the wheat tree. Some of the people of the Yemen, on the authority of Wahb b. Munabbih the Yemenite, used to say that it was the wheat tree, but the fruit from it in the Garden was like the kidneys of the cow, softer than butter and sweeter than honey. The People of the Torah would say that it was the wheat tree. Yaʿqub b. ʿUtbah related that it was the tree which the angels used to touch in order to live forever.

On the authority of Layth b. Abu Sulaym, who got it from Taus the Yamanite, Ibn ʿAbbas said that the Enemy of God, Iblis, presented himself to the animals of the world to see which one of them would carry him into the Garden to talk with Adam and his wife. All of the animals refused until he talked with the serpent. He said to her, I will protect you from the children of Adam; you will be under my protection if you get me into the Garden. So she placed him between her two fangs. Then she went in with him, and the two of them spoke from her mouth. She was graceful, walking up on all fours, but God, the Most High, afflicted her and made her walk on her belly. Ibn ʿAbbas used to say, Kill her wherever you find her, and watch out for the protection of the Enemy of God over her.

Some scholars said that when Adam, peace be upon him, entered the Garden, saw the noble things in it and what God had given him out of it, said, If only we could live forever. When the Devil heard that from him, he discovered his weakness and came to him offering eternal life. The first of the Devil's plots against Adam and Eve was that he wept over them, mourning them. When they heard it, they said to him, What makes you to weep? He said, I weep for the two of you, because you will die and leave the pleasure and honor you are in. That struck their very souls. Then the Devil came to them and whispered to them, saying, O Adam, "Shall I lead you to the tree of eternal life and the power of not growing old?" [Q 20:120] "Your Lord did not keep you from this tree except that you would become two angels or that you would become immortal. And, he swore to the two of them: I am one of the well-wishers for you" [Q 7:20–21], that is, you two will become angels or you will live forever. Even if you are not two angels, you will not die while in the pleasure of the Garden. This is according to God's words, "He led them with vanities" [Q 7:22].

Saʿid b. al-Mussayib said on the authority of Yazid b. ʿAbdullah b. Qusayt, I heard him swear by God that there was no doubt that Adam did not eat from the tree while he had all his senses. Eve plied him with an intoxicating beverage. When he became drunk, she led him to the tree, and he ate of it. When Adam and Eve sinned, God expelled them from the Garden and denied them the pleasure and honor which they had. He flung them down and caused enmity on the earth between them, Iblis, and the serpent. Their Lord said to them, Go down as enemies, some of you against the other.

Ibn ʿAbbas and the People of the Torah said that the Devil came to Adam and his wife with God's authority, which He had given to him, to test Adam and his progeny and that he comes to the son of Adam in his sleep, while awake, and in every state. The Devil comes to call him to rebellion and put lust in his soul, but he is not seen.

God said, "The Devil whispered to the two of them and caused them to go out of what they were in" [Q 7:20, 2:36 conflation]. And He said, "O Children of Adam, do not let Satan seduce you as he expelled your parents from the Garden and tore their clothes off of them to show them their shame. He sees you, he and his tribe, from whence you see them not. We have made devils protectors to those who do not believe" [Q 7:27].

God said to His Prophet, upon him be prayers and peace, "Say, I seek refuge in the Lord of the people, the King of the people . . . up to the end of the chapter" [Q 114:1–6]. Then he mentioned the account which was transmitted about the Prophet, the prayers and peace of God be upon him, that the Devil flows in mankind's bloodstream. Ibn Ishaq said, The son of Adam was instructed about what was between him and the Enemy of God just as it was commanded between him and Adam. God said, "Go down from it; it is not for you to show pride here; so go out; you are of the debased" [Q 7:13]. Then the Devil went to Adam and his wife to talk with them, as God told us in their story: "The Devil whispered to him, saying, O Adam, shall I lead you to the tree of eternity and the power of not growing old?" [Q 20:120] The Devil went to them as he has gone to Adam's offspring ever since, they unable to see him. And, God knows best, they repented to their Lord.

The People of the Torah said, Adam fell down in India on a mountain called Wasim in a valley called Bahil between ad-Dahnaj and al-Mandal, two areas in the land of India. Eve fell to Jiddah in the land of Mecca. Adam fell on the mountain, and with him were leaves from the Garden. He spread them on that mountain, and from them was the root of all good things and all fruit found nowhere but India. When Adam, upon him be peace, was cast down to the earth, he grieved about missing what he used to see and hear of God's worship in the Garden. So God gave him a place to live in the Holy House and commanded him to travel to it. He journeyed to it, never making camp without God's providing a spring of water for him, until he came to Mecca. He remained there worshiping God at that house and circumambulating it, and it did not cease to be his home until God buried him there.

It reached me that Iblis, after he was expelled from the Garden, married the serpent whose mouth he entered when he spoke to Adam, upon him be peace, and they had offspring.

According to some scholars of the People of the First Book, Adam, upon him be peace, had been having sexual intercourse with Eve in the Garden before the sin, and she bore him Cain, the son of Adam, and his twin sister.

She did not crave certain foods during pregnancy, nor was she uncomfortable, nor did she experience labor pains when she bore the two of them. And she did not menstruate because of the purity of the Garden. After the two of them ate from the tree, rebelled, fell to the earth, settled down and had intercourse, she bore Abel and his twin sister. With the two of them, she craved certain foods and experienced discomfort. She had labor pains when she bore them, and she saw blood with them. And Eve, according to what they say, never bore any children except twins, one a male and one a female. Eve bore Adam forty children, male and female, in twenty pregnancies.

There was a man who wished to marry no one but his twin who was born with him, but she was not licit to him. That was because there was not a woman at the time except their sisters and their mother Eve. On the authority of some of the scholars of the First Book, Adam commanded his son Cain to marry the twin of Abel, and he ordered Abel to marry the twin of Cain. Abel agreed to that and was pleased, but Cain refused, hated to show generosity to Abel's sister, and loathed to have his own sister with Abel. He said, We are Children of Paradise, and they are Children of the Earth; I have more right to my sister. Some of the scholars of the First Book say that, on the contrary, Cain's sister was one of the most beautiful people, and he begrudged her to his brother and wanted her for himself, and God knows which is so. His father said to him, O my son, she is not licit for you. But Cain refused to accept that on his father's authority, so his father said to him, O my son, offer a sacrifice, and your brother Abel will offer a sacrifice. Which of the two of your sacrifices God accepts, he has the greater right to her.

Cain was a sower of the earth, and Abel a tender of flocks; Cain offered wheat, and Abel offered the firstlings of his sheep and goats, and some say he even sacrificed a cow. God, the Mighty and the Powerful, sent a white fire which consumed Abel's sacrifice, leaving the sacrifice of Cain. That was how God, the Mighty and the Powerful, accepted sacrifices. When God accepted Abel's sacrifice, judging in his favor about Cain's sister, Cain became angry. Pride vanquished him, and the Devil urged him on. So he followed his brother Abel while he was out walking and killed him. They are the two about whom God told Muhammad, may the prayers and peace of God be upon him, in the Quran. He said, "Tell them," that is, the People of the Book, "the account of the two sons of Adam in truth, when they offered sacrifices, and it was accepted from one of them . . . to the end of the story" [Q 5:27ff].

When Abel fell before Cain, Cain did not know how to conceal him. According to what is asserted, that is because this was the first killing among Adam's children. "So God sent a raven to dig up the earth to show him how to hide the genitals of his brother. He said, Woe is me. I am not able to be as this raven and hide the genitals of my brother . . . up to His saying . . . Then many of them after that became prodigals on the earth" [Q 5:31–32].

The People of the Torah assert that God said to Cain when he killed his brother Abel, Where is your brother Abel? He said, I do not know; I am not his guardian. And God said to him, The voice of the blood of your brother calls to me even now. You are cursed on the earth which opened its mouth and received the blood of your brother from your hand. Since you did this on the earth, it will not yield its tilth to you, so that you will become frightened and lost on the earth. Cain said, My sin has become so great that you cannot forgive it, for you have expelled me today from the face of the earth, from your presence, and I will be frightened and lost on the earth. Anyone who meets me will kill me. And God, the Mighty and the Powerful, said, That will not be so. It will not be that everyone who kills will be recompensed by seven for that one, but he who kills Cain will be accounted for by seven. And God placed a sign on Cain lest anyone who found him would kill him. So Cain went out from the presence of God, the Mighty and the Powerful, from the east of the Garden of Eden.

The total number of children that Eve bore Adam was forty males and females in twenty pregnancies. The names of some of them have reached us, and some have not reached us. The names of those which reached us are fifteen men and four women, among them Cain, Abel, Liyudha, Ashuth, the daughter of Adam and her twin brother, Seth and his twin sister, Hazurah and her twin brother, born when Adam was one hundred and thirty years of age. Then Iyad, and his twin sister, Jaligh and his twin sister, Ithathi and his twin sister, Tubah and his twin sister, Bunan and his twin sister, Hayyan and his twin sister, Darabis and his twin sister, Hadhar and his twin sister, Sandal and his twin sister, and then Bariq and his twin sister. Each man of them had a woman born with him in the same pregnancy in which he was carried.

On the authority of Daud b. al-Husayn, who got it from ʿIkrimah, Ibn ʿAbbas said, Eve bore children to Adam, and he devoted them to the service of God, the Mighty and the Powerful. He named them ʿAbdullah [the Servant of God] and ʿUbaydallah [the Servant of God], and so on like that, and they died. So Iblis came to her and to Adam, upon him be peace, and said, If the two of you would name them other than what you named them, they would live. So she bore him a boy, and the two of them named him ʿAbdu-l-Harith [the servant of al-Harith]. God, the Mighty and the Powerful, sent down a message about this: "He is the one who created you from one soul . . . up to His words . . . the two of them ascribed partners to Him in what He had given them . . . to the end of the verse" [Q 7:189–190].

According to what they allege, and God knows best, when Adam's death was near, he called his son Seth, entrusted him with his legacy, taught him the hours of the night and day, and instructed him in the worship of the Creator in every hour of them. He told him that every hour has a particular characteristic for His worship. He said to him, O my son, the Flood will be upon the earth, lasting for seven years. Then he wrote his will, and Seth, according to what is mentioned, was the executor of the estate of his father Adam, upon him be peace. The leading position went to Seth after the death of Adam. According to what is transmitted on the authority of the Messenger of God, may the prayers and peace of God be upon him, God sent down fifty sheets to him.

After Adam, the prayers of God be upon him, wrote his will, he died, and the angels gathered around him because he was a friend of the Merciful. The angels, Seth and his brothers buried him east of Paradise in a village which was the first village on the earth. The sun and the moon were eclipsed seven days and nights on account of him. When the angels gathered around him, the will was taken and placed on a ladder along with the horn which our father Adam took from Paradise in order not to neglect the mention of God, the Mighty and the Powerful.

Yahya b. ʿAbaad, who got it from his father, said, I heard him say that when Adam died, upon him be peace, God sent material from the Garden to enshroud him and embalm him. Then the angels came to his grave and buried him so that the earth covered him.

On the authority of al-Hasan b. Dhakwan, who heard it from al-Hasan b. Abu-Hasan, Ubayy b. Kaʿb said, the Messenger of God, may the prayers and peace of God be upon him, said that your father Adam, may the prayers and peace of God be upon him, was as tall as a tall palm tree, sixty cubits, and very hairy, covering his genitals. When the sin touched him, his shame became apparent to him, and he fled in the Garden. A tree grabbed him and took hold of his forelock. His Lord called to him, Do you flee from me, O Adam? He said, No, by God, O Lord, except out of shame before you for what I have done. So God cast him down to the earth. But when his time of death came, God sent him the materials from Paradise to embalm and enshroud him.

When Eve saw the angels, she tried to go in to Adam without them. He said, Go away from me and the messengers of my Lord. I would not have encountered what I encountered except for you, and what happened to me would not have happened except for you. When he died, they washed him with the leaves of the lote and water separately, and wrapped him in a single garment. Then they dug a grave for him and buried him. Then they said, This is the precedent for the children of Adam after him.

Seth married his sister Hazurah, the daughter of Adam. She bore him Enosh, the son of Seth and Niʿmah, the daughter of Seth. Seth was at this time one hundred and five. He lived beyond the time he sired Enosh eight hundred and seven years. Enosh, the son of Seth, married his sister Niʿmah, the daughter of Seth, and she bore him Cainan when he was ninety years old. Enosh lived after he sired Cainan eight hundred and fifteen years, and he sired sons and daughters. And the lifespan of Enosh was nine hundred and five years.

Then Cainan, the son of Enosh, at the age of seventy married Dinah, the daughter of Barakil, the son of Mahuil, the son of Enoch, the son of Cain. She bore to him Mahalail, the son of Cainan. And Cainan lived eight hundred and forty years after he sired Mahalail. The lifespan of Cainan was nine hundred and ten years. At the age of sixty-five, Mahalail, the son of Cainan, married his maternal aunt, Sim'an, the daughter of Barakil, who was the son of Mahuil, the son of Enoch, the son of Cain, the son of Adam. She bore him Yarad at eight hundred and thirty; and sons and daughters were born to him. The lifespan of Mahalail was eight hundred and ninety-five years, and then he died.

Cain married his sister Ashuth, the daughter of Adam, and she bore him men and women, Enoch, the son of Cain, and Eden, the daughter of Cain. Enoch, the son of Cain, married his sister, the daughter of Cain, and she bore him men and women: 'Irad, the son of Enoch, Mahuil, the son of Enoch, Abushil, the son of Enoch, Mawlith, the daughter of Enoch. Abushil, the son of Enoch, married Mawlith, the daughter of Enoch, and she bore to Abushil a man whose name was Lamech. Lamech married two women: The name of the first was 'Ada, and the name of the second was Sala. 'Ada bore him Tulin, the son of Lamech, and he was the first to dwell in a structure with a cupola and acquire property, and Tuyish, and he was the first to play the cymbals. And she bore him a son whose name was Tubalcain, and he was the first to work copper and iron. Their children were giants and tyrants, and they had been given great size, so that a man, according to what they allege, would be thirty cubits.

Now the children of Cain died out, and they only left a few after them. And all of the genealogies of Adam's descendants are unknown, and their line has been cut off, except what was from Seth, the son of Adam. From him is the line and the genealogy of all the people today, excluding his father, Adam, who is really the father of mankind.

The People of the Torah say that Cain married Ashuth, and she bore him Enoch, and Irad was born to Enoch, and Irad sired Mahuil, and Mahuil sired Abushil, and Abushil sired Lamech, and Lamech married 'Ada and Sala, and the two of them bore him the ones I mentioned, and God knows best. Then at the age of one hundred and twenty-six, Yarad married Barkana, the daughter of ad-Darmasil, the son of Mahuil, the son of Enoch, the son of Cain. She bore him Akhnukh, the son of Yarad, and Akhnukh was Idris, the prophet. He was the first of the children of Adam who was given prophethood, and he wrote with the pen. Yarad lived after Akhnukh was born to him eight hundred years and sons and daughters were born to him. The lifespan of Yarad was nine hundred sixty-two years; then he died.

Then Akhnukh, the son of Yarad, married Hadanah, and, it is said, Adalah, the daughter of Bawil, the son of Mahuil, the son of Enoch, the son of Cain, the son of Adam. He was sixty-five years old when Methuselah, the son of

Akhnukh was born to him. He lived three hundred years after Methuselah was born to him, and he sired sons and daughters. The lifespan of Akhnukh was three hundred sixty-five years; then he died.

Then according to what Ibn Ishaq said, Methuselah married Araba, the daughter of Azrail, the son of Abushil, the son of Khanukh, the son of Cain, the son of Adam, when he was one hundred thirty-seven years old. Lamech, the son of Methuselah, was born to him and he lived seven hundred years after Lamech was born, and sons and daughters were born to him. The lifespan of Methuselah was nine hundred and nineteen years; then he died.

Lamech, the son of Methuselah, married Cainush, the daughter of Barakil, the son of Mahuil, the son of Enoch, the son of Cain, the son of Adam, upon him be peace. He was one hundred eighty-seven years old when Noah, the prophet, may the prayers and peace of God be upon him, was born to him. Lamech lived five hundred and ninety-five years after Noah was born to him, and his lifespan was seven hundred and eighty years; then he died. Noah, the son of Lamech, married Amrurah, the daughter of Barakil, the son of Mahuil, the son of Enoch, the son of Cain, the son of Adam, and he was five hundred years old when his sons Shem, Ham, and Japheth were born to him.

Sources

at-Tabari, *Ta'rîkh* 31, 32, 83, 91, 93, 103, 105, 108–109, 109–110, 120–121, 125–126, 139–140, 140–142, 146–147, 149, 153, 161, 161–162, 164, 165, 166, 167–168, 172-173, 176, 177–178

at-Tabari, *Tafsîr* 1:149–150, 1:193, 1:224, 1:199, 1:207, 29:205, 1:229–230, 1:231, 1:237, 1:236, 1:237, 1:238–239, 6:188, 6:194, 6:198

al-Maqdisi 1:149–150, 2:1, 2, 5, 38, 2:53, 1:169, 2:83–84, 2:81, 2:93–94, 1:99

al-Azraqi 1:9–10

ath-Tha'labi 19, 25, 26, 29

al-Baghdadi 1:448

al-Sijistani 1:4

Noah and His Issue

The story of Noah follows the Quran closely, utilizing extensive quotations and references to this popular Islamic prophet. As has been observed by both Muslim and non-Muslim scholars, the figure of Noah is conceived as a prefiguration of Muhammad. This is because he is understood as a new Adam, ushering in a new age, a view of Noah that Muslims share with Christians and Jews.

We have already noted the similarity between the rabbinic version and the Islamic version of the Noah story. This is the case particularly for the story of Noah's son Yam, but many more details can be cited throughout the whole of the account. The figure of Og ('Uj) in this Islamic version of the Noah legend also appears in rabbinic stories of this giant. He is supposed to have been born before the flood [*Niddah* 61a] and survived by riding on the ark [Pirke de R. Eliezer].

The Quranic passage "We opened the gates of heaven with pouring water and we caused the earth to gush forth springs, and the waters met according to a preordained command" [Q 54:11–12] presupposes the notion of the undoing of the original act of creation as described in Genesis, when the waters were divided. Here, the primordial waters come together, and only a few humans survive. On the number of passengers on the ark, Ibn Ishaq lists Noah, his wife, Shem, Ham, and Japheth, their wives, and six more believers. In various Muslim versions of the Noah legend the number varies between seven and eighty people, but in Ibn Ishaq's variation the passenger manifest lists enough humans for a *minyan*, the Jewish religious quorum.

The stories of the Devil's trick to enter the ark and the etiological stories of the first cats and the first pigs are similar in type to those told by early Muslim street preachers, the Qass. The early Muslim street preachers began to appear around the time of the caliph 'Umar I (634–644 C.E.), preaching on street corners and in mosques. They soon acquired considerable popular followings and sometimes had more authority among the Muslim rank and file than the learned scholars. It appears that these preachers were purveyors of a wide variety of stories, some of which appear in rabbinic literature. The popularity of the preachers helped assimilate these stories into general use in sermons and Quran commentaries [see Newby, "Tafsir Isra'iliyat"].

Other details to note in the story of Noah are the extensions of the genealogies and the system of chronology beyond the usual biblical parameters. By including the pre-Islamic ancestors of the Arabs, Ibn Ishaq succeeds in integrating the Arabs into the biblical panorama. It is a panorama that appropriates in a distinctly Islamic key successive periods of reckoning human history that end with the era of Muhammad. Ibn Ishaq underscores the emergence of Islam as the result of an inevitable historical progression.

Text

In the name of God, the Merciful and the Compassionate

Ibn Hamid related on the authority of Salamah, from Muhammad b. Ishaq, on the authority of one who is not to be doubted, from ʿUbayd b. ʿUmayr al-Laythi, that ʿUbayd used to say that it reached him that they used to attack him, meaning the people of Noah against Noah, and they would choke him until he would pass out. When he would recover, he would say, O Lord, forgive my people for they are unknowing. This went on until they spread rebellion, and sin became great on the earth because of them. Events turned against them, and affliction increased against Noah because of them. He waited for son after son, but every age was more wicked than the one before, until it was the last. All the while he would say, This madness was with our fathers and our uncles.

Noah's people would not accept anything from him, so Noah complained about their situation to God, the Mighty and the Powerful. He said, as God, the Mighty and the Powerful, told us in His Book, "Lord, I have called my people night and day, but my calling does not add anything but defection . . . up to the end of the story . . . when he said, Do not leave one of the unbelievers on the earth, for if you leave them, they will lead your servants astray, and I will sire not . . . up to the end of the story" [Q 71:5–27].

When Noah complained about them this way to his Lord, and asked His help against them, God, the Mighty and the Powerful, inspired him, "Build a ship under our eyes and inspiration, and do not preach to me about those who sin, for they are drowned" [Q 11:37]. So Noah accepted the building of the ship and renounced his people. He began cutting the wood and beating the iron and arranging the tackle of the ship with pitch and other things which no one could do well except him. His people began passing by him while he was working, scoffing at him and deriding him. He would say, "Though you mock us, we mock you as you are mocking, and you will know to whom a punishment which will debase him will come and upon whom a punishment which will undo him will be set" [Q 11:38–39]. And they would say, according to what reached us, O Noah, have you become a carpenter after being a prophet? So, God closed the wombs of the women [of the generation of the Flood], and they did not bear.

The People of the Torah assert that God, the Mighty and the Powerful, commanded him to build the ship of teak, that he make it curved, that he coat it with pitch inside and out, that he make its length eighty cubits, its width fifty cubits, and its height thirty cubits, that he make it with three decks, a lower, a middle, and a top, and that he put a window in it.

So Noah did as God, the Mighty and the Powerful, commanded him, until he finished it. God promised him, "When our command comes and the oven gushes forth water, then load it with two of every kind, a pair, and your household, except him to whom the word has gone forth already, and those who believe, and no one believed except a few" [Q 11:40]. The oven was set as a sign between them. He said, when the command comes, then load it with two of every kind, a pair, and depart.

When the oven gushed forth water, Noah took into the ship the ones whom God had ordered, and they were few, as He said. And he took in it a pair of every kind, animal and vegetable, male and female. He took his three sons, Shem, Ham, and Japheth, and their wives, and six who believed in him. They were ten people, Noah, his sons plus their wives. Then he took aboard what beasts God commanded him. But he left behind his son Yam, who was an unbeliever.

Ibn Hamid said, on the authority of Salamah, from Ibn Ishaq, from al-Hasan b. Dinar, from ʿAli b. Zayd, from Yusuf b. Mihran, from Ibn ʿAbas: I heard him saying that the first animal Noah took on board the ship was the ant and the last was the ass. When the ass entered and got its breast in, Iblis, may God curse him, grabbed on to its tail, and it could not pick up its feet. Noah began to say, Woe unto you, enter, even if the Devil is with you. The words slipped from his tongue. When Noah said it, the Devil let the ass go on its way, and it entered, and the Devil entered with it. Noah said to him, What caused you to come on board with me, O Enemy of God? He said, Did you not say Enter, even if the Devil is with you? He said, Depart from me, O Enemy of God. The Devil said, There is no way out for you but to carry me, and he was, according to what they assert, in the back of the boat.

When Noah had provisioned the ship and put in it all who believed in him—and that was in the month of the year after the six-hundredth year of his life, in the seventeenth night of the month—and when he entered and took with him whom he took, the springs began to pour forth water in a great flood. The gates of heaven opened, as God said to His prophet, may the prayers and peace of God be upon him: "We opened the gates of heaven with pouring water and we caused the earth to gush forth springs, and the waters met according to a preordained command," [Q 54:11-12]. Noah and those with him entered the ship and concealed themselves on the decks. Between the time God sent the water and when the water bore the ship away were forty days and forty nights.

Then the water rose up, just as the People of the Torah assert, and became great and strong and raised up, according to the saying of God, the Mighty and the Powerful, to His prophet, Muhammad, may the prayers and peace of God be upon him: "We carried him on a thing of planks and nails which ran by our sight as a recompense for him who was ungrateful" [Q54:14]. And the word for nail means peg, pegs of iron. The ship was made to go with him and those with him on a wave like a mountain.

Noah called his son who was destroyed along with those who were destroyed while he was in seclusion. When Noah saw what he saw of the truth of the promise of his Lord, he said, O my son, ride with us and do not be among the ungrateful. He was a rogue who harbored ingratitude in his heart. He replied, I will go to a mountain which will protect me from the water. It had been the duty of the mountains to be a protection against the rain, and he thought it was as it had been. Noah said, There is no protection today against the command of God, except out of mercy. The waves came between them, and he was among the drowned.

The water increased and raged and raised up over the mountains, as the People of the Torah assert, fifteen cubits, so the creatures on the face of the earth, everything animal and vegetable, perished. No creatures remained except Noah and those with him in the ship except ʿUj b. Aʿnaq, according to what the People of the Book assert. Between the time God sent the flood and the recession of the water was six months and ten nights.

We were told on the authority of Ibn Hamid, from Salamah, from Ibn Ishaq, from al-Hasan b. Dinar, from ʿAli b. Zayd b. Ja ʿdan, that when the people's waste offended Noah on the ship, he was commanded to stroke the tail of the elephant. So he stroked it, and two pigs came forth from it, and he was freed from it [because they ate it]. The mouse gave birth on the ship, and when they troubled him, he was commanded to order the lion to sneeze, and two cats came forth from the nostrils which ate the mice.

God, the Blessed and Most High, sent the flood in the six-hundredth year of Noah's life, and Noah lived, according to the People of the Torah, after he disembarked from the ship, three hundred forty-eight years. Noah's total lifespan was one thousand years less fifty when God made him die.

It is related from ʿAli b. Mujahid, from Ibn Ishaq, from az-Zuhri, from Muhammad b. Salih, and from ash-Shaʿbi that when Adam fell from the Garden, and his children spread out, his descendants reckoned dating from the Fall of Adam. That was the system of dating until God sent Noah. Then they dated from the advent of Noah until the flood, and those were destroyed who were destroyed on the face of the earth. The dating was then from the flood to the fire of Abraham, and from the fire of Abraham to the advent of Joseph, and from the advent of Joseph to the coming of Moses, and from the advent of Moses to the kingdom of Solomon, and from the rule of Solomon to the advent of Jesus, and from the advent of Jesus the son of Mary to the time of the advent of the Prophet of God, may the prayers and peace of God be upon him.

When Noah and his offspring and all who were in the ship went down onto the land, he divided the land among his sons in thirds. He gave Shem the middle third of the earth, and in it is the Holy Temple, the Nile, the Euphrates, the Tigris, Sihan, Jihan, and Fishun, and what is between the Fishun to the east of the Nile, and what is between the origin of the south wind to the origin of the north. He gave Ham his portion west of the Nile and what is behind it to the origin of the west wind. He assigned Japheth the portion in the Fishun and what is behind it to the origin of the east wind.

Gomer, the son of Japheth, was, according to Ibn Ishaq, the father of Gog and Magog, Marih, Wail, Hawan, Tubil, Hushil, Taras, and Shabkah, his daughter. Among the sons of Japheth were Gog and Magog, the Slavs and the Turks, according to what they assert. The wife of Ham, the son of Noah, was Yahlab, the daughter of Marib, the son of ad-Darmasil, the son of Mahuil, the son of Enoch, the son of Cain, the son of Adam. She bore him three sons, Cush, the son of Ham, Qut, the son of Ham, and Canaan, the son of Ham. Cush, the son of Ham, the son of Noah, married Qarnabil, the daughter of Batawil, the Son of Tarnas, the son of Japheth, the son of Noah, and she bore him Copt, and Copt is Egypt according to what they say.

Canaan, the son of Ham, the son of Noah, married Arsal, the daughter of Batawil, the son of Taras, the son of Japheth, the son of Noah, and she bore him black Nubia, Fazzan, Zanj, as-Zaghawah, and all the people of the Sudan. Ibn Hamid said on the authority of Salamah from Ibn Ishaq that the People of the Torah assert that this was not so because of a curse Noah called down on his son Ham. That was because Noah slept, and his private parts were uncovered, and Ham saw them and did not cover them. Shem and Japheth saw them and threw a cloak over them and covered his private parts. So, when he awoke from his sleep, he knew what Ham, Shem, and Japheth had done. He said, Cursed is Canaan, the son of Ham; as a slave he will be to his brothers. And he said, May God, my Lord, bless Shem, and may Ham be a servant to his two brothers. And may God advance Japheth and allow him the dwelling places of Shem, and Ham will be a servant to them.

The wife of Shem, the son of Noah, was Saliha, the daughter of Batawil, the son of Mahuil, the son of Enoch, the son of Cain, the son of Adam. She bore him sons: Arpakhshad, Ashudh, Laudh, and ʿAwilam, the sons of Shem. And Aram was of Shem. I do not know whether Aram belongs to Arpakhshad and his brothers or not. Laudh, the son of Shem, the son of Noah, married Sabakah, the daughter of Japheth, the son of Noah, and she bore him Fars and Jurjan, and the people of Persia. Along with Fars, Tasm and ʿAmaliq were born to Laudh, and I do not know whether he is of the mother of Fars or not.

ʿAmaliq is the father of the Amalekites, all of them, a people scattered over the land. The people of the East and the people of Oman and the people of the Hijaz and the people of Syria and the people of Egypt are of them. And from them are the giants in Syria who were called Canaanites. From them are the pharaohs of Egypt, the people of Bahrein and Oman, a people called Jasim. They used to inhabit Medina. Of them are B. Haff, Saʿd b. Hazzan, the B. Matr, and the B. al-Azraq. The people of Nejd are of them, and Badil, Rahil, Ghaffar, and the people of Teima are of them. The king of the Hijaz, whose name was al-Arqam, was one of them, and they were inhabitants of Najd. The inhabitants of at-Taif were the B. ʿAbd b. Dakhm, a tribe of the ʿAbbas al-Awal. The sons of Umaym, the son of Laudh, the son of Shem, the son of Noah, were the people of Wabar in the land of ar-Raml, and Raml of ʿAlij. They became many and prosperous there. And God took vengeance on them because of frowardness, and they were destroyed. Only a remnant remained called an-Nusnas.

Tasam, the son of Laudh, dwelt in al-Yamamah and its environs, and they became many and prosperous, extending as far as Bahrein. Tasam and the Amalekites and Umaym and Jasim were an Arab people in language who were born into the Arabic language. Fars was of the people of the East of the land of Persia who spoke Persian. Aram, the son of Shem, the son of Noah, sired ʿAws, the son of Aram, and Ghathir, the son of Aram, and Huil, the son of Aram. Ghathir, the son of Aram, sired Thamud, the son of Ghathir, and Judays, the son of Ghathir. They were an Arab-speaking people speaking the language of Mudar. The Arabs used to call these people true Arabs because of their language into which they were born, and they used to call the descendants of Ismail, the son of Abraham, arabicized Arabs because they only spoke the language of these people when they dwelt in their midst. ʿAd, Thamud, the Amalekites, Umaym, Jasim, Jadis, and Tasam were Arab. ʿAd was in this country as far as Hadramaut and all the Yemen. Thamud was in al-Hijr, between al-Hijar and Syria to Wadi al-Qura and environs. Jadis clove to Tasam and was with them in al-Yamamah and environs to Bahrein. The name of al-Yamamah was Jaww. Jasim dwelt in Oman.

Sources

at-Tabari, *Taʾrîkh* 188-190, 190-192, 196, 198, 200-201, 211-212, 212-213, 213-215.

at-Tabari, *Tafsîr* 8:213, 12:36, 12:42, 12:36-37, 12:37

Al-Maqdisi T.3:16-17, 3:72

Al-Azraqi 1:65

Hud

The story of Hud and the following narrative about Salih introduce the reader to the first "Arabian" prophets who do not have a biblical analogue. Because of the lack of biblical "corroboration," many non-Muslim scholars have asserted that the stories were derived from the Arab imagination. Julius Wellhausen, for example, contended that the tribe of ʿAd was a personification of the idiomatic expression in Arabic *min al-ʿad*: "from ancient times." Following that line of reasoning, it is also possible to see the story of Luqman (one of Hud's people) and the vulture Lubad as expansions of folk aphorisms. Even the name Hud has been regarded as derived from the *root h-w-d*, a root used in the Quran as a name for the Jews (e.g. Q. 2:111), rendering the prophet as merely an allegorical figure. The allegorical view of these Arabian prophets coupled with the view that the Quran is Muhammad's creation has also led non-Muslim scholars to see clues to the life and experiences of Muhammad in the stories of Hud and Salih.

For the Muslim, Muhammad in his role of Seal of the Prophets embodied all previous prophetic activity, but not necessarily in a causal relationship; one did not need to look at previous prophets to understand Muhammad, but with the appearance of Muhammad and the advent of Islam, all prophets become revalorized. Rather, Muhammad, by reason of his selection by God, was a member of the elite brotherhood of messengers chosen to carry God's word. Correlations between Muhammad and Hud or Muhammad and Salih would naturally arise, but they would not necessarily indicate that specific events in the lives of the two prophets would correspond to recorded events in Muhammad's life.

In the literary scheme of the biography a number of points in the narrative of Hud show strong resonance with Muhammad's life. Hud's people are idolaters who worshiped at the Kaʿbah at Mecca. Some, like the Hanifs from just before Muhammad's time, followed monotheism, and some, like the early followers of Muhammad, practiced their religion in secret. Hud is also like Noah, a prophet whose unheeded warnings call down destruction on an unbelieving people.

Luqman appears in Ibn Ishaq's narrative as a member of the tribe of ʿAd. In chapter 31 of the Quran, Luqman is a pre-Islamic author of wise sayings and proverbs, and later Islamicate legends ascribe all manner of wisdom literature to him. Indeed, modern studies have shown that the figure of Luqman has attracted a prodigious body of wisdom literature derived from such works as the *Alphabet of Ben Sira* and *Akhikar*. But here Luqman is merely a *muʿam-mar*, a person of extremely long life, his long life usually taken to be a sign of devotion and piety.

The list of idols worshiped by the people of ʿAd probably reflects the names of the idols worshiped in Arabia in pre-Islamic times. For example, the idol Sumud is found not only in this form but in the compound epithet, *samad*, as in the second verse of Quran 112: *allahu as-samadu*. This parallels Canaanite pagan praxis where we see the names *smdl* and *smdbʿl* (see Newby, "*Sûrat alʾ-Ikhlâs*: A Reconsideration"). In this story Mecca's close association as a cultic center is further confirmation of its abiding importance even before Islam. This connection also parallels statements elsewhere in the *Kitâb al-Mubtadaʾ* that it is the *locus venerationis* for all prophets.

Text

In the name of God, the Merciful and the Compassionate

Ibn Hamid said on the authority of Salamah, from Ibn Ishaq, from Muhammad b. ʿAbdullah b. Abu Saʿid al-Khuzai, from Abu at-Tufayl ʿAmir b. Wathilah, who said, I heard ʿAli b. Abu Talib, upon him be peace, saying to a man from Hadramaut, Did you see a red sandhill made up of a mixture of red clods of earth, having arak and lote trees, in such-and-such a direction in the land of Hadramaut; did you see it? He said, Yes, O Commander of the Faithful; you have described it as one who has seen it. He said, No, but I have been told about it. The Hadramauti said, What is its importance, O Commander of the Faithful? He said, Hud, the prayers of God be upon him, is buried in it.

Ibn Ishaq said, the dwelling place of ʿAd and their company was al-Ahqaf when God sent Hud to them. Al-Ahqaf is a land between Oman, in the direction of Hadramaut, and the Yemen. They had ranged all over the land and had vanquished its people by their strength which God had given them. They were idolaters, worshiping idols instead of God: an idol called Sada, an idol called Sumud, and an idol called al-Hiba. So God sent Hud to them. He was one of the best of them in lineage and the highest in rank. He ordered them to worship God alone, not place other gods along with Him, and refrain from oppressing mankind. He did not order them to do anything else according to what was mentioned, but God knows best. But they refused him and disbelieved in him and said, Who is stronger than we in power?

A group from among them followed Hud, and they were few, concealing their belief. Among those who believed in him and regarded him as truthful was a man of ʿAd called Marthad b. Saʿd b. ʿUfayr, who was concealing his belief. When ʿAd raged against God and called their prophet a liar and increased scandal in the land and acted haughtily and built useless, vain monuments on every high place, Hud spoke to them and said, "Do you build on every high place a monument which is in vain, seeking strongholds, so that you might last forever? When you seize by force do you seize as tyrants? Fear God and follow'' [Q 26:128–131]. They said, O Hud, you have not brought us clear evidence, and we are not going to forsake our gods on your word, for we do not believe in you. We say nothing but that some of our gods have possessed you with evil, that is, ''this which you have brought is nothing but dementia with which some of our gods have touched you, these which you denounce. He said, I call God as witness, and you bear witness that I am innocent of what you associate with other than Him. So plot against me altogether and do not delay . . . up to His words . . . a straight path'' [Q 11:53–56]. And when they did that, God withheld rain from heaven from them for three years, according to what they assert, until it wore them down.

When a trial or vexing thing happened, the people in that time sought relief from it with God. Their rogation of God was at His Holy House in Mecca, be they Muslims or polytheists. So people of many diverse religions gathered in Mecca, all of them venerating Mecca, acknowledging its sanctity as a place of God. Ibn Ishaq said, In that time the Temple was known, its place and sanctity established. According to what they say, the people of Mecca were Amalekites. They were named Amalekites because their ancestor was ʿAmliq b. Laudh b. Muʿawiyyah b. Bakr. His father was alive at that time, but he had grown old, and his son was the head of his people. The as-Suaddad and the ash-Sharaf are of the Amalekites, according to what is asserted among the people of that house. The mother of Muʿawiyyah b. Bakr was Kalhadah, the daughter of al-Khaybari, a man from ʿAd.

When the rain was withheld from ʿAd and they were worn out, they said, Prepare a delegation from among you to go to Mecca. Let them seek rain for you, lest you be destroyed. So they send Qayl b. ʿAyr and Luqaym b. Hazal b. Huzayl and ʿUqayl b. Dadd b. ʿAd al-Akhbar and Marthad b. Saʿd b. ʿUfayr, a Muslim keeping his Islam secret, and Jalhamah b. al-Khaybari, the maternal uncle of Muʿawiyyah, the brother of his mother. Then they sent Luqman b. ʿAd, the son of so-and-so, the son of so-and-so, the son of Dadd b. ʿAd al-Akhbar. Each man of these people left with a troop of his folk, so that the number of their delegation reached seventy men.

When they came to Mecca, they camped with Muʿawiyyah b. Bakr. He was outside of Mecca, out of the sacred precinct. He settled them and honored them because they were his relations and in-laws. When the delegation of ʿAd settled with Muʿawiyyah b. Bakr, they stayed a month drinking wine while two fine singing girls belonging to Muʿawiyyah b. Bakr sang to them. Their journey had been a month and their stay a month. When Muʿawiyyah b. Bakr saw the length of their stay and that their people had sent them to seek aid for their affliction, it grieved him. He said, My relatives and my in-laws are being destroyed while these stay with me. But they are my guests, settled with me. By God, I do not know what to do with them to order them to go out to do what they were sent for. They will think I am poor, while those left behind are destroyed from fatigue and thirst, or words to that effect. So he complained about it to his two fine singing girls. They said, Recite a poem to be sung to them, the author of which they will not know. Perhaps that will move them. So when they suggested it to him, Mu'awiyyah b. Bakr, said:

> Indeed, O Tribe, woe to you; rise and murmur; perhaps God will give us
>   water in affliction
> And water the land of 'Ad. Indeed, 'Ad has become lean, not speaking
>   clearly.
> From strong thirst there will not be saved an old man or a youth.
> Their women had been among the best, but their women have become lean
>   over the years.
> The wild beast comes to them openly and does not fear the arrows of one
>   of 'Ad.
> You are here for what you crave, your days and nights completed.
> Your delegation is shameful as a delegation of a people; they will not meet
>   with welcome or a word of peace.

When Mu'awiyyah recited that poem, the two girls sang it to them. When the people heard what they sang, they said to one another: O people, your folk sent you to seek aid against the affliction which has come upon them, and you have delayed. So enter the sacred precinct and seek water for your people.

Marthad b. Sa'd b. 'Ufayr said to them, By God, you will not be watered by your prayers, but if you follow your prophet and repent to him, you will be given water. And, at that, his Islam became evident. When Jalhamah b. al-Khaybari, the maternal uncle of Mu'awiyyah b. Bakr, heard his speech and knew he followed the religion of Hud and believed in him, he said to them:

> Abu Sa'd, you are of a tribe which possesses honor and your mother is
>   from Thamud.
> We will not follow you, what remains of us, and we do not do what you
>   wish.
> Do you command us to leave the religion of the Rafd and Raml and the
>   people of Dadd and al-'Abud,
> And that we abandon the religion of wise ancestors, possessors of wisdom,
>   and that we follow the religion of Hud?

Rafd, Raml, and Dadd are tribes of 'Ad, and al-'Abud is of them. Then they said to Mu'awiyyah b. Bakr and his father, Bakr, Keep Marthad b. Sa'd away from us and do not let him go with us to Mecca, for he follows the religion of Hud and has left our religion.

Then they departed for Mecca to seek water there for ʿAd. When they came near Mecca, Marthad b. Saʿd left the camp of Muʿawiyyah b. Bakr to catch up with them before they called on God for anything. When he got to them, he called on God in Mecca at the same time there was a delegation of ʿAd which had assembled to pray. He said: O God, grant me my request alone, and do not involve me in anything which the delegation of ʿAd requests from you.

Qayl b. ʿAyr was the head of the delegation of ʿAd, and the delegation of ʿAd said: O God, grant Qayl what he asks you and put our request with his request. Luqman b. ʿAd was absent from the delegation of ʿAd when it prayed, and he was a lord of ʿAd. So, when they finished their rogation, he stood up and said, O God, I have come to you alone in my need. Grant me my request. And Qayl b. ʿAyr said, when he prayed, O our God, if Hud be right, give us water, for we are destroyed. And God caused three clouds to appear to them, a white one, a red one, and a black one. Then a herald called to him from the clouds: O Qayl, choose from these clouds for yourself and your people. He said, I have chosen the black cloud, for it is the most abundant in water. And the herald announced to him:

> You have chosen ashes burning
> From ʿAd no one's remaining
> Neither parents left nor offspring
> Except they will be rotting

The ones excepted from this are the B. al-Ludhiyyah al-Muhaddi, and the B. al-Ludhiyyah were the sons of Luqaym b. Hazal b. Hazilah b. Bakr. They were dwelling in Mecca with their relatives, and they were not with ʿAd in their land; they are the other ʿAd, the ones whose progeny remains of ʿAd.

According to what they say, God drove the black cloud which Qayl b. ʿAyr had chosen in which there was vengeance toward ʿAd so that it appeared to them from a wadi called Succor. When they saw it, they began to take it as a good omen. "They said, this is coming to bring us rain," all the while God was saying, "Nay, it is that which you sought to hasten, a wind in which is a painful torment, destroying all things by the command of its Lord" [Q 46:24–25], that is, everything it was commanded.

According to what they mention, the first of those who saw it and knew it was a wind was a woman from ʿAd who was called Muhaddid. When she was sure what was in it, she screamed and was struck unconscious. When she recovered, they said, What did you see, O Muhaddid? She said, I saw a wind in which is a flame of fire which men are leading. God mocked them seven trying nights and eight days, as God said. It did not skip anyone of ʿAd, but all were destroyed.

55

According to what they mention, Hud was separated along with those believers with him in an enclosure, so that he and they were not touched by the wind except lightly on the skin and sweetly on the breath. It passed through ʿAd with a thrust between heaven and earth, and branded them with stones.

The delegation of ʿAd went out of Mecca until they passed by Muʿawiyyah b. Bakr and his father, and they camped with him. While they were with him, suddenly there came a man on a she-camel on a moonlit night on the third evening of the event of ʿAd, and he told them the story. They said, Where did you leave Hud and his companions? He said, I left them on the shore of the sea. It was as though they were transfixed by what he told them.

Huzaylah bt. Bakr said, He told the truth, by the Lord of Mecca, and Muthawwib b. Jaghfar, the nephew of Muʿawiyyah b. Bakr was with them. According to what they say, and God knows best, Marthad b. Saʿd and Luqman b. ʿAd and Qayl b. ʿAyr were told when they prayed in Mecca: You have been given your wish, so choose for yourselves, except there is no way to live forever, and no escape from death.

Marthad b. Saʿd said, O Lord, give me probity and truth, and he was given that. Luqman b. ʿAd said, Give me life, and it was said to him, Choose for yourself—except that there is no way to eternal life—either the length of life of a mountain sheep in a rugged mountain which only the rain meets, or that of seven vultures; when a vulture passes away, you will pass over to another vulture. So Luqman chose the vultures for himself, and he lived, according to what they say, the lifespan of seven vultures, taking the chick when it came from its egg and taking the male to strengthen him, until, when he died, he would take another one. He did not cease doing that until he came to the seventh. And each vulture, according to what they said, would live eighty years.

When only the seventh remained, a nephew said to Luqman, O uncle, only the lifespan of this vulture remains of your life. Luqman said to him, O my nephew, this is Lubad (and Lubad in their tongue is Fate). When the vulture of Luqman matured, and its life ended, the vultures flew in the early morning from the top of the mountain, but Lubad did not rise up. These vultures of Luqman would not hide from him when they were designated for him. So when Luqman did not see Lubad rise with the vultures, he went up to the mountain to see what Lubad did. Luqman found himself weak in a way he had not found himself before. When he came to the mountain, he saw his vulture Lubad fallen among the vultures. So he called to him, Rise, Lubad, and Lubad tried to rise, but he was not able, his feathers having fallen out, and the two of them died together.

It was said to Qayl b. ʿAyr, when he heard what was said to him in the cloud, Choose for yourself as your companions have chosen. He said, I choose that there happen to me what befalls my people. It was said to him that it was destruction. He said, I do not care; there is no need for me to remain after them. So the punishment happened to him that happened to ʿAd, and he perished. Marthad b. Saʿd b. ʿUfayr said, when he heard the speech of the rider who told him about ʿAd and its destruction:

> ʿAd was hard on their messenger, so they became thirsty, heaven not
> wetting them.
> Their delegation was sent forth for a month to seek water, the heavy
> clouds riding behind them, thirsty.
> By their public display of disbelief in their lord, the traces of ʿAd were
> obliterated.
> Did not the God take away the forbearance of ʿAd, for their hearts were an
> empty wasteland?
> By a clear account, He promised, and what would be the gain of sincerity
> or wretched behavior.
> My soul, my two daughters, and the mother of my offspring are ransom
> for the soul of the prophet, Hud.
> He came to us, and the hearts were stopped up with sin, and brightness
> had gone.
> We had an idol called Samud, which stones and dirt will receive.
> Those who frequent it, pondered it, misfortune reaches him who lied about
> it.
> I will join the people of Hud and his sister when night falls.

In another version Ibn Ishaq said, When the wind stormed, a group of ʿAd remained, seven in the north, of whom six were the strongest and biggest of ʿAd; of them were ʿAmr b. al-Hali, al-Harith b. Shaddad, al-Halqam, Ibnatiqan, Khaljan b. Asʿad. They set their families out at night in a ravine between the two mountains. Then they formed a line at the mouth of the ravine to turn back the wind from the dependents in the ravine. The wind began to subdue them man by man, and a woman of ʿAd said:

> Fate came to ʿAmr b. Hali and the Time
> Then to al-Harith and al-Halqam, striving in the passes
> Which the wind closed on us on the days of Trial.

On the authority of al-ʿAbbas b. al-Walid al-Bayruti, who got it from his father, who heard it from Ismail b. ʿAyyash, Ibn Ishaq said, When the wind came out from the wadi against ʿAd, seven of them, one of whom was al-

Khaljan, said, Let us go up to the edge of the wadi, and we will turn it back. The wind went under one of them and bore him up. Then it threw him, broke his neck and left him just as God, the Mighty and the Powerful, said, "Overthrown as they were hollow trunks of palms" [Q 69:7], so that no one of them remained except al-Khaljan. He turned to the mountain and took hold of its side and shook it, and it swayed in his hand, and he recited:

There does not remain anyone except al-Khaljan himself; O what a day for calamity to overtake me.
By the fixity of the low ground, strong and fierce, if it had not come to me, I would have gone to it spying.

Hud said to him, Woe to you, O Kaljan; submit so that you can be saved. He said to him, What do I get from your Lord if I submit? He said, Paradise. He said, What are these which I see in the clouds as though they were Fortune? Hud said, These are the angels of my Lord. He said, If I submit, will your Lord protect me from them? He said, Woe to you; do you see an angel which protects from His army? He said, Would that He would do what I wish. Then the wind came and put him with his comrades.

Hud lived as long as God wished, and then he died, and his lifespan was a hundred and fifty years.

Sources

at-Tabari, *Ta'rîkh* 234–239, 239–241, 242
at-Tabari, *Tafsîr* 8:217, 8:217–220, 27:98–99, 27:99
Al-Maqdisi 3:30, 3:36–37
Al-Baghdadi 2:101, 2:1023

Salih

Salih and the people of Thamud are third in the sequence of the stories of divine destruction following Noah and Hud. Thamud occurs as a name of pre-Islamic inhabitants in the Hijaz as far back as Assyrian times. Some scholars, seeing the people of Thamud as related to the Lihyanic peoples, date their demise to a century or so before Muhammad's birth and say that the visible remains of their civilization provided the inspiration for Muhammad's stories about them.

Salih was a warner to his people, the Thamud, who demanded clear proof that he was a prophet and messenger of God and not just an ordinary man. They set up a contest where they would call on their gods and Salih would call on God. If Salih could get God to produce a she-camel, then they would believe in him. Even this sure sign failed to bring about a general conversion, however, mostly because of opposition by those who were in charge of their idols. One is reminded here of the contest which introduced Judaism into Yeman [see Ibn Hisham]. In that story the king had rabbis undergo a fire ordeal with the pagans, and when the rabbis won, the Yemenites converted to Judaism.

Thamud's demands of Salih parallel the demands made by the Meccans of Muhammad in Q 17:90–92: "We will not believe in you until you make an abundant spring to come forth from the earth or you have a garden of date palms and grapes and cause rivers to flow, or cause the heaven to fall on us in pieces as you have claimed, or bring God and the angels as proof." Salih's camel not only came forth miraculously, but, when it was allowed to drink freely, it provided abundant milk for the tribe. The abundant milk of Salih's camel is meant as a sign of God's favor just as the abundant milk of Muhammad's foster mother and her camel was a sign of God's favor during Muhammad's childhood. The destruction of Salih's camel brings about the expected destruction of the tribe of Thamud: their faces turn first yellow, then red, and then black, all colors of disease, sin, and death. Salih's escape to Ramlah in Palestine belongs to the hagiographic traditions in which various towns claim holy persons and thus become centers of veneration.

Text

In the name of God, the Merciful and the Compassionate

When God destroyed ʿAd, and their affairs were finished, Thamud lived after them and followed them on the land, settled in it and propagated. Then they became insolent toward God, and when their evil conduct became open and they worshiped other than God, he sent Salih to them as a messenger. They were an Arab people, and Salih was truly of their lineage and the best of them in position. Their dwelling was al-Hajar up to al-Qarh, which is al-Qura, between there and eighteen miles into the area between the Hijaz and Syria.

God sent them a young boy, and he called them to God until he turned gray and became old, no one following him except a few of the weak ones. When Salih pestered them with his preaching and multiplied the warnings of God for them, the punishment and the vengeance, they asked him to show them a sign which could be believed about what he was calling them to. So he said to them, What sort of sign do you wish? They said, Come out with us to our festival. They had a festival in which they would go out with their idols and the things they worshiped beside God on a certain day in the year. You call on your God, and we will call on our gods. If He answers you, we will follow you, and if he answers us, then you follow us. Salih said to them, Yes; so they went out to their idols at their festival, and Salih went out with them to God. They called on their idols and asked of them that Salih should not be answered in anything. Then Junduᶜ b. ʿAmrad b. Harrash b. ʿAmr b. ad-Damil, who was then the lord of the Thamud and the mightiest of them, said to him, O Salih, extract for us from this rock—which was a monolith in the direction of al-Hajar called al-Kathibah—a she-camel, extracted free and clear, not resembling a Bactrian camel. Then Thamud said to Salih what Junduᶜ b. ʿAmrad said. If you do this, we will believe in you, regard you as truthful and bear witness that what you have come with is true. Salih took their pledge: If you do this and if God does this to prove me true, will you believe in me? They said, Yes, and they gave him their promise on that. So Salih called on his Lord that He bring out for them from that hill what was described.

Yaᶜqub b. ʿUtbah b. al-Mughirah b. al-Akhnas was told that they looked at the hill when Salih called on God with what he asked Him: May you bring forth a she-camel bearing a foal. The hill moved, and then down dropped a she-camel. As they described it, a foal of which only God knew the greatness broke from the she-camel, free and clear at her side. Junduᶜ b. ʿAmrad believed in him, as well as those with him under his command, those of his group.

The nobles of Thamud wished to believe in him and regard him as truthful, but Dhuab b. ʿAmr b. Labid and al-Habbab, the lord of their idols, and Rayyab b. Samᶜar b. Jalhas forbade them, and they were of the nobles of the Thamud.

They turned its nobles from Islam and from entering the mercy and redemption Salih had invited them to.

Junduᶜ had a nephew, who was called Shihab b. Khalifah b. Makhlah b. Labid b. Jawwas, who wished to become a Muslim, but this party dissuaded him from that, and he followed them. He was of the nobility of the Thamud and their finest. A man of Thamud called Mahus b. ᶜAnmah b. ad-Damil, who was a Muslim, said:

> A party of the people of ᶜAmr had been invited to the religion of the
>   prophet by a flame,
> The noble of Thamud, all of them together, and they started to answer;
>   would that they had answered.
> Salih had become noble among us, but Dhuab did not act fairly with his
>   comrades,
> And the temptation of the folk of Hajar caused them to take power after
>   their right guidance, like jackals.

The she-camel which God had brought forth for them remained with her young male, newborn foal in the land of Thamud, pasturing on the trees and drinking the water. Salih, peace be upon him, said to them, "This is God's she-camel for you as a sign, so let her eat on God's land. Do not touch her with evil, for a painful torment will take you" [Q 7:73]. God said to Salih that the water was divided among them, each drink being taken in turn; that is, the water is in two parts; they have a day, and she has a day [see Q 54:28]. That is the meaning, and on her day do not omit her drink. So he said, She has a drink, and you have a drink on a fixed day.

According to what reached me, and God knows best, when she appeared and would drink avidly, she put her head in a well in al-Hajar called the She-Camel-Spring. They assert that when she would drink, she would come, put her head in it, and not raise it until she would drink all the water in the wadi. Then she would raise her head and spread wide, meaning she would put herself in a position to be milked, and she would lactate as much milk as they wanted. They would drink it and store some away until all the vessels were filled. Then she would go out, but not through the pass through which she appeared because of its being too narrow for her, and she would not return until the morning after it was their day. They would drink what they wished of the water and store what they wished for the day of the she-camel. Because of all this, they had great abundance.

According to what they mention, the she-camel would spend the summer when it was hot at the top of the wadi, and the cattle, the sheep and the goats, the cows, and the camels, would flee from her and would go down into the inside of the wadi, in its heat and barrenness. That was because the cattle had an aversion to her when they saw her. She would pass the winter in the inside of the wadi, when it was winter, and the cattle would flee to the top of the wadi into the cold and barrenness. That was harmful to their cattle because of the distress and trial, and, according to what they allege, all that grazed in the wadi of al-Hajar were afraid of her. That became a grave thing for them, and they became recalcitrant against the command of their Lord, and their opinion became united against the she-camel.

There was a woman of the Thamud called ʿUnayzah bt. Ghanam b. Majaz, with the nickname of Mother of Sheep. She was of the B. ʿUbayd b. al-Muhall, the brother of Damil al-Muhall, and she was the wife of Dhuab b. ʿAmr. She was advanced in age, had fine daughters and much wealth in camels, cows, sheep and goats. There was another woman called Saduf bt. al-Muhayya, the lord of the B. ʿUbayd and the chief of their idols in former times. The wadi was called the Wadi of al-Muhayya, who was al-Muhayya the Elder, the grandfather of al-Muhayya the Younger, the father of Saduf. Saduf was of the best of her people. She was wealthy, possessing camels, sheep, goats, and cows. The two were the strongest women in Thamud in their enmity to Salih and the greatest disbelievers in him. The two wished to wound the she-camel because of their disbelief in him. So when their cattle were distressed, Saduf was with a nephew of hers called Santam b. Harawah b. Saʿd b. al-Ghatrif of the B. Hulayl. He had become a Muslim, and his Islam was proper. Saduf had entrusted her wealth to him, and he had dispersed it to those who were Muslims with him of the companions of Salih so that the wealth had diminished. Saduf knew of that because of his Islam, and she reproved him for that. He divulged his religion to her and called her to God and to Islam, but she refused him and reviled his birth and took his sons and daughters from him and led them away among the B. ʿUbayd, since they were from her womb. Santam was her spouse from the Banu Hulayl and her nephew. He said to her, Return my children to me. She said, Not until I dispute with you among the B. Sanʿan b. ʿUbayd or the B. Junduʿ b. ʿUbayd. Santam said to her, Nay, I say, among the B. Mardas b. ʿUbayd, and that was because the B. Mardas b. ʿUbayd had been quick to become Muslims, and the others had been slow. She said, I will not dispute with you except among those I have called you to. The B. Mardas said, By God, you will give him his children willingly or unwillingly. And when she saw that, she gave them to him.

Then Saduf and ʿUnayzah plotted to wound the she-camel because of the distress which had befallen. Saduf called a man from Thamud called al-Habbab to wound the she-camel and offered herself to him if he would do that. He refused, so she called in a paternal nephew she had named Masdaʿ b. Mahraj b. al-Muhayya and put herself forward to him on the condition that he wound the she-camel. She was among the most beautiful and was very wealthy. So he agreed to that. And ʿUnayzah bt. Ghanam called Qaddar b. Salif b. Junduʿ, a man from the people of Qarh. Qaddar was a short, bright red man. They say he was the offspring of the fornication of a man called Sahyad and that his father was not Salif by whom he was called, but that he had been born on Salif's bed and thereby named for him and connected with his genealogy. She said, I will give you whichever of my daughters you wish on the condition that you wound the she-camel. ʿUnayzah was a noble woman of the Thamud, and her spouse was Dhuab b. ʿAmr of the most noble men of the Thamud. Qaddar was regarded as strong among his people, so Qaddar b. Salif and Masdaʿ b. Mahraj went out and incited the riffraff of Thamud. Seven individuals followed them so that they were nine. One of those who followed them was a man named Hawil b. Milagh, the uncle of Qaddar b. Salif, the brother of his mother by her father and mother, and he was a strong man among the folk of Hajar. And there was Duʿayr b. Ghanam b. Daʿir, and he was of the B. Halawah b. al-Muhall, and Dab b. Mahraj, the brother of Masdaʿ b. Mahraj, and five [sic] of their names are not preserved.

They lay in wait for the she-camel when she appeared for water. Qaddar hid at the base of the rock on her path, and Masdaʿ hid at the other base. She passed by Masdaʿ, and he shot an arrow at her, and the muscle of her leg was injured by it. Then Mother of Sheep, ʿUnayzah, came out and ordered her daughter, who had one of the most beautiful faces, to uncover her face for Qaddar and show it to him. Then she reproved him so that he violently attacked the she-camel with his sword and laid bare her hamstring. The she-camel fell down and gave out one foaming cry, warning her foal. Then he pierced her heart and killed her. Her foal left until it came to an inaccessible mountain. He came to a rock on the summit of the mountain, exhausted, and sought shelter there. The name of the mountain, according to what they say, was Sur.

Salih came to them, and when he saw that the she-camel had been wounded, he said, You have defiled a sacred thing of God; are they happy about the punishment of God and His vengeance? They said to him, mocking him, And what is this, O Salih; what kind of sign is this?

They used to name their days: Sunday as Awwal, Monday as Ahwan, Tuesday as Dabbar, Wednesday as Jabbar, Thursday as Muanis, Friday as al-ʿArubah, Saturday as Shayyar, and they wounded the she-camel on Wednesday.

Salih said to them when they said that, You will wake up in the morning of Muanis, meaning Thursday, and your faces will be yellow. Then you will wake up on al-ʿArubah, meaning Friday, and your faces will be red; then you will wake up on Shayyar, meaning Saturday, and you will wake up and your faces will be black. Then the punishment will come to you on the morning of al-Awwal, meaning Sunday. When Salih had said that to them, the nine who had wounded the she-camel said, Come, let us kill Salih. If he is truthful, we will hasten him on before us, and if he is lying, we will have inflicted on him what we inflicted on his she-camel. So they came to him at night in order to hatch a plan against him among his people, but the angels triumphed over them with stones.

When they were late in coming to their comrades, they went to the house of Salih and found them crushed, having been smashed by the stones. So they said to Salih, You killed them, and they started toward him. But his people stood up in front of him, put weapons on and said to them, By God, you will never kill him. He has already warned you that the punishment will come upon you in three days, and if he is right, then you will not add anything but anger from your Lord, and if he is lying, then you are beyond what you wish. So they left him that night. The party which the angels crushed were the nine whom God, the Mighty and the Powerful, mentioned in the Quran in his words: "There were in the district a party of nine who had made mischief in the land and did not reform . . . up to His words . . . a sign for people who know" [Q 27:48–52].

They awoke the morning after the night they had left Salih, their faces were yellow, and they were certain of the punishment and knew that Salih had told them the truth. So they sought to kill him. Salih left, fleeing from them, and seeking refuge in the center of Thamud among the B. Ghanam. He settled with their chief, a man called Nufayl, nicknamed Abu Hadab, who was a polytheist. Nufayl hid him, and they were unable to get to Salih, so they went to the companions of Salih and tortured them to lead them to him. A man from the companions of Salih called Mayda⁵ b. Haram said, O prophet of God, they are punishing us in order to make us lead them to you. Shall we lead them to you? He said, Yes. So Mayda⁵ b. Haram led them to him, and when they knew Salih's location, they came to Abu Hadab and spoke to him. He said to them, Salih is with me, and there is no way to him for you. So they turned away from him and left him.

The punishment God sent distracted Thamud from Salih, and they began to talk to one another about what they were seeing on their faces when they awoke the morning of Thursday; that was when their faces had become yellow. Then they got up on Friday and their faces were red; and they got up on Saturday and their faces were black, so that, when it was Sunday night, Salih left their midst along with those who had become Muslims and went to Syria. He settled in Ramlah in Palestine.

A man from his companions called Mayda⁵ b. Haram stayed behind and settled in Qarh, which is called Wadi al-Qura; and between Qarh and al-Hajar is eighteen miles. He camped with their chief, a man called ⁵Amr b. Ghanam, who had eaten the flesh of the she-camel but had not participated in her killing. Mayda⁵ b. Haram said to him, O ⁵Amr b. Ghanam, leave this country, for

Salih said that he who remains in it will be destroyed, and he who leaves will be saved. ʿAmr said, I did not participate in her wounding, and I was not pleased with what was done to her.

When it was Sunday morning, a great cry overtook them, and there did not remain of them great or small but they were all destroyed, all but a crippled slave girl called ad-Dariʿah, who was a Kalbite, the daughter of as-Salaq, who had been a disbeliever, strong in enmity to Salih. God freed her legs after she saw the punishment, and she left as fast as one would ever see until she came to some living persons and told them of what she had seen of the punishment and what befell Thamud. Then she asked for water. They gave it to her, and when she drank it, she died.

Sources

at-Tabari, *Tafsîr* 8:225–226, 8:226–229, 19:173
Al-Maqdisi 3:40
ath-Thaʿlabi 39–43

Abraham, The Friend of God

The story of Abraham is one of the richest in the whole of the *Kitâb al-Mubtadaᵓ* for both narrative detail and plot structure. While it follows the Quranic versions of the story, it weaves them together into a comprehensive treatment of one of the most important prophets for Muslims. The figure of Abraham occupies a central position in Muhammad's polemical arguments with the Jews of Medina. Muhammad's position is illustrated by the passage from Q 3:56–68: "O People of Scripture, why do you argue about Abraham? The Torah and the Gospels were not revealed until after him. Don't you understand? You are people who argue about that of which you have some knowledge. Why do you argue about that of which you have no knowledge? God knows, but you do not know. Abraham was not a Jew nor a Christian but a pure monotheist [Arabic *hanif*], one who submitted to God [Arabic *Muslim*], and not one of the idolaters." Abraham was a prototype for the proper monotheist, the founder of the Religion of Abraham [Arabic *Millat Ibrahim*], and free from sectarian claims. As Q 3:69 asserts, the person with the best claim to Abraham was Muhammad, and the people with the claim to the Abrahamic heritage are the followers of the restored Abrahamic religion, the religion of Islam, restored, as Muslims claim, by Muhammad after the people of the world fell away from the proper worship of God. A function of the prophetic office is to restore correct worship and lead the community of faithful back to God. Abraham restored the worship Adam had initiated, and Muhammad renewed what Adam and Abraham had done. The theme of renewal [Arabic *tajdid*] makes Muhammad the new Adam and Abraham in the scheme of the *Kitâb al-Mubtadaᵓ*.

Abraham's association with the Kaᶜbah is another central feature of this narrative, because it is around this theme that Islam's great revisionism of world history is built. As we learned in the story of Adam, the first worship of God was at Mecca by Adam. He laid the foundations of the Kaᶜbah and instituted the rites of worship there. Some Muslim authors say that during the period of the flood, the Kaᶜbah was taken up into heaven to protect it from the waters, and that it was later restored to its proper place. By the time of Abraham there was little left of the original site, and he was commanded along with his first-born son, Ishmael, to rebuild the temple, called the House of God, and to restore proper worship (Q 2:125–128).

While Abraham is the restorer of the true religion, Ishmael is prominently featured as the heir to the Abrahamic legacy. Ishmael is credited with the discovery of the well of Zamzam when he and his mother Hagar are expelled from the Holy Land. Zamzam is no ordinary well, however, for we are told that had Hagar not stopped it, it would have flowed forever. Ishmael had tapped into a spring of the primordial waters near the Ka'bah. Ishmael, rather than Isaac, is depicted as the intended sacrificial victim, and Ishmael helps his father build the Ka'bah, although the crucial cornerstone is supplied by divine intervention. And Ishmael is the son through which the Arabs are connected to the biblical genealogy. The underlying claim of the text is that there is a new dispensation and a new line of inheritance. Just as the Christians had claimed that after Jesus the church was the New Jerusalem, so Islam laid claim to biblical panorama.

The details of the Ka'bah take on importance because they help connect it to features formerly associated with the Temple in Jerusalem. We are told of footprints on the stone at the Ka'bah like the footprints on the Foundation Stone in Jerusalem, and the Shechinah, God's Spirit, speaks to Abraham through the Adamic foundations. When the restoration of the Ka'bah takes place in Muhammad's time, we are told that attempts at the removal of the Foundation Stone caused the entire earth to shudder, further confirmation that Mecca was the site of the foundation of the world, not Jerusalem.

Much of the detail of the narrative of Abraham can be found in Jewish sources. Some of these sources received their final editing after the time of the rise of Islam, and some scholars have argued that details which are common to both traditions could have come from Islam into Judaism. Regardless of the ultimate origin, the *Kitâb al-Mubtada*꜄ is replete with material that continues the rabbinic Haggadic traditions, showing that the early Muslim exegetes were well acquainted with the methodology of Haggadic commentary as well as with the particular stories.

The first theme is the foretelling of Abraham's birth by the astrologers of Nimrod. One is immediately reminded of the stories of Moses and Jesus, the story of Moses being the *locus classicus*. Abraham's argument against natural phenomena as divine, and the trick he played on the idol worshipers—claiming that the idols destroyed each other and then having the idol worshipers admit that that could not be possible—are two delightful examples of the polemical use of the Abraham account. Both stories expand on the Quranic version of his life, but they have a rabbinic base (e.g., *Bereshit Rabbah* 38).

In the story of the cutting apart of the four birds and their restoration to life, we find a conflation of several features present in rabbinic literature. In our version Abraham quarters four birds and places a piece of each bird on the top of four mountains which represent the cardinal points of the compass. He then prays to God, and the four birds are restored to their original shape and made to fly. In rabbinic traditions Abraham is commanded by God to offer a certain order of sacrifices, thus establishing Temple worship. When he divided the sacrificial victims, he laid the pieces of the animals against each other, at which point the animals became alive. While it could be argued that the narratives derive from a post-Islamic version of Midrash, the interpretation rests on a particular reading of the Hebrew text of Genesis. Genesis 15:11 reads, "And the birds of prey came down on the carcasses, and Abram drove them away." The Midrash that makes Abraham bring the animals to life interprets the word "them," the object of the verb "to drive away," as "carcasses" rather than "birds of prey," indicating that Abraham drove the carcasses away, perforce alive.

Abraham also becomes the *locus* for a story that is similar to the story of the companions of Daniel, Hananiah, Mishael, and Azariah, who were cast into the fiery furnace. This and the ministrations of the angels to Abraham are found in the old sources of *Genesis Rabbah* 4 et passim. As Muslim authors became less dependent on external sources, rabbinic texts, though known to scholars, could not prevail against the commonly held view of Abraham, Ishmael, and other biblical figures. As part of the process whereby Muslim authors develop their own modes of discourse about these figures, they include aetiological words and phrases that focus on and explain purely Arabic or Islamic items. The Ka'bah in Mecca is called Cube [Arabic *ka'bah*] because of the dimensions given it by Abraham. Similarly, the place name 'Arafah was said to be the place where Abraham finally knew [Arabic 'arafa] the rites of the Pilgrimage. They still use the methodology of the rabbinic sources, however, as well as preserving some of the content, and so continue to make Midrash in Islamic guise.

Text

In the name of God, the Merciful and the Compassionate

Abraham was the son of Azar, that is, Tarikh, the son of Nahur, the son of Sarugh, the son of Arghu, the son of Faligh, the son of 'Abir, the son of Shalikh, the son of Qaynan, the son of Arfakhshad, the son of Shem, the son of Noah. Muhammad b. Ishaq told me that Azar came from the district of Kutha in the district of Kufah, which was, at that time, the eastern kingdom of Nimrod, who was called al-Hasir. According to what has been alleged, his kingdom encompassed the eastern and western portions of the earth while he lived in Babylon. His kingdom and his people were in the east before the time of the Persians. It is said that no king united the whole earth, and no people made the earth into one kingdom, except three kings: Nimrod the son of Arghu, Dhu-l-Qarnayn, and Solomon the son of David.

When God wished to send Abraham, the Friend of God, as evidence to his people and as a messenger to his servants (there were no prophets between

Noah and Abraham except Hud and Salih) and when the time for Abraham approached, Nimrod's astrologers came to him and said: Know that by our science we have found that a youth will be born in such-and-such a month and such-and-such a year in this city of yours who will be called Abraham. He will cast your religion asunder and break your idols. So when the year came which the astrologers had described, Nimrod sent for all pregnant women in his city and imprisoned them, except the mother of Abraham, the wife of Azar. Azar did not know of her pregnancy, because she did not talk about it.

So it happened that every boy born to a woman in that month in that year was ordered to be slaughtered. When the mother of Abraham was parturient, she went out at night to a nearby cave and bore Abraham in it. Then she set everything in order for the newborn, blocked up the cave, and returned to her house. She went back to the cave to inspect him, and she found him alive, being suckled by wild beasts. It is alleged, and God knows best, that God provided for his suckling. According to what they assert, Azar asked Abraham's mother what happened to her pregnancy. She said, I bore a youth which died, and he believed her and kept quiet.

According to report, a day for Abraham in his infancy was like a month and a month like a year. Abraham did not stay in the cave more than fifteen months until he said to his mother, Take me out so I can look around. So she took him out in the evening, and he looked and thought about the creation of the heavens and the earth and said, He is my Lord who created me and provided for me and fed me and gave me drink; what would I be without Him? He looked at heaven, saw a star, and said, This is my Lord. Then he followed it with his gaze until it set. When it set, he said, I do not like things which set. Then the moon rose. He saw it coming out, and he said, This is my Lord. Then he followed it with his gaze until it set. When it set, he said, If my Lord does not guide me, I will become one of the people of error. When day came, and the sun rose, he saw the power of the sun, and he saw something with stronger light than anything he had seen before, so he said, "This is my Lord; this is the greatest. And when it set, he said, O people, I am free from your polytheism; I have set my face toward the One who created the heavens and the earth, as a monotheist, and I am not one of the polytheists" [Q 6:78–79]. Then Abraham returned to his father, Azar. His direction remained true, and he knew his Lord. He was free from the religion of his people but he did not extirpate them for that belief. He told his father that he was his son, and Abraham's mother told Azar that he was his son, and she told him what she had done. Azar was happy at that and rejoiced greatly.

Now Azar used to make the idols his people would worship. Then he would give them to Abraham to sell, and Abraham would go out with them and, according to what they assert, would say to him who bought one that it would not hurt him or help him. So no one would buy from him. When this activity proved unprofitable to him, he went to the river with the idols and immersed their heads in it. He said, Drink, mocking his people and their error so that his shaming them and mocking them spread among his people and the rest of the people of the city until it reached Nimrod, the king.

When it became clear to Abraham that he should declare his break with his people openly and declare his situation with God and his prayers to Him, he saw a vision in the stars, and he said, "I am sick; so they turned their backs on him" [Q37:89–90]. (His statement, I am sick, means stricken with sickness.) They went away from him when they heard him. Abraham wanted them to go away so he could do what he wanted with their idols. When they left him, he went to the idols which they worshiped instead of God and brought food to them. Then he said, reviling them for their condition and mocking them, "Do you not eat? What is the matter with you that you do not speak?" [Q 37:91–92] Then he came up to them, as God said, striking them with his right hand, and began breaking them with an ax which was in his hand until only the largest idol remained. Then he fastened the ax to its hand and left.

When the people returned, they saw what had been done to their idols. It frightened them, and they were amazed by it. They said, Who did this to our gods; he is one of the sinners. Then they remembered and said, We heard a youth called Abraham finding fault with them and mocking them, and we have not heard anyone say that except him. He is the one whom we think did that.

The affair came to the attention of Nimrod and the nobles of his people, and they said, Bring Abraham before the leaders of the people that perhaps they will bear witness about what we should do with him. When he was brought and his people were gathered against him before their king, Nimrod, they said, "Did you do this to our gods, Abraham? He said, Nay, their chief did this; so ask them, if they can speak" [Q 21:62–63]. He became angry that you worship these small ones along with him. He is bigger than they; so he shattered them.

Keeping an eye on him, they gathered apart from him to discuss the breaking, and they said, We have wronged him, and we do not see that it is other than as he said. Then knowing that the idols neither harmed nor helped and could not strike, they said, "You know that these do not speak" [Q 21:65], that is, they do not talk; so tell us who did this with them and why you struck them, and we will believe you. At that, when the proof came to them by their words, You know that these do not speak, Abraham said, "Do you worship what will not help you or harm you instead of God? Fie on you and what you worship instead of God. Do you not have any sense?" [Q 21:66–67] And with that, his people disputed with him about God, and they argued with him to show that their gods were better than what he worshiped. So he said, "Do you dispute with me about God when he has guided me . . . up to his statement . . . Which of the two factions has more right to safety, if you know"

[Q 6:81–82], offering them parables and fending off interpretations to teach them that it is more right to fear and worship God than what they worshiped.

It was told us, and God knows best, that Nimrod said to Abraham, What is this God of yours whom you worship, invite to His worship, and tell of His might, which you assert is greater than anything else. Abraham said, My Lord who gives life and death. Nimrod said, But I give life and death. And Abraham said, How do you give life and death? He said, I take two men worthy of killing in my judgment, and I kill one of them, and I have given death to him. I forgive the other and release him, and I have given him life. Abraham said to that, "Show me how you give life to the dead. He said, Do you not believe? He said, Yes, but I ask in order that my heart be at ease" [Q 2:260] from any doubt in God or His power. He wished to know that, and his heart yearned for it. "He said, take four birds and bring them to you. Then place a part of each on each mountain. Then call them. They will come to you quickly. Know that God is Mighty and Wise" [Q 2:260].

The People of the Book said that he took four birds, a peacock, a cock, a raven, and a dove. He cut each bird into four pieces, and went to four mountains, placing a quarter of each bird on each mountain, so there was on each mountain a quarter of the peacock, a quarter of a cock, a quarter of the raven, and a quarter of the dove. Then he called to them and said, Come, with the permission of God, as you were. Each quarter joined with its mate until they were reassembled, and each bird was as it was before it had been cut. Then they came to him quickly, just as God had said. It was said, O Abraham, thus God gathers His servants and gives life to the dead in the resurrection of the East and the West and the North and the South. So God showed him the quickening of the dead by His power, so that he would know that instead of what Nimrod said in lying and error. And Abraham said to them, "Indeed, God is the one who raises the sun from the East, so you bring it from the West" [Q 2:258], so that I will know if it is as you say. Nimrod was abashed at this and did not respond, and he knew that he could not do that. In the words of the Most High, "The sinner was abashed" [Q 2:258], meaning the proof fell on him, Nimrod, "and God does not guide a sinful people" [Q 2:258].

Then Nimrod and his people gathered around Abraham and said, "Burn him and stick by your gods if you are men of action" [Q 21:68]. Ibn Hamid told me on the authority Salamah, who got it from Muhammad b. Ishaq, who got it from al-Hasan b. Dinar, that Layth b. Abu Sulaym, who got it from Mujahid, said, I recited this verse to ʿAbdullah b. ʿUmar, and he said, Do you know, O Mujahid, who ordered the burning of Abraham by the fire? I said, No. He said, A man from the Arabs of the Persians. I said, O Abu ʿAbd-ar-Rahman, do the Persians have Arabs? He said, Yes, the Kurds; they are the Arabs of the Persians, and one of them was the one who ordered the burning of Abraham in the fire.

Abraham, the Friend of God

Nimrod commanded that they bring him firewood, so they made a cross of all sorts of firewood. There was a woman from Abraham's town who had vowed because of her religion that if she came across Abraham, she would gather the firewood for the fire in which he would be burned. When they wished to throw him in, they brought him and kindled the wood which they had gathered on all sides. When the fire ignited, and they gathered to throw him in it, heaven and earth and all the creatures in it except men and Jinn cried out to God with one cry: Our Lord, there is no one in your land who worships you except Abraham, and he is being burned by fire. Give us permission to save him. They mention, and God knows best, that when they said that, God said, If he asks for rain from you or prays for it, it will save him. I have given permission to him for that, if he does not pray to anyone but me, for I am his protector. So leave the affair between me and him. I will protect him. So when they threw him in it, He said, "O fire, be coolness and peace for Abraham" [Q 21:69]. So it was as God said, and God sent the Angel of Shade in the image of Abraham, and he sat by his side amusing him.

Now Nimrod waited a few days, not doubting that the fire had consumed Abraham and was finished with him. Then he rode out and passed by where the fire was burning all the firewood that they had gathered, and he looked at it. He saw Abraham sitting in it with a man like him at his side. So Nimrod came back from his ride and said to his people, I have just seen Abraham alive in the fire, but this seems doubtful to me. Build me a tower that will take me up over the fire so that I can be certain. So they built him a tower, and he climbed up it over the fire, and he saw Abraham sitting in the fire, and he saw the angel sitting at his side in his image. Nimrod called out to him, O Abraham, great is your God whose power and might reaches to the extent I see so that you are not harmed. O Abraham, are you able to come out of there? He said, Yes. Nimrod said, Are you afraid that if I leave you in the fire you will be harmed? He said, No. Nimrod said, Rise and come out. So Abraham got up and walked in the fire until he came out. When he came out to Nimrod, Nimrod said, O Abraham, who was the man in your image I saw with you, sitting at your side? He said, That was the Angel of Shade which my Lord sent to be with me and to amuse me. He placed coolness and peace over me. So Nimrod said, according to what I was told, O Abraham, I am going to sacrifice to your God because of what I have seen of His might and power, and because of what He did for you when you insisted on His worship and His unity. I will sacrifice four thousand cows for Him. Abraham said to him, God will not accept a sacrifice from you because of your religion unless you break with it. He said, O Abraham, I am not able to abandon my kingdom, but I will sacrifice them to Him. So Nimrod sacrificed them, and he kept away from Abraham. Thus God guarded Abraham from the torment.

From Ibn Hamid, who got it from Salamah, who got it from Muhammad b. Ishaq, who got it from ʿAbd-ar-Rahman b. Abu az-Zanad, who got it from his father, who got it from ʿAbd-ar-Rahman al-Aʿraj, Abu Hurayrah said, I heard the Messenger of God say, Abraham never said anything that was not true except three times: his saying that he was ill when he was not; his saying that the chief of the idols did that, so ask them, if they are able to talk; and his saying to Pharaoh, My sister, when Pharaoh asked him about Sarah, Who is this woman? Abraham never said anything that was not so except those. On the authority of Saʿid b. Yahya, who got it from Ubayy, who got it from Muhammad b. Ishaq, who got it from Abu az-Zanad, who got it from ʿAbd-ar-Rahman al-Aʿraj, Abu Hurayrah said, The Messenger of God said that Abraham never lied except thrice; then he narrated something like the above.

Abraham set out on a Hijrah for his Lord, and Lot went with him. He married Sarah, the daughter of his paternal uncle, and left, fleeing, until, because of his religion, he settled in Harran, seeking safety in the worship of his Lord. He remained there as long as God wished, and then he went to Egypt. On the authority of Muhammad b. Ishaq, who got it from ʿAbdullah b. Kaʿb, who got it from Malik al-Ansari, the Messenger of God said, When you conquer Egypt, treat its people well, for they have protection and mercy. So I asked az-Zuhri what the mercy was which the Messenger of God mentioned, and he said, Hagar, the mother of Ishmael, whom Abraham took from Egypt to Syria was from there.

Then Abraham left Egypt for Syria. He settled a seventh of the land of Palestine, which was the Syrian desert. Lot settled in al-Mutafikah, and it is a seventh of the land of Palestine, a day and a night's journey or nearer. Then God made Abraham a prophet. Because he feared the king that was there at the time and was apprehensive about his evil intentions, he settled a seventh of the land of Palestine, dug a well there, and established a place of worship. The water of this well was an open spring, and his flock would return to it.

Abraham remained there for seven years. Then his people annoyed him, so he left and settled in an area of the land of Palestine between Ramlah and Aylah in a land called Qattah. When he went away from there, the water of the spring dried up and went away. The people were called together about what to do, and they said, We have expelled a good man. So they followed him until they found him and asked him to return. He said, Why should I return to a land from which I have been expelled? They said, The water which you drank and we drank with you has dried up and gone away. So he gave them seven goats from his flock and said, Go, take these with you, and when you place them before the well, the water will appear as it was. Drink from it, and do not let a menstruating woman come near it. So they left with the goats, and when they stopped by the well, the water appeared, and they drank from it. This continued until a menstruating woman came and scooped out some water from the spring. The water in it has been stagnant to this day. Abraham stayed in his country, playing host to whoever settled there, God having amply provided him with sustenance, property, and servants.

When God wished to destroy the people of Lot, He sent His messengers to tell Lot to leave them, and He commanded the messengers to go to Abraham to announce the glad tidings of Isaac and Jacob to him and to Sarah. So the messengers came down to Abraham. When he saw them in the form of men, Abraham was pleased with them and regarded them as guests whose beauty and grace he had not seen before. So he said, No one go out to these people but me. He went out and brought an expensive calf which had been roasted by Hagar, gave it to them, and they grabbed it. He said to them, Will you not eat? And when he saw them not partaking of it, he did not know who they were. And he feared them, because they would not eat any of his food. They said, O Abraham, we will not eat food except when we pay a price for it. He said, Here is the price. They said, What is it? He said, That you mention the Name of God at the beginning of the meal and that you praise Him afterward. Gabriel looked Michael and said, It is right that his Lord took him as a friend. Then they said, Do not fear; we are sent to the people of Lot. His wife, Sarah, was standing apart from them while Abraham was seated with them, and when they told him about why they were sent and about the glad tidings of Isaac and Jacob, Sarah laughed.

Hagar was a good-looking servant girl whom Sarah had given to Abraham and said, I think she is a pure woman, so take her. Perhaps God will provide you with a son by her. Sarah was barren, and she did not bear for Abraham until she was old. Abraham prayed to God that He give him the benefits of a son, but the prayers were of no avail until Abraham grew old, for Sarah was barren. Then Abraham slept with Hagar, and she bore Ishmael to him.

From Ibn Hamid, who got it from Salamah, who got it from Muhammad b. Ishaq, who got it from al-Hasan b. ʿUmrah, who got it from Sammak b. Harb, who got it from Khalid b. ʿArʿarah, ʿAli b. Abu Talib, peace be upon him, said: When God commanded Abraham to visit the Kaʿbah and call mankind to the Pilgrimage, Abraham left Syria with his son Ishmael and Ishmael's mother, Hagar. And God sent the Shechinah with him, a wind which had a tongue with which Abraham could talk in the morning, and travel with so that it brought him to Mecca. When it came to the place of the Kaʿbah, the Shechinah went around it. Then it said to Abraham, Build over me; build over me; build over me. So Abraham laid the foundations and raised up the Temple, he and Ishmael, until they stopped at the place of the cornerstone. Abraham said to Ishmael, O son, get me a stone that I can make as a sign to mankind. So he brought a stone, but Abraham was not satisfied with it and said, Get me another. Ishmael went to get a stone, and he brought it, but one had already been placed in its place, so he said, O Father, who brought you this stone? He said, He who did not entrust one to you, O my son.

When Abraham was sent to settle in the environs of the Temple, Gabriel went with him, and they would not pass by a town but he would say, Is this the place, O Gabriel? And Gabriel would say, Pass it by, until he came to Mecca. At that time Mecca was rocky and thorny, with a people there called Amalekites living just outside Mecca and its environs. The Temple was a small, brown hill. Abraham said to Gabriel, Is this the place? And he said, Yes. So Abraham went with Ishmael and his mother, Hagar, to the place of the stone and settled them there. Abraham ordered Hagar, the mother of Ishmael, to make a hut. "My Lord, I have settled some of my progeny in an uncultivable valley near your Holy House . . . up to the words . . . that they may be thankful"[Q 14:37]. Then he left them at the Temple and departed for his other family in Syria.

Ishmael developed a strong thirst, so his mother went out to get water, but she did not find any. She heard a voice, as you might hear a voice, urging her to get a drink for him, and she heard it as a voice coming from as-Saffa. So she went there, but she did not see anything. It is alleged that, on the contrary, she went up to as-Saffa and asked God to send rain to Ishmael. Then she went to al-Marwah and did the same. Just then she heard the cries of the beasts of the valley in the direction where she had left Ishmael, so she went toward him very distressed, and she found him scratching up water with his hand from a spring which had burst forth under his hand, and he drank from it. The mother of Ishmael came to it and made it drinkable. Then she filled her waterskin for Ishmael, and if she had not done that, the spring Zamzam would not have ever stopped pouring out its water.

Sa'id b. Salim, who got it from 'Uthman b. Saj, who got it from Muhammad b. Ishaq, told us: It reached me that an angel came to Hagar, the mother of Ishmael, after Abraham settled her in Mecca, before Abraham and Ishmael raised up the edifice of the Temple, and showed her the Temple, which was a round, red hill, and said to her, This is the first temple made for mankind on earth, and it is the Temple of God. Know that Abraham and Ishmael will erect it for mankind.

From Sa'id b. Salim, who got it from 'Uthman b. Saj, Muhammad b. Ishaq said, When God commanded Abraham, the Friend of God, to build the Holy Temple, Abraham came from Armenia on Buraq, along with the Shechinah, which was like a gentle wind and had a face which would talk. With Abraham was an angel which guided him to the place of the Temple, so that he came to Mecca. And there was Ishmael, who was twenty, his mother having died before that, and she was buried in al-Hijr. He said, O Ishmael, God has commanded me to build a temple for Him. Ishmael said to him, Where? And the angel showed him the place of the Temple. The two of them began digging, and there were only two of them, and Abraham reached the first foundation of Adam. He dug around the Temple and found a stone great enough that three men could not surround it. Then he built on the first foundation of Adam. The Shechinah flitted about the first foundations as though it were alive and said, O Abraham, build on me. So he built on it, and for that reason the Arabs do not circumambulate the Temple without seeing the Shechinah on it.

He built the Temple, making its height seven cubits, and its depth in the early thirty-two cubits from the Black Stone to the Syrian corner. From the Syrian corner to the western was twenty-two cubits, and from the western corner to the Yemenite corner, thirty-one cubits. Its southern side from the Black Stone to the Yemenite corner was twenty cubits, and for that reason it was called Cube.

When Abraham, the Friend of God, finished building the Holy Temple, Gabriel came to him and said, Circumambulate it seven times. So he went around it seven times, he and Ishmael, touching the corners on each circuit. When they had completed the seven, they prayed two prostrations. Gabriel stayed with Abraham and showed him all the rites of the Pilgrimage, as-Safa, al-Marwah, Mina, Muzdalifah, and ʿArafah. When he entered Mina and came down from the height, Iblis appeared to him on the height, and Gabriel said to him, Throw at him. Abraham threw seven pebbles, and Iblis disappeared. Then Iblis appeared at the lowest part, and Gabriel said to Abraham, Throw at him. So he threw seven pebbles, and Iblis disappeared. Then Abraham performed his Pilgrimage. Gabriel stopped him at the stations and taught him the rites until he came to ʿArafah. When he arrived, Gabriel said to him, Do you know the rites? And Abraham said, Yes; so it was named ʿArafah because of his statement that he knew the rites.

Then God commanded Abraham to announce the Pilgrimage to mankind. Abraham said, O Lord, my voice will not reach. God said, Announce and it will reach. So he raised his voice up over the place until it went to the tops of the mountains and along their length. The earth, its plains, its mountains, its dry land and sea, its men and Jinn gathered that day so that they all heard it together. He put his fingers in his ears and turned his face to the south and the north, and east and the west. He began with the south, saying, O mankind, the Pilgrimage is ordained for you in the ancient Temple, so respond to your Lord. And they responded from the seven limits and from the east and the west, from the ends of the earth: At your service, O God, Labayka.

The stones were as they are today, except that God wished to make the place a sign, and Abraham's footprints are there today. Everyone who makes the Pilgrimage today is of those who answered Abraham. He who performs the

Pilgrimage twice answers twice, or thrice, likewise, and the traces of the two footprints of Abraham are a sign in the place, and that is because of His words, "In it are clear signs of the Place of Abraham, and he who enters it is safe"[Q 3:97].

Ibn Ishaq said, It reached me that Adam, upon him be peace, had established the foundations before Abraham, and that Isaac and Sarah made the Pilgrimage from Syria. Abraham, upon him be peace, used to make the Pilgrimage every year on Buraq. The prophets and mankind made the Pilgrimage after that. Muhammad b. Ishaq said, Some of the scholars told me that 'Abdullah b. az-Zubayr said to 'Ubayd b. 'Umayr al-Laythi, How did you learn that Abraham, upon him be peace, issued the call to the Pilgrimage? He said, It reached me that when Abraham and Ishmael raised the foundations and finished what God wished of them, Abraham faced the Yemen and invited mankind and Jinn to God, the Mighty and the Powerful, and to the Pilgrimage. The answer was Labayka, O God, Labayka. Then he faced the east and invited mankind and Jinn to God and to the Pilgrimage, and the answer was Labayka, Labayka, and then to the west likewise, and toward Syria likewise. Then he performed the Pilgrimage with Ishmael and those Muslim neighbors who were with him, dwelling with Ishmael in the sacred precinct at that time. They were his kith, and he prayed with them the noon, the afternoon, and the sunset and evening prayers at Mina. Then he spent the night with them until morning. He prayed the morning prayer and then breakfasted with them. He remained with them at 'Arafah in the mosque of Abraham until the sun passed midway between noon and mid-afternoon. Then Abraham journeyed with his kith to the stopping place at 'Arafah, and stopped with them. When the sun set, he went to al-Muzdalifah, where he combined the sunset and evening prayers. Then he spent the night until dawn, at which time he prayed the morning prayer. Then he stayed at al-Muzdalifah until the sky was no longer yellow. Then he demonstrated how to fast until he finished with the Pilgrimage. Abraham gave permission for the Pilgrimage to mankind, and then he left, returning to Syria, where he died, may the prayers and peace of God be upon him and on all the prophets of God and the messengers.

On the authority of 'Abd-ar-Rahman b. Abu Bakr, who got it from az-Zuhri, who got it from al-'Ala b. Jariyyah ath-Thaqafi, who got it from Abu Hurayrah, who got it from Ka'b, and 'Abdullah b. Abu Bakr, who got it from Muhammad b. Muslim az-Zuhri, who got it from Abu Sufyan b. al-'Ala b. ath-Thaqafi, a client of the B. Zuhrah, who got it from Abu Hurayrah, Ka'b al-Ahbar said that Isaac was the one of the sons whom Abraham was commanded to sacrifice. Ibn Ishaq said, I heard Muhammad b. Ka'b al-Qurazi say that the son whom God commanded Abraham to sacrifice was Ishmael. I found that in the Book of God in the story of Abraham and his being commanded to sacrifice his son, Ishmael. That is because, when he finished with the story of the sacrifice of the son of Abraham, God said, "We gave him the glad tidings of Isaac as a prophet of the righteous" [Q 37:112], and "We gave her the glad tidings of Isaac, and after Isaac, Jacob" [Q 11:71], saying a son and a grandson, and He did not command him to sacrifice anyone except Ishmael.

From Buraydah b. Sufyan b. Farwah al-Islami, Muhammad b. Kaʿb al-Qurazi said that he mentioned the above story to Ibn ʿAbdu-l-ʿAziz, when he was caliph, when he was with him in Syria, and ʿUmar said to him that it could not be as I had said. So he sent for a man who was with him in Syria who was a Jew. He greeted him—and he could be seen to be one of the learned men of the Jews—and ʿUmar b. ʿAbdu-l-ʿAziz asked him about that. Muhammad b. Kaʿb al-Qurazi said, I was with ʿUmar b. ʿAbdu-l-ʿAziz, and ʿUmar said to him, Which of the two sons was Abraham commanded to sacrifice? He said, Ishmael; by God, O Commander of the Faithful, the Jews know that, but they are jealous of the Arabs because it was your ancestor about whom God issued the command for sacrifice, and to whom God referred when He mentioned his patience about what he was ordered to do. So they say it was Isaac, because Isaac was their ancestor. From al-Hasan b. Dinar and ʿAmr b. ʿUbayd, al-Hasan b. Abu al-Hasan al-Basri said, There is no doubt that Ishmael was the one of the two sons of Abraham who was ordered to be sacrificed.

According to what they say, when Abraham visited Hagar, he was carried on Buraq, breakfasting in Syria, or Mecca, and going from Mecca and spending the night with his people in Syria, until the ordeal came which nearly took his soul and his hope when he pondered his service to his Lord and the enormity of His holiness, seeing in a dream that he was to sacrifice his son. According to some scholars, when Abraham was commanded to sacrifice his son, he said to him, O son, take the rope and the butchering knife and go with us to this mountain to gather firewood for your people, without mentioning anything to him about what he had been commanded. When he turned toward the mountain, the Enemy of God, Iblis, in the form of a man, tried to dissuade him from what God had commanded. He said, Where are you going, old man? Abraham said, I am going to this mountain for a reason. Iblis said, By God, I see that the Devil has come to you in your dreams and commanded you to sacrifice your son, and you wish to sacrifice him! Abraham knew him, and he said to him, Get away from me, Enemy of God. By God, I will carry out the command of my Lord.

When Iblis, the Enemy of God, gave up on Abraham, he turned to Ishmael, who was behind Abraham carrying the rope and the knife, and he said to him, O youth, do you know where your father is going with you? He said, To gather firewood on this mountain for our people. Iblis said, By God, he only wishes to sacrifice you. He said, Why? Iblis said, He asserts that his Lord commanded him to do that. He said, Then he should do what his Lord has commanded, willingly and obediently.

So when the boy put him off, Iblis went to Hagar, the mother of Ishmael, who was in her house, and said to her, O mother of Ishmael, do you know where Abraham went with Ishmael? She said, He went with him to gather firewood in that mountain. Iblis said, He only went to sacrifice him. She said, No, he is more merciful than that and loves him more than that. But if his Lord commanded him to do that, then he should accept the command of God.

So the Enemy of God returned enraged, not getting anything he wanted from the family of Abraham. He had been deterred from Abraham and the family of Abraham by the aid of God. They agreed to the command of God willingly and obediently.

When Abraham had gone up with his son into the mountain, which was, according to what they say, the mountain of Thabir, he said to him, O my son, I have seen in a dream that I should sacrifice you. He said, "O my father, do what you are commanded; you will find me, if God wills, among the enduring ones"(Q 37:102). Muhammad b. Ishaq said on the authority of some scholars that Ishmael said to him, O my father, if you desire my sacrifice, nothing is imposed on you from me, and my bloodwit is diminished; make my bonds fast, for if the death is hard, I do not believe I will be able to endure it when I feel death's touch. Hone your knife so that you can finish me off and release me. When you lay me down to sacrifice me, lay me on my face; do not lay me on my side, for I fear that if you look at my face, you will turn soft and abandon the command of God. If you wish, return my shirt to my mother, for it might be a consolation to her. So do it! Abraham said, Yes, you are a great help in the command of God. So he bound him as Ishmael had ordered and made him fast. Then he honed the knife and placed him on his face, wary of the look on his face. Then Abraham placed the knife to Ishmael's neck. But God turned it up, seizing it from his hand, and moved it away to save Ishmael. Then a call came: O Abraham, you have believed the vision. Here is your sacrifice as a ransom for your son; so sacrifice it instead of him (see Q 37:103-107).

From the Kitâb al-Mubtada᾿ by Muhammad b. Ishaq, according to Ibn ᶜAbbas, the name of the wife of Ishmael was ᶜUmarah bt. Saᶜid b. Usamah, Abraham came from Syria to Mecca, and he found Ishmael's wife, and asked her about him. She said, He is absent, and her voice was not soft. So Abraham said to her, Say to Ishmael, A certain old man has come looking for you, and he gives you greetings and he says to you, Without blame on your house, I am not pleased with her. Ishmael, whenever he came, would ask his people, and his wife said, An old man came looking for you, and she described him. Ishmael said to her, Did you say anything to him? She said, No. He said, Did he say anything to you. She said, Yes, greet him and tell him, without blame on your house, I am not pleased with her for you. Ishmael said, You are the blame of my house; return to your people. And he returned her to her people and married another woman.

Abraham tarried as long as God wished him to tarry. Then he returned and found Ishmael absent and found another woman, so he stopped and offered greetings. She returned the greetings, and invited him to come into the house, and offered him food and drink. He said, What is your food and drink? She said, Meat and water. He said, Is there no grain or any other kind of food? She said, No. He said, May God bless you in meat and water. From Ibn 'Abbas, the Messenger of God, may the prayers and peace of God be upon him, said, If he had found any grain with her that day, he would have included it in the blessing and the land would have been a land of herbage. Then Abraham left and said, Say to him that a certain old man has come for him who said he found the threshold of this house well, and he is delighted with it. Ishmael returned to his family and said, Did anyone come for me? She said, Yes, a certain old man came for you. He said, Did he say anything? She said, Yes, that he found the threshold of your house well and is delighted in it.

According to Ibn Ishaq, when Sarah, the daughter of Aaron, the wife of Abraham, died, Abraham married Qatura, the daughter of Yuqtan, a Canaanite woman, and she bore him six sons; Yaqqas Zamran, Midian, Yasbaq, Suh, and Basar. The total of Abraham's sons was eight counting Ishmael and Isaac. Ishmael was the firstborn, the oldest of his children.

Yaqqas, the son of Abraham, married Ra'uwwah, the daughter of Zamar, the son of Yuqtan, the son of Ludhan, the son of Jurhum, the son of Yuqtan, the son of 'Abir, and she bore to him al-Barbar and Laqqaha. Zamran, the son of Abraham, sired a group of people who are unknown. The people of Midian were born to Midian, the people of Shu'ayb, the son of Mikail, the prophet, and he and his people were among the children to whom God, the Mighty and Powerful, sent a prophet.

He said, Twelve men were born to Ishmael, the son of Abraham, and their mother was as-Sayyidah, the daughter of Madad b. 'Amr al-Jurhumi: Nabit, Qaydar, Adabil, Mubasha, Masma', Dama, Mas, Adad, Watr, Nafis, Tama, and Qaydman. According to what they say, the lifespan of Ishmael was one hundred and thirty years. From Nabit and Qaydar, God made the Arab. And God, the Mighty and the Powerful, made Ishmael a prophet and sent him to the Amalekites, according to what they say, and to the tribes of the Yemen.

Isaac, the son of Abraham, married Rebecca, the daughter of Bethuel, the son of al-Yas, and she bore him Esau, the son of Isaac, and Jacob, the son of Isaac. They say that they were twins, and that Esau was the older of the two of them. Then Esau, the son of Isaac, married his cousin, Basmah, the daughter of Ishmael, the son of Abraham, and she bore him Rum, and all the yellow-skinned people are of his offspring. Some of the people allege that al-Ashban is from him, but I do not know whether he is of a daughter of Ishmael or not.

Jacob, the son of Isaac, who was Israel, married a cousin of his, Leah, the daughter of Laban, the son of Bethuel, the son of al-Yas, and she bore him Rubil, the son of Jacob, who was the eldest of his children, and Simeon, the son of Jacob, and Levi, the son of Jacob, and Yehudah, the son of Jacob, and Zebulon, the son of Jacob, and Issachar, the son of Jacob, and Dinah, the daughter of Jacob. Then Leah died, and Jacob had offspring from her sister Rachel, the daughter of Laban, the son of Bethuel, the son of al-Yas. She bore him Joseph, the son of Jacob, and Benjamin, the son of Jacob, and he was Shaddad in Arabic. From two concubines, the name of one of whom was Zilpah and the name of the other Bilhah, four men were born: Dan, Naphtali, Gad, and Asher, the sons of Jacob. The sons of Jacob were twelve.

Some of the People of the Torah say that Rebecca was the wife of Isaac and that she was the daughter of Nahor, the son of Azar, the paternal uncle of Isaac, and that she bore him two sons, Esau and Jacob, in one pregnancy, and that Isaac commanded his son, Jacob, that he should not marry a Canaanite woman, and that he should marry a woman from the daughters of his maternal uncle, Laban, the son of Nahor. So when he wished to marry, Jacob went to his uncle, Laban, the son of Nahor, seeking marriage. Night overtook him along the way, and he spent the night using a rock as a pillow. In his sleep he saw that there was a ladder at his head, raised up to one of the gates of heaven, and angels were descending and rising up it.

Jacob went to his uncle and proposed to him for his daughter Rachel. Laban had two daughters, Leah, the elder, and Rachel, the younger. He said, Do you have some wealth so that I can marry you? Jacob said, No, but let me serve you for a wage so that you can receive a dower for your daughter. He said, The price is that you serve me for seven Pilgrimages. Jacob said, Marry me to Rachel; she is the one I stipulate, and for her I serve you. His uncle said, That is between me and you. So Jacob tended flocks for him for seven years. But when he discharged his obligations to him, Laban gave him his eldest daughter, Leah, and he sent her to him in the night.

When he awoke in the morning and found other than what he had stipulated, Jacob went to him while he was with his people, saying to him, You have beguiled me, duped me, misappropriated my labor for seven years, and swindled me out of my wife. His uncle said to him, O my nephew, do you wish to bring shame and disgrace on your uncle even though he is your uncle and your parent? When have you seen people marrying the younger before the elder? Serve me seven more years, and I will marry you to her sister. (The people at that time could have two sisters together until Moses was sent and the Torah came down to him.) So Jacob tended flocks for his uncle for seven more years, after which Laban gave him Rachel. Leah bore him four sons: Rubil, Yehudah, Simeon, and Levi. Rachel bore him Joseph and his brother, Benjamin, and sisters to the two of them. Laban had given handmaidens to his two daughters when he had got them ready for Jacob, and they presented the two handmaidens to Jacob. Each one of them bore him three tribes.

Jacob left his uncle and returned to settle with his brother, Esau. Some say that Zilpah, the servant of Rachel, bore him Dan and Naphtali because Rachel had given her to Jacob and had asked that he seek a child from Zilpah when a child was late in coming from her. Some also say that Leah had given her handmaid, Bilhah, to Jacob in competition to Rachel with her handmaid, and that she asked him that he seek a child from her. So she bore him Gad and Asher. Then Rachel bore him Joseph and Benjamin after all hope had been abandoned. And Jacob departed with his children and his women to the dwelling place of his father in Palestine out of fear of his brother, Esau, although he had never seen anything but good from him.

Esau, according to what has been told, cleaved to his uncle, Ishmael, and married his daughter, Bismah, and took her to Syria. She bore him a number of children, and they increased until they overcame the Canaanites. They traveled to the sea in the direction of al-Iskandariyyah and then to Rum. Esau, according to what was mentioned, was named Adam because of his ruddy complexion, and for that reason his children are termed yellow.

Now Rebecca, the daughter of Bethuel, had borne to Isaac, the son of Abraham, his two sons, Esau and Jacob, twins in one birth, after Isaac was sixty years old. Esau led the two of them coming out of the belly of his mother. According to what has been reported, Isaac gave preference to Esau, and Rebecca, their mother, preferred Jacob. They say that Jacob cheated Esau in a sacrifice which was made at the command of their father, Isaac, after Isaac had become old and his sight was weak. Most of the blessing went to Jacob, and the blessing was turned to him by his father, Isaac. That angered Esau, and he promised to kill Jacob, so Jacob fled from Esau to his uncle, Laban, in Babylon. Laban took him and married him to his two daughters, Leah and Rachel. He went with the two of them, and with their handmaidens, and with his children, the twelve tribes, and their sister, Dinah, to Syria, the dwelling place of his forefathers. He associated with his brother, Esau, until Esau left the land. He changed his residence from Syria to the coasts. Then he crossed to Rum and dwelt there. Kings came from his children who are the Greeks.

Sources

at-Tabari, *Ta'rīkh* 253, 254-261, 262-263, 264-265, 269, 270-271, 277, 278-279, 287-288, 292, 298-299, 303-306, 345-346, 351-352, 354-358 at-Tabari, *Tafsîr* 7:248-251, 7:254, 7:258, 17:39, 17:40, 17:41, 17:42, 3:27, 3:48, 3:57, 3:27, 17:43, 17:47, 1:544, 1:548, 23:81, 23:82-83, 23:84-85, 23:87, 23:88

Al-Baghdadi 2:26, 2:336

ath-Tha'labi 46, 47-48

Al-Azraqi 1:36-37, 1:43, 1:24-25, 1:46ff.

Ibn Sa'd 1:25

Lot

This story of Lot is really part of the Abraham narrative and may have occurred as a digression in the original versions. Like Noah, Hud, and Salih, Lot is regarded as a prophet of punishment. The narrative follows the Quran closely and in this version has little in common with the Haggadic legends of the rabbis or the more extensive treatments in later Muslim writers. The graphic description of Gabriel's carrying Sodom up to heaven and then dropping it is most likely derived as a gloss on the Quranic words, "We brought it low" (Q 11:82). The stones of baked clay are, like the stones in the Surah of the Elephant (Q 105), heavenly seals of the official death decree (see Newby, "Abraha and Sennacherib: A Talmudic Parallel to the Tafsir on Surat al-Fil").

Text
In the name of God, the Merciful and the Compassionate
Ibn Hamid said on the authority of Salamah, who got it from Ibn Ishaq: "When the fear went from Abraham, and the glad tidings came to him" [Q 11:74] of Isaac and Jacob, born of Isaac, and that he was safe from what he had been fearing, he said, "Praise be to God who gave me Ishmael and Isaac in old age; my Lord is the Hearer of prayer" [Q 14:39]. God said, "He argued with us about the people of Lot" [Q 11:74], meaning that Abraham argued with God and His messengers about the people of Lot in order to turn the punishment away from them.

The People of the Torah assert that Abraham said in his debate with God's messengers, when he argued with them about the people of Lot to avert their punishment: If you see that there are a hundred believers among the people of Lot, will you destroy them? They said, No. He said, If you see that there are eighty? They said, No. He said, If you see that there are sixty? They said, No. He said, If you see that there are fifty? They said, No. He said, If you see that there is one Muslim man? They said, No. And when they did not mention to Abraham that there was one believer among them, "He said, Lot is among them" [Q 29:32], eliminating the punishment from them because of Lot. "They said, We know best who is among them. We will save him and his people, except his wife, who is among the ones passed over" [Q 29:32]. They said, O Abraham, turn away from this. The command of your Lord has been given, and a punishment will come to them which cannot be averted.

According to what the People of the Torah assert, the messengers left Abraham and went to Lot in disguise. When the messengers came to Lot, he was vexed by them "and he was uneasy about them" [Q 11:77] because of his fear that his people would dishonor his guests. So he said, "This is a distressful day" [Q 11:77] that is, a day of trial and tribulation. "And his people came to him, running to him—and they used to do evil things—and he said, My people, here are my daughters; they are purer for you" [Q 11:78]. When the messengers came to Lot, his people came running to Lot when they were told of the messengers. They assert, and God knows best, that Lot's wife was the one who told them of the messengers's location. She said: There are two guests of ours with Lot who are more comely and handsome than I have ever seen.

The people of Lot used to lust after men instead of women for fornication as no one else in the world had before. So when they came to Lot, they said, "Have we not forbidden you from anyone?" [Q 15:70] That is, Did we not say to you that no one was to come near you, and that if we found anyone with you, we would fornicate with him? "He said, O people, here are my daughters; they are purer for you" [Q 11:78]. I ransom my guests from you by them. (He did not make the offer to them except as permission for marriage.) "So fear God and do not degrade me among my guests. Is there not among you a rightly guided man" [Q 11:78] that is, a man who knows the truth and denies abomination? They said, "You know what we desire" [Q 11:79]; that is, our desire is other than being rightly guided. When his speech did not put them off or dissuade them, and when they did not accept anything about his daughters that was offered them, "He said, Would that I had the power to go against you or that I had recourse to strong support" [Q 11:80], that is, a clan to defend me or a party to aid me and intervene between you and these guests.

The messengers were listening to what he was saying and what was said to him and perceived what distress he was in. So when they saw what had come to him, "They said, O Lot, we are messengers of your Lord; they will not reach you" [Q 11:81], that is, with anything you despise. "So travel with your family part of the night and do not let anyone of you turn around, except your wife, for that which smites them will smite her. Their appointed time is in the morning. Is not the morning near?" [Q 11:81] That is, the punishment will come down on them on the morning of this night; so depart as you have been commanded.

Muhammad b. Ka'b al-Qurazi related that the messengers flapped their wings in the faces of those of Lot's people who had come to him attempting to seduce him from his guests, and the people became blind. God said, "They sought to seduce his guests from him, and we blinded them" [Q 54:37]. I was told that the Prophet, may the prayers and peace of God be upon him, said, God sent Gabriel, upon him be peace, in disguise to the town of Lot, upon him be peace, which Lot was in, and he carried it off with his wings. He ascended with it until the people of the sublunary sphere heard the barking of its dogs and the voices of its cocks. Then he turned the town on its face. After that, God followed it with stones, God saying, "Then we brought it low and rained stones of baked clay on it" [Q 11:82]. God destroyed the town and the evil that was around it. There were five evil townships: Sanʿah, Saʿwah, ʿAthrah, Duma, and Sodom, which was the biggest township. God saved Lot and those of his family who were with him, except his wife, who was among the ones destroyed.

Sources

at-Tabari, Tafsîr 12:77, 12:79-80, 12:82, 12:85, 12:86, 12:87, 12:92-93, 12-98
at-Tabari, *Taʾrîkh* 342-343

Job

Job in the Bible is not a prophet but the long-suffering servant of God. For some of the rabbis Job had come to be regarded as a pious Gentile and a prophet to the Gentiles (*Baba Bathra* 15b). In the *Kitâb al-Mubtadaʾ*, Job is said to have come from Rome (*Rum*), reflecting the notion in the apocryphal *Testament of Job* that he was a descendant of Esau. By Muhammad's time, however, Job was regarded as a righteous prophet.

The text that Ibn Ishaq chose to include in the *Kitâb al-Mubtadaʾ* reflects both the end result of long Midrashic development and a considerable literary polishing. The rhetorical style of the story of Job seems different from many of the other narratives in this collection. In the story of creation, for example, one can distinguish many of the short, pithy stories and anecdotes that were knit together into the longer narrative. The narrative of creation is closer to the *Akhbar* or anecdotal style of historical writing. The story of Job appears as a unified whole and with a higher level of rhetorical sophistication than much of the rest of the material in the *Kitâb al-Mubtadaʾ*. It is likely that Ibn Ishaq's story of Job is based on some of the written versions we assume to have been available in early Abbasid times in the booksellers' stalls. As we have seen, Ibn Ishaq had recourse to written versions of much material from Jewish and Christian circles. Because the story of Job was so important, a great body of literature and discussion grew up. The Talmudists frequently discussed Job's origin, role, manner of suffering, his piety and purity, the cause of his affliction, and his ultimate restoration to God's favor. Much of the rabbinic discussions are reflected in the well-known Greek apocryphal *Testament of Job*. We can only surmise about the existence of translations into Arabic before Ibn Ishaq's time.

Some of the narrative details of the story of Job as found in the *Kitâb al-Mubtadaʾ* are paralleled in the *Testament of Job*, but the actual relationship between the two is very problematic. What is of more importance for our concerns is the way in which the ideas of Job as a prophet are stated. The youth in the *Kitâb al-Mubtadaʾ*, who corresponds to Elihu in the Book of Job, states Job's claim as a prophet. The argument that the youth advances reinterprets the notion that punishment of a messenger is because of sin or wrongdoing, and states that it is because of God's favor that Job is punished. This is parallel to the argument found in Q 3:184: "If they regard you [Muhammad] as false, they have regarded as false messengers who came before you with the

Psalms and the Illuminating Book.'' In other words, rejection and affliction are the lot of the righteous, a means and a sign of purification, a guarantee of salvation.

With the aid of the story of Job, Muhammad's persecution and the afflictions and persecutions of the rest of his community can be read as negative signs of God's favor and guarantees of future success. Just as in the Bible, the message in the Quran is that the good will be rewarded and the bad will be punished. The exception is when the righteous suffer. The narrative of Job in the *Kitâb al-Mubtada* goes beyond the biblical answer and shows that rejection and punishment are the fate of God's elect prophets. It is one of the ''burdens'' of prophethood that proved so heavy for Jonah to bear.

Text

In the name of God, the Merciful and the Compassionate

On the authority of Salamah, who received it from Muhammad b. Ishaq, who got it on the authority of one who is not to be suspected, who took from Wahb. b. Munabbih the Yemenite and others of the people of the First Book, Ibn Hamid said that Job was from Rum. God had singled him out, elevated him, tempted him with wealth, many children, and much property, offered him the world, and was generous to him in divine blessings. Job owned al-Bathaniyyah in Syria, both its heights and valleys, its plains and mountains. Job had all kinds of property: camels, cattle, sheep and goats, horses and asses, which were finer and more numerous than those of any other man. God had given him family and children, both sons and daughters. He was pious, reverent, merciful to the poor, feeding the indigent, relieving the burdens of widows, providing for orphans, honoring guests, and aiding travelers. He was thankful for God's gifts to him, realizing God's truth in wealth, and acknowledging that He had prevented the Enemy of God, Iblis, from afflicting him in the way he afflicts wealthy persons with fame, foolishness, neglect, and distraction from God's commands by the things of this world.

Now Job had three people who trusted him, regarded him as a friend, and knew the extra favor which God had given him. One of them was a Yemenite called Eliphaz, and the other two were from his own country, one called Zophar and the other called Bildad, both middle-aged men.

Iblis, the Enemy of God, dwelt outside the seventh heaven. Every year he would arrive and ask to come in. One day he climbed up to heaven, and God said to him (or he was told), Do you have any power over my servant Job? Iblis said, O Lord, how could I have any power over him? If you had not given him prosperity, luxury, wealth, vigor, and granted him family, property, children, independence, a health body, a family, and made him rich, then he would not thank you, worship you, and be obedient to you. But you have done that for him. If you were to afflict him by removing what you gave him, then he would not obey you but something else. (Or, this is something like what the Enemy of God said.)

God said, I give you power over his family and his wealth. Now God knew more than the Devil. He only granted Iblis power over Job out of mercy, to increase Job's reward after the trial, to make Job an example for the forbearing and make him a reminder to servants in tribulation so that they would be consoled and would hope that the result of patience in this world would be recompense in the next because of the way God favored Job.

The Enemy of God quickly descended and gathered the demonic Jinn and the giant devils in his army and said, I have been given power over Job's family and wealth. What can you do? One of them said, I am a whirlwind with fire; I will pass by his wealth and destroy it. The Devil said, Do that! So he went out to Job's camels and shepherds and completely burned them. Then the Enemy of God in the guise of an overseer came to Job while he was at prayer and said, O Job, a fire came, overtook your camels and burned them and all with them except me. I have come to tell you that. But Job knew the Devil and said, Praised be to God who gave them and took them. He rescued you from them as he brings darnel from worthless seeds.

Then the Devil left Job and began to attack his wealth, bit by bit, until he destroyed the last of it. Whenever a portion of his wealth was destroyed, Job praised God, lauded Him even more, accepted the judgment, and made his soul patient with the trial. When none of Job's wealth remained, Iblis came to Job's family and children and their maidservants and manservants in their castle. He assumed the guise of a violent wind and lifted the castle off its foundations. Then he cast it upon Job's family and children and crushed them under it. The Devil came to Job in the form of one of their butlers, with a crushed face, and said, O Job, a violent wind came and bore the castle off its foundations. Then it cast it on your family and your offspring and crushed all except me. I have come to tell you that.

Job had not mourned anything that had befallen him, but he mourned his family and his offspring. He took dirt and placed it on his head. Then he said, Would that my mother had not borne me and that I was nothing. The Enemy of God was delighted with that, and he ascended to heaven, exuberant. But Job repented of what he had said, and he praised God, and his repentance got to God ahead of the Enemy of God, so when Iblis came and mentioned what he had done, he was told, Job's repentance and his return to God have preceded you.

The Enemy of God said, O Lord, give me power over his body. God said, I give you power over his body except for his tongue, his heart, his breath, his hearing, and his sight. So Iblis went to Job while he was praying and blew a breath into his body which burned from his head to his feet like a flame. Then warts broke out on his body the size of sheep buttocks. Job scratched with his nails until the nails came out; then he scratched with pottery, and then with stones, until his flesh came off and nothing remained except veins and sinews and bones. His eyes wandered about his head, and his heart tried to understand. Nothing came out of his bowels because he ate and drank only enough to preserve them. He stayed in this condition as long as God wished.

Al-Hasan used to say on the authority of Ibn Dinar that Job remained seven years and six months with that affliction, lying on a rubbish heap near the city. Wahb. b. Munabbih said that none of his family survived except one woman who stayed with him and would get things for him. And the Enemy of God was not able to extract from Job what he wanted, whether great or small.

When the affliction had lasted a long time for Job and the woman, people became weary of her feeding him and giving him drink. Wahb b. Munabbih said, I was told that one day she asked for something to feed Job, but she did not find anything, so she cut her hair and sold it for a loaf of bread which she brought to him and with it kept him alive. Job remained afflicted for some years until someone passed by and said, If this one had done anything worthwhile, then God would deliver him from this condition. Wahb. b. Munabbih said that Job remained in that condition exactly three years.

When Job had prevailed over the Devil and the Devil was still not able to make any headway against him, he went to Job's wife disguised in size, shape, and height like a man, riding on a great splendid, beautiful beast unlike the beasts of men. He said to her, Are you the companion of Job, the man who is afflicted? She said, Yes. He said, Do you know me? She said, No. He said, I am the god of the earth, and I am the one who is responsible for what happened to your spouse. This came about because he worshiped the god of heaven, and left me out and angered me. If he were to bow down to me one time, I would return to him and to you all the wealth and children you two had. I have that ability. Then, in the middle of the wadi in which he met her, he showed her a vision of what he promised. Wahb b. Munabbih said, I have heard that the Devil said, If your spouse will only eat food without reciting the name of God over it, he will be delivered from his affliction, but God knows best if that is so. The Enemy of God wished her to take his part with Job, so she returned to Job and told him what the Devil had said to her and what he had showed her. He said, The Enemy of God has only come to you to tempt you away from your religion. Then he swore that if God would deliver him, he would beat her with a hundred strokes.

When the affliction had lasted for a long time, the group which had been with Job, had believed in him, and had regarded him as veracious came to him. A young boy was with them who also had believed in him and thought him to be truthful. They sat with Job, looked at his state of affliction, were distressed at it and found him repulsive. Job, may the prayers of God be upon him, was worn out from his pains. That was at the time God wished to grant him relief from his condition. So when Job saw that his condition distressed them, he said, O Lord, for what did you create me? Would that I had been blood that my mother cast away. Would that I had died in her belly. I do not know anything, and you have not informed me what sin I have committed and what I have done that has turned your gracious face from me. Would that you would cause me to die and make me to join my forefathers. Death would be more attractive to me. The powerful are a model for me, those against whom armies are arrayed. They beat with swords, wish to stave off death, and hope for their endurance. They wake up crouching in their graves, thinking they will live forever. This is the model for me of kings who store up treasures, gather in grain and collect things. They think they will live forever. And I have the model of tyrants who build cities and castles and live in them for hundreds of years; then they are destroyed, becoming the dwelling places of wild beasts and the refuge of devils.

Eliphaz, the Taymite, said, We are at out wits' end about your problem, O Job. If we speak with you, we do not hope for conversation from you while you are in this condition, and if we are silent with you because of what we see of your tribulation, it is in spite of ourselves. Indeed, we have seen your deeds, deeds which we had hoped would get you a good reward and not what we see. Man reaps what he sows and is rewarded for what he does. Call upon God whose power is incomprehensible, the number of whose favors cannot be counted, who sends down the waters from heaven and quickens thereby the dead, raises up the lowly and strengthens the weak, at whose wisdom the wisdom of the wise vanishes and at whose knowledge the knowledge of the learned disappears, so that you see them powerless in darkness, wandering to and fro. The one who hopes in the aid of God is the powerful one, and he who trusts in Him is satisfied, because He is the one who destroys and restores, who wounds and heals.

Job said, I am silent and I bite my tongue at that. I have lowered my head because of my bad service to God, because I know that His punishment has taken away the light of His face and that His power has removed the power of my body. I am His servant. What He has decided for me has happened to me. I have no power except what He causes me to have. Were my bones of iron, my body of brass, and my heart of stone, I could not bear this. He has tried me, and He will relieve me. You have come to me angry; you are fearful before fear was invoked in you, and you have wept before you were smitten. Just imagine if I were to say to you, Give alms for me with your wealth so that perhaps God would redeem me, or offer a sacrifice for me that perhaps God would accept it from me and be pleased with me. When I am awake, I wish for sleep, hoping to find rest, and when I am asleep, my soul almost gets better. My fingers have been cut off, so I raise a morsel of food with both my hands together, but only by my great effort do they reach my mouth. My soft palate has fallen out, and my head and what is between my ears has rotted so that you can see one of my ears through the other. My brains flow from my mouth; my hair has fallen out. It is as though my face were burned with fire. The pupils of my eyes hang down on my cheeks. My tongue has become so swollen that it has filled my mouth, and I am not able to put any food in that does not choke me. My lips have become swollen so that they cover the top of my nose and the bottom of my chin. My intestines have been destroyed in my belly, so that, if I put food in, it comes out as it entered. I do not feel the food, and it does not benefit me. The strength of my legs has left, and they are like two waterskins filled with water which I am unable to carry. I carry my wrap in my hands and my teeth, but I am unable to lift it unless someone carries it with me. Wealth has gone, and I have come asking for sustenance. He whom I used to feed with a single morsel feeds me and gives it back to me. The destruction of my sons and daughters reviles me. If one of them were to have remained, he could have aided me in my affliction and assisted me. Punishment is not the punishment of this world, which goes away from mankind; they die. But it is a blessing for one to have rest in a household in which its people do not die and do not depart from their dwelling place. The happy one is he who is fortunate therein, and the miserable one is he who is troubled therein.

Bildad said, How does your tongue stand this speech and how are you so eloquent? Do you say that the just person strays or that the strong becomes weak? Weep over your sins and beseech your Lord that he might possibly be merciful to you and disregard your offense. Perhaps, if you are guiltless, He will store this up for you for your afterlife. If your heart has become cruel, then our words will not benefit you and will have no effect on you. It is preposterous that reeds grow in the desert. It is impossible that papyrus grows in the arid waste. How can he who trusts in weakness hope that it will defend him, and how does he who disavows the truth hope that his truth will redeem him?

Job said, Indeed, I know that this is the truth. The servant will not be separated from his Lord, nor is he able to litigate against him. What words do I have against Him even if I had the power? He is the one who, alone, vaulted the heavens and established them. He is the one who removes the heavens when He wills, and they roll up for Him. He is the one who spread out the earth, and He alone leveled it and erected towering mountains on it. He is the one who will shake them to their foundations by earthquake, so that they will return with their heights made low. If I have speech, what sort of speech do I have against Him who by one word created the great throne which He made wide enough to hold the heavens, the earth, and all their creatures? He is the one who spoke to the sea, and it understood His speech. He commanded it, and it did not go against Him. He is the one who taught the animals, the birds, and all the beasts, and He is the one who speaks to the dead. His speech resurrects them. It is He who speaks with the rocks, and they understand His speech. He commands them, and they obey Him.

Eliphaz said, What you say is so great, O Job, that the flesh crawls just remembering your words. Indeed, what happened to you happened because of a sin which you committed, like this rage and this speech. God has put you here because of the greatness of your sin. Those who made claims against you were numerous. You robbed the wealthy of their money. You were clothed while they were naked, and you ate while they were hungry. You barred the weak from your door, kept your food from the hungry and your knowledge from the litigant. You have kept those evil deeds secret, hidden them in your house, and revealed only your good deeds. Those are what we saw you doing. You thought that God would not recompense you for your deeds. You thought that God would not bring forth what you hid in your house. How would He not bring it forth? He knows what the Jordan hides and what is under the deeps and beyond the air.

Job, may the prayers and peace of God be upon him, said, If I talk, speech does not help me, and if I am silent, you do not excuse me. My cunning works against me, and my Lord is angry with my sins. My enemies are on guard, and He puts them on my neck. They subject me to trials and torment me with disease without pause. Tribulation follows me on the heels of tribulation. Was I not a shelter to the homeless, an abode to the poor, a patron to the orphan and a caretaker to the widow? Whenever I saw a stranger, I was an abode in the place of his abode or a dwelling instead of his dwelling. Whenever I saw a poor person, I gave wealth to him in place of his wealth and was family instead of his family. I did not see an orphan but I was a father to him instead of his father. I did not see a widow but I was a guardian in place of her husband. I was the servant of the lowly. When I did good deeds, there was not a word from me about my beneficence, because gracious giving belongs to my Lord and not to me. If I have done badly, then my punishment is in His hand. Troubles have fallen on me which, if they had fallen on a mountain, would be too much for it to bear. How shall my weakness bear it?

Eliphaz said, Do you argue with God, O Job, about His authority? Do you wish to demand justice while you are a sinner or be considered guiltless while you are without innocence? He created the heavens and the earth in truth and numbered the creatures in them. How would He not know what you hid, and how would He not know what you did and punish you for it? God set the angels in rows around His throne and in the vastness of His heavens. He veiled them with light, but their appearance is like darkness with respect to Him, and their strength is weakness compared to Him. Their majesty is lowliness with respect to Him. And you claim that all would be well if only He would argue and dispute with the wisdom you have. Do you see Him so that you can demand justice from Him? Do you hear Him so that you can argue with Him? We know His judgment of you. Indeed, He is the one who wishes to raise up the lowly. The one who humbles himself to God, He raises up!

Job, may the prayers and peace of God be upon him, said, If He destroys me, then who among His servants can go against Him and question His authority? Nothing will avert His anger but His mercy. Only beseeching Him benefits His servant. Lord, come near me with your mercy and inform me what sin I committed or what thing turned your noble face from me and made me like an enemy to you, since you used to honor me. Nothing is concealed from you. You count the drops of rain, the leaves of the trees, and the grains of the earth. I awoke with my skin like rotten clothes; whenever I touch it, it falls in my hands. Make me a sacrifice and release me from my trials by the power with which you send men's deaths and lay waste the countryside. Do not destroy me without my knowing what my sin is. Do not spoil the work of your hands. If you are independent of me, then you do not need to be tyrannical in your judgment or hasty in your punishment. Only the weak resort to tyranny, and only those who fear escape resort to haste. You have not mentioned my sin and my transgression to me. Remember how you created me from clay; you took a small bit, made it into bones, and covered the bones with flesh and skin. You made nerves and veins, and because of that it was a strong body. You fed me and caused me to grow from small to large. Then I guarded your pledge and did your command. If I have sinned, enlighten me and do not destroy me with affliction. Inform me of my sins; if I have not pleased you, I am worthy of your punishment. If I am among your creatures, give me an account of my deeds. I seek your forgiveness, but you do not forgive me. If I have done well, I have not raised my head, and if I have caused evil, you have not held back your rage. You have not told me of my slip. You have seen my weakness under you and my imploring you. Why did you create me, or why did you bring me forth from my mother's womb? Would that I were one who was not; that would be best for me. The world is nothing to me with your anger. My body does not stand up to your punishment. Have mercy on me. Let me taste the food of amnesty before I go to the narrowness of the grave, the darkness of the earth and the affliction of death.

Zophar said, You speak, O Job, but no one is able to comprehend what your mouth utters. You assert that you are guiltless, but what benefit is it to you that you are blameless while He who counts your deeds has power over you? You assert that you know God will forgive your sins. Does the roof know how far heaven is? Do you know the depth of the air or which land is the widest, or do you have any power to master it? Do you know which sea is the deepest, or do you know the count of all things? If you know this, or even if you do not know, God created it, and He reckons it. If you left behind many traditions, sought your Lord and repented so that He be merciful to you, by that you could bring forth His mercy. If you are steadfast in your sin, yet raise up your hand to God in need while you are resolute in your sin, steadfast as running water on a slope which cannot be dammed, making requests of the Merciful, remember that evil deeds will cause disgrace. He will be happy to grant the needs of those who have abandoned carnal appetites; their abstinence is an adornment before their Lord. They come in supplication to seek the rightness of mercy. They are the ones who suffer at night, keep away from the bed and watch the daybreak. These believers are the ones who do not fear or wrong or grieve. What is your situation, O Job, compared with theirs?

A youth was with them and heard what they said. They had not noticed him or paid any attention to him, for God had sent him to them while they were being excessively outrageous in their talk. God wished to use the youth to humble them. When the youth spoke, he would stretch out his speech adding nothing but wisdom. The people were submissive and eager to hear him when he admonished or preached. So he said, You spoke before me, O you mature ones, and you were truer in your speech and more entitled to speak than me. Your years have given you the right. Because you gained experience before me, and you saw and know what I do not know, you refrained from saying that which is more beautiful than what you did say, from expressing an opinion more appropriate and from telling of affairs more lovely and of lessons more wise. Job has more right than you and a better claim than you described. Do you know, O you mature ones, the truth about the one you disparaged and the holiness of the one you revile? Do you not know about the man with whom you find fault and accuse, O you mature ones? Job is the prophet of God and is the best and purest person on earth in your day. God chose him to inspire him, save him, and give him the prophethood. Do you not know, did God not make you aware that He was enraged at something at the time this happened to Job and not because He took away from him anything with which He honored him? It is not the case that Job has altered the truth while you have kept him company today. If it is a trial, God is the one who upbraids him among you and humbles him. You know that God tries His prophets, His righteous ones, His martyrs, and His pious. His trials are not for the errant with whom He is angry, and they are not for His degrading them, but they are an honor and goodness for them. Would that Job were not in this relationship to God, not a prophet, not in God's favor nor in His grace and honor, but a brother you loved for his company. It is not proper for the wise man to blame his brother in tribulation and reprove him in disaster about which he knows not, while the brother is anguished and grieved. He should have mercy on him, weep with him, seek forgiveness for him, grieve with his grief, guide him rightly, and not judge and guide him from ignorance. For God, O you mature ones, is also the God of your souls.

Then the youth approached Job, may the prayers and peace of God be upon him, while Job was praising and magnifying God and remembering death, and said, May your tongue not be cut off, nor your heart broken, nor your deeds forgotten. Do you not know, O Job, that there are servants of God whom fear silenced into inexpression and dumbness? Indeed, they could articulately express God's distinguishing characteristics and His signs. But when they mentioned the greatness of God, their tongues were cut out, their blood was curdled, their hearts were broken, and their senses departed while they were praising, magnifying, and glorifying God. When they recovered, they outdid each other before God in doing good deeds, counting themselves among the wrongdoers, the sinners, the neglectful, and the niggardly, even though they were among the able and the powerful. They did not regard an abundance of good actions as enough for God. They were not satisfied with only a little for God. They were not full of pride before Him for their actions. Whenever you saw them, O Job, they were frightened, terrified, distressed, humble, apprehensive, submissive, and confessing.

Job said, Indeed, God in His mercy plants wisdom in the hearts of the small and the great, and when it grows in the heart, God makes it appear on the tongue. There is no wisdom before age, nor in youthfulness, or before long practice. When God makes a servant wise through fasting, He does not abolish his position among the wise. They see the light of God's nobility around him. But you have been vain and thought that you were saved by your good conduct. There you have acted outrageously and pridefully. If you were to see what is between you and your Lord, then your souls would attest to the truth, for you would find that you have faults which God forgave. I awoke today, and I had nothing to say to you except that you should hear my words and know my truth, while I was appealing for justice against my opponent, forceful against him who coerces me to flee my place. At that, men listen and oppress me. I awoke this morning with my hope cut off, and my guard lifted. My family was tired of me, my kin disrespectful of me, my acquaintances alienated from me, and the people of my house ungrateful to me. I renounced my rights and forgot my duties. I called for help, but they did not aid me. I apologized, but they did not forgive me. God's decree is what humbles me, humiliates me, and debases me. His power makes me ill and emaciates my body. If only my Lord would remove the fear in my heart and soften my tongue so that I could speak with the fullness of my mouth, then it would be proper for the servant to argue for his soul. I had hoped that I would be cured from what is in me, but He cast me away and raised Himself away from me while He looked at me, but I did not see Him. He heard me, but I did not hear Him. He did not look at me to have mercy on me and did not come near me or approach me or grant my forgiveness or speak of my innocence. I litigate for myself.

The Making of the Last Prophet

96

When Job said that with his companions nearby him, the clouds darkened so that his companions thought a punishment was coming. A voice called to him: O Job, God says, Am I the one who has already been near you? I have never ceased being close to you. Rise up. Express your excuse. Speak of your innocence, argue for yourself and gird your loins. Rise to the stature of a colossus, for it is not fitting that any but a colossus argue with me. It is not appropriate for any to argue with me but one who puts a bridle in the mouth of a lion, a lamb in the mouth of a griffin, meat in the mouth of a dragon, measures the weight of light, calculates with weight of wind, binds up the sunshine, and returns tomorrow to yesterday. Your soul grants you the power that is beyond your capacity. Would that when your soul grants you that and induces you, you remember what goal you were aiming at. Do you intend to argue with me about your injustice, or do you wish to debate me about your sins, or do you wish to vie with me in your weakness? Where were you when I created the earth and put it on its foundations? Do you know the extent of its power? Or are you able to traverse its borders? Or do you know the distance of its corners or on what I placed its sides? Is the load of water of the earth under your obedience, or is the earth covered with water by your wisdom? Where were you on the day I raised heaven as a roof over the air, without a support above it or a buttress below it? Is it through your judgment that its light flows or its stars course. Does night follow day at your command? Where were you on the day I caused the ocean to overflow and the rivers to gush? Did you decree that the floods subside to their limits, or was it your order that wombs open when they reach their term? Where were you on the day I poured water on the earth and raised up the lofty mountains? Do you have the span to grasp their weight, or do you know their measure or where the water is I sent from heaven? Do you know the mother who bears it or the father who sires it? Does your judgment count the drops and divide the nourishment, or is it your order that swirls the clouds and causes rain? Do you know the voice of thunder or by what thing lightning ignites? Have you seen the depths of the seas, or do you know the distance of the air? Have you stored up the souls of the dead? Do you know where the treasure house of snow is, or where the vault of cold is, or where the mountains of cold are? Do you know the stores of night and day and where day is at night or the path of light or in what language the trees speak or where the wind hides and how to bar it? Who gave understanding, hearing, and sight? Who humbled the angels to His sovereignty, conquered the tyrants with His might, and set the nourishment of the beasts with His wisdom? Who gave the lions their provision and gave the birds their way of life and disposed them to their chicks? Who released the wild animals from service and made their dwelling places in the wastes, untamed by voice or frightened by power? Was it from your sagacity that their mothers were favorably disposed to their young so that they brought out food for them from their bellies and trained them for life? Was it from your judgment that the eagle got its sight and attained its place? Where were you on the day I created Behemoth in its place in the ends of the earth and Leviathan which bears the mountains and the villages and cities, whose ears are like pine trees in length, whose heads like mountain hills, whose thighs like pegs of iron, as though their skin were split rocks, and their bones like pillars of brass? They are the first among my deadly creatures. Did you fill their skin with flesh or their heads with brains, or did you have a partner in their creation? Did you have the power to create them with two hands, or did you attain your power to muzzle them or put your hands on their heads or set them on their way, harness them or turn them from their power? Where were you on the day I created the [sea creature called the] Tinnin and fed it in the sea, causing it to dwell in the cloud, its eyes striking fire, its nostrils giving forth smoke, its ears like circles of clouds trailing fire like the raging whirlwind, its center burning, its foam like boulders, the creaking of its teeth like the crash of thunder, and the glance of its eyes like the fire of lightening? It does not worry. Armies pass by it, and nothing frightens it, for pieces of iron are like straw for it, and brass like thread. It does not fear arrows, and it does not feel the fall of boulders on its body. It laughs at the lance. It travels in the air like a sparrow and destroys all it passes, the king of beasts. I bestowed on it the power over my creation. Did you take it with your ropes and tie it with its tongue or put a bridle in its mouth? Do you think it will keep your command or praise you out of fear of you? Do you calculate its term of life, or do you know its reward or its nourishment, or do you know what it has destroyed on the earth or what it will destroy in what remains of the rest of its life? Can you comprehend its anger when it is angered or command it and have it obey you?

Job, may the prayers and peace of God be upon him, said, I desist from what you have set before me. Would that the earth would split and I would depart with my trouble. I did not speak of anything about which my Lord is displeased, but He gathers tribulation on me. My God, you have made me like an enemy to you. You used to honor me and know my good faith. You knew that which I mentioned was the work of your hands and the management of your wisdom. Whatever more you have wished, you have done. Nothing makes you incapable, and nothing makes you fear. Nothing is hidden from you. Who is it that thinks that he can keep a secret from you? You know what occurs in my heart. In my trial I learned from you what I did not know. When I was afflicted, I became afraid more than I have ever been. I used only to hear your power, but now I see it. I only spoke of your forgiving me and was silent about your having mercy on me, a slip of the tongue which I will not do again. I have placed my hands on my mouth, grabbed my tongue with my teeth, put my cheek in the dust, and made my face humble. I am silent as you were silent with me about my sins. Forgive me for what I said, and I will never again do that which you hate.

God, the Blessed and the Most High, said, O Job, my knowledge has penetrated you. Because of my graciousness, my anger is turned form you. When you sinned, I have forgiven you, and I have returned to you your family and what you had and the like of them with them. So wash with this water, for it is your restoration. Sacrifice for your companions and seek forgiveness for them, for they opposed me for you, but my mercy outstrips my anger. Hurry with your feet and drink, for it is your cure. I have given you your family and the like of them with them and what you had and the like of it with it. For you will be a sign to the people of trial and a solace to the patiently enduring.

So Job ran off, and a spring burst forth. He entered the water, washed, and God removed all his tribulation from him. Then he got out and sat down. His wife came searching for him in his sleep, but she did not find him, so she got up like one in grief, perplexed. Then she said to him, O servant of God, do you know of a man in affliction who was here? He said, No. Then she smiled and knew him and laughed and hugged him.

On the authority of some of the scholars who got it from Wahb b. Munabbih, ʿAbdullah b. ʿAbbas said: they embraced. And ʿAbdullah said, By the One who has ʿAbdullah's soul in his hand, she did not let go of his neck until all the wealth and children passed by. I heard some of the ones who mention tradition say that Job called her when she asked about him and said to her, Would you know him if you saw him? She said, Yes, why would I not? He smiled and said, I am he, for God has removed that condition from me, and at that she embraced him. Wahb said, God inspired him: "Take a branch in your hand, strike with it and do not break your oath" [Q 38:45], that is, keep your oath with your right hand. God, the Most High, said, "We found him steadfast, an excellent servant, ever turning" [Q 38:45]; "We gave to him his people and the like of them with them as a mercy from us and a reminder to those of understanding" [Q 38:44].

Sources

at-Tabari, *Taʾrîkh* h. 361
at-Tabari, *Tafsîr* 17:65-66, 17:59-62, 17:67-68, 17:68-69

SHUᶜAYB

Another prophet of punishment, Shuᶜayb is often identified with the biblical Jethro, although there is no basis in the Quran for that assertion. He exhorted his people to correct behavior, which included moral business practices, and to abandon their habits of shortweighting. This has led some scholars to see parallels between Shuᶜayb's experiences with his people and Muhammad's experiences with the Meccans. He is said to have been sent to the people of the Thicket, *al-Aykah*, but this may be no more than an expansion on the root of the name Shuᶜayb, which can mean "branch" or "twig." The name of the dog ar-Raqim occurs once in the Quran, in association with the Companions of the Cave (Q 18:9), where it is glossed by the Muslim commentators as the name of a dog, the name of the mountain containing the cave, or a word meaning "inscription."

Without a clear development in the Quran, Shuᶜayb's prophetic personality is hard to determine. But Ibn Ishaq has picked out one salient feature which seems to parallel Muhammad's experience. He states, "But, when they called him a liar and threatened him with stones and banishment from his country, and raged against God, God punished them with the Day of Gloom." Here is a characteristic "trial" that many pre-Islamic prophets endure. They are regarded as liars, threatened with physical harm, and frequently suffer banishment. It is the banishment of Shuᶜayb from his land that suggests a graphic parallel with Muhammad's experience in the Hijrah.

Even in this short passage it is implied that the community of those who believed in Shuᶜayb's message were saved, and they were saved precisely because they were a believing community. Seldom noted but critical to the prophetic experience is the building of communities. Prophets to be acknowledged and remembered as prophets must coalesce a group of followers into a community. [Arab. *ummah*].

Text
In the name of God, the Merciful and the Compassionate

Muhammad b. Ishaq said, Shuᶜayb was the son of Mikail, the son of Issachar, the son of Midian, the son of Abraham, and his name in Syriac is Yatrun. His mother was Mikil, the daughter of Lot. Shuᶜayb, upon him be peace, was blind. We know that because of God's word: "We see that you are weak among us" [Q 10:91], that is, blind. He was called the Orator of the Prophets

99

because of his eloquence among his people. So God, the Most High, sent him as a prophet to the people of Midian, who possessed al-Aykah, and al-Aykah means a thicket.

God mentioned the story of Shuʿayb and his people in the Quran. They were a folk who, because of their disbelief in God, would shortweight people. And they would call their prophet a liar when he invited them to worship God and abandon the sin of shortweighting. He exhorted them truthfully: "I do not desire to do behind your backs that which I ask you not to do. I desire nothing but reform as long as I am able. My welfare is only in God. In Him I trust and to Him I turn" [Q 11:88].

Ibn Ishaq said that according to Yaʿqub b. Abu Salamah, the Prophet of God, may the prayers and the peace of God be upon him, said when he mentioned Shuʿayb: He was the Orator of the Prophets because of the beauty of his exhorting his people. But when they called him a liar and threatened him with stones and banishment from his country, and raged against God, God punished them with the Day of Gloom. It was the punishment of an awful day [cf. Q 26:189]. I heard that a Midianite called ʿAmr b. Jalha said when he saw it:

> O people, Shuʿayb was sent and Samir and ʿImran b. Shaddad were
> scattered from you.
> Indeed, I see a cloud, O people, which has risen, inviting with a voice on
> the edge of the wadi,
> And you will not see the dawn in it tomorrow except ar-Raqim will be
> walking amidst the calamity.

Samir and ʿImran were two of their soothsayers, and ar-Raqim was their dog.

I heard, and God knows best, that God inflicted them with heat until they were well cooked. Then He caused gloom to come on them like a black cloud. When they saw it, they rushed to it seeking the coolness of its rain from the heat they were suffering, so that when they were under it, it closed over them and destroyed them completely. God saved Shuʿayb and those who believed with him out of His mercy. Shuʿayb was struck with sadness over his people when he saw the vengeance of God. Then he said, consoling himself with what God mentioned: "O my people, I delivered my Lord's messages to you and gave you good advice, so how can I be sad for a people who disbelieved?" [Q 7:93]

Sources

at-Tabari, Taʾrikh. 367

at-Tabari, *Tafsîr*. 9:4, 9:6
ath-Thaᶜlabi, 95, 96

Joseph

The story of Joseph in the twelfth chapter of the Quran is described as "the best of narratives" (Q 12:3). There has been much discussion among Muslim commentators about what "best narrative" might mean, but almost all agree that the story is the most complete of all the stories in the Quran. That is, the details of the story are in one place and combined to form a coherent narrative. The story of Joseph in the *Kitâb al-Mubtada*ʾ is constructed to follow the Quranic account closely, and it seems in many places that Ibn Ishaq is merely supplying transitional glosses to the Quranic text, much in the manner that later Muslim exegetes of the Quran clarified grammar and syntax when writing Quran commentary.

The Quranic story of Joseph is elliptical in places for all its completeness, and Muslim exegetes were often at great pains to clarify some of the passages in the story. They made use of some material which can be traced back to rabbinic sources and some which has no parallel with Jewish or Christian sources. The Quranic story is itself replete with details found in antecedent rabbinic literature. For example, the dramatic incident with Potiphar's wife, in which the young Joseph is tempted but prevented from sin by the vision of his father, is found in *Bereshit Rabbah* 87.7. In the biblical narrative Joseph is given Potiphar's daughter, Asenath, to marry, and this is the version found in the extant rabbinic versions. There is a strain of commentary among the rabbis, however, that makes Joseph guilty at least in spirit of sin with Potiphar's wife (*Bereshit Rabbah* 87.7; *Pirke De Rabbi Eliezer* 39). Philo, in *De Josepho,* makes the assertion that Joseph's innocence was proved by his garment, and the Quran further refines the argument by asserting that the proof of Joseph's innocence was that the garment was torn from behind, the commentators contending that a man does not approach a woman backwards.

Ibn Ishaq's exegetical sources show that Midrash making continued, producing material that has no parallel in rabbinic sources. For example, when Joseph's brothers are shown the cup which had been hidden in Reuben's saddlebags, they exclaim, "If he steals, then a brother of his has stolen before him" (Q 12:77). To explain the passage, a parallel story is offered, the story of Joseph's aunt hiding Isaac's girdle on Joseph in order to be able to keep him with her. Unable to make a claim for Joseph, Jacob is forced to leave the child with his aunt until she died. Of course, neither Reuben nor Joseph actually stole anything.

Joseph

103

The story of Joseph in the *Kitâb al-Mubtada²* is careful to stress Joseph's innocence in the face of temptation. Muslims view prophets as human, subject to normal human temptations but prevented from committing error because they are rightly guided from birth. This means that their conduct can be a model for human behavior. The notion of prophet as paradigm becomes central in Islamic notions of behavior where Muhammad's actions [Arab. *sunnah*] form the pattern for proper conduct. Another point of correspondence between Joseph and Muhammad is that both function as temporal rulers concerned with practical politics and management: Joseph over Egypt and Muhammad over his community in Arabia.

To round out the Joseph story in the *Kitâb al-Mubtada²*, Potiphar is described as a man who would not have intercourse with women. His wife remained a frustrated virgin, whose sexual drive is channeled properly only when she marries Joseph. The rabbis also describe Joseph as a person without sexual blemish and, following the usual pattern, place the blame for the temptation on the fact that Potiphar's wife was a descendant of Eve. In this androcentric view female sexuality, unless controlled, leads to evil and destruction.

Text
In the name of God, the Merciful and the Compassionate

Abu ꜥAbdullah ath-Thaqafi reported on the authority of ꜥUmar b. Ahmad b. ꜥUthman, who got it from Muhammad b. Sulayman, who got it from Muhammad b. Hamid ar-Razi, who got it from Salamah b. al-Fadl, who got it from Muhammad b. Ishaq, who got it from Rawh b. al-Qasim, who got it from ꜥUmarah, who got it from Abu Saꜥid al-Khudari, that the Prophet of God, may the prayers and peace of God be upon him, said to some companions: On the night of my nocturnal journey, I went to heaven and saw Joseph. I said, O Gabriel, who is that? He said, This is Joseph. The Companions said, How did he appear, O Prophet of God? He said, Like the full moon at night.

When Joseph's mother, Rachel, bore him, Jacob, her spouse, gave him to his sister to protect him. Now the state of affairs for him and his aunt, who was protecting him, was as Ibn Hamid, who got it from Salamah, who got it from Ibn Ishaq, who got it from ꜥAbdullah b. Najih, who got it from Mujahid, said: The first trial to afflict Joseph that I know about concerned his aunt, the daughter of Isaac, the eldest of Isaac's children. She had Isaac's girdle which used to be bequeathed to the eldest. The person to whom it was assigned could do whatever he wished with a person who stole it.

When Joseph was born to him, Jacob had given him to be raised by his aunt. He was with her, and no one loved anything as much as she loved him. When he grew up and reached his majority, Jacob came to her and said, O my little sister, give me Joseph, for, by God, I cannot bear that he is absent from me for an hour. She said, By God, I will not give him up. But leave him with me for a few days, and I will look at him and then go away from him. Perhaps that will cheer me up from losing him, or so she said. When Jacob left her, she bound Isaac's girdle around Joseph under his clothes. Then she said, I have lost Isaac's girdle. Look for the one who took it or caused something to happen to it. So they searched, and she said, Undress the people of the house. So they undressed them and found it on Joseph. She said, By God, I am free to do with him what I want.

Jacob came to her, and she told him the story. He said to her, For heaven's sake, if he did that, then he is yours; I am not able to go against that. So she took Joseph, and Jacob had no authority over him until she died. This is the situation to which Joseph's brother referred when he did what he did with his brother: "If he steals, then a brother of his stole before"[Q 12:77].

At the time the Prophet of God, may the prayers and peace of God be upon him, saw the injustice and envy of his own people when God, the Mighty and the Powerful, honored him with prophethood, God, in order to console him, told Muhammad the story of Joseph, the injustice of his brothers toward him, and their envy of him when he described his vision: "When they said, Joseph and his brother are dearer to our father than we, and we are one group. Indeed, our father is in clear error. Kill Joseph or cast him in a land to turn your father's face toward you. Afterwards you can be a righteous people. One of them said, Do not kill Joseph; throw him in a pit; some caravan will find him, if you must do anything" [Q 12:8–10]. It was mentioned, and God knows best, that the one who said that was Rubil, the eldest of Jacob's sons. He was the wisest of them. "They said, O our father, what is with you that you will not trust us with Joseph . . . up to His words, . . . for a low price, a number of dirhams, and they regarded him as worthless" [Q 12:11–20]. They sold him, but the price they sold him for was less than an ounce. At that time the people used to sell in ounces, and what fell short of an ounce was counted, as God said, ". . . and they sold him for a low price, a number of dirhams" [Q 12:20], that is, less that an ounce. "He of Egypt who bought him said to his wife, Treat him with honor . . . up to His words, . . . and most of mankind did not know it" [Q 12:21]. When he said, Honor his place of abode, he was saying, Treat the place he stays with honor. That is because wherever one resides is called the abode of so-and-so in such-and-such a place.

The one who sold him in Egypt was Malik b. Dhiʿr b. Thuwwayb b. ʿAnqa b. Midian b. Ibrahim. Muhammad b. as-Saib, who got it from Abu Salih, who got it from Ibn ʿAbbas, said, The name of the man who purchased him was Qatfir. It is also said that his name was Atfir b. Ruhayb, and he was called al-ʿAziz. He was in charge of the storehouses of Egypt. The king at that time was ar-Rayan b. al-Walid, an Amalekite. His wife's name, according to what was mentioned, was Raʿil bt. Ruʿail.

According to the reports, Atfir was a man who did not come to women, while his wife, Ra'il, was the most beautiful woman in the world. "And when he reached his majority . . . up to His words . . . Wrongdoers never prosper" [Q 12:22–23]. When Joseph reached his majority, she, whose house he was in, asked him to do an evil act. The wife of al-ʿAziz said, Come here, meaning, Come to me. He said, He is my lord, meaning al-Atfir. He made me safe in his house and among his family. "She desired him . . . up to His words . . . He was one of our chosen servants" [Q 12:24]. The woman threw herself at him, enticing him with her beauty, good looks, and fortune, inviting him to the pleasures of the flesh. He was a young man who had the lusts that men do, so he was sympathetic to her because of her affection for him, and he was not afraid of her until he desired her, and she desired him.

According to what has reached me, some scholars say that the Burhan which Joseph saw and which turned him from evil and disgrace was a vision of Jacob biting his fingers. When he saw him, he fled. But some say that it was the sight of Atfir, his master, when he approached the door. We know that, because when Joseph fled from her and she followed him, he found her master at the door: "And they raced one another . . . up to His words . . . a painful doom" [Q 12:25]. She put the evil deed onto Joseph, fearing that he would accuse her of participating in the ugly affair. So he said, telling the truth, "It was she . . . up to His words . . . and he is of the truthful" [Q 12:26–27]. The witness was a counselor, a man of Atfir's people, and he made use of his intellect. He said, I testify that if his shirt is torn from the front, she is truthful, and he is of the liars, because a man makes for a woman front-wards. But if his shirt is torn from behind, she lied, and he is among the truthful. That is because a man does not come to a woman backwards. He said, It is not possible for it to be any other way. So when Atfir saw his shirt torn from behind, he knew that it was one of her wiles and said, "Lo, this is of the guile of you women . . . up to His words . . . We behold her in plain aberration" [Q 12:28–30]. He said, The report spread throughout the town, and the women talked about his situation, saying, "The wife of al-ʿAziz is asking an evil act of her slave boy" [Q 12:30], that is, her servant. As for the title al-ʿAziz, it means king in the language of the Arab. On that point are the words of Abu Daud:

A trader plunges after a pearl;
On a day of presentation
It is brought out for al-ʿAziz

meaning by al-ʿAziz the king, for he is the one with power.

When it became clear from what the women were saying that the wife was seducing her servant, she plotted to show them Joseph, who had been described to them as handsome and good-looking. "And when she heard . . . up to His words . . . couch," a dinner couch, "and she brought each one a knife" to cut up food, and she said to Joseph, "Go out to them." He went out to them, "and when they saw him, they praised him." When they saw him, their wits left them in astonishment, and they began cutting their hands with the knives which they had, unaware of what they were doing, "and they said, By God, this is not a human being . . . up to His words . . . and verily shall be one of those brought low" [Q 12:31–32].

Turning to his Lord and asking His aid for what He revealed to him, Joseph said, "My Lord, prison is dearer to me than that which they urge me" [Q 12:33], that is, prison is preferable to me than that I do what I hate, "and, unless you turn from me their wiles," that is, what I fear from them, "then I will incline to them and be one of the evildoers" [Q 12:33], that is, acting in a wrong manner while being disobedient to you. "So his Lord answered his prayer and fended off their wiles from him" [Q 12:34], that is, He saved him from acting wrongly among them and sent down something to guard against them. "And it seemed good to them to imprison him for a time, even after they had seen signs" [Q 12:35] of his being cleared of the guilt by the appearance to them of the rend in his shirt from behind. So Joseph was cast into prison. And two youths who belonged to the great king, ar-Rayan b. al-Walid, entered prison with him because of the king's annoyance at the two of them. One of them was in charge of the king's drink and the other over some of his affairs. The name of one of them was Mujalith and the other Nibu, and Nibu was the one in charge of the drink. When the two youths saw Joseph, they said, By God, O youth, we liked you as soon as we saw you.

On the authority of ʿAbdullah, who got it from Ibn Najih, who got it from Mujahid, Ibn Ishaq said: When they said that to him, Joseph said to them: I adjure you by God not to love me, for, by God, no one has ever loved me without my being tried by his love. My aunt loved me, and from her love I was tried. Then my father loved me, and I was tried by his love. Then the wife of my master loved me, and this trial came to me, so do not love me. May God bless the two of you. But they insisted on his love and intimacy whenever possible, and they began to be amazed at what they saw of his understanding and intelligence.

The two of them saw a vision when they entered prison. Mujalith saw that he was carrying bread on his head from which birds were eating, and Nibu saw that he was pressing wine. So they sought an interpretation of the dreams and said to him, "Announce to us the interpretation, for we see that you are of the good" [Q 12:36] if you were to do it. Joseph said to them, "The food which you are given will not come to you before I announce to you its interpretation'' [Q 12:37], meaning what the interpretation was and what would happen in regard to what they saw in their sleep of the food they dreamed was brought to them. ''This is of that which my Lord has taught me . . . up to His words . . . but most men do not give thanks'' [Q 12:37–38].

Then Joseph invited them to God and to Islam and said, ''O my fellow prisoners, are divers lords better, or God, the One, the Almighty?'' [Q 12:39] That is, is it better that you worship one deity or different deities who will not assist you in anything? He said to Mujalith, As for you, you will be crucified, and birds will eat from your head. Then he said to Nibu, As for you, you will return to your occupation, and your master will be pleased with you. ''Thus is decided the case about which you sought an opinion'' [Q 12:41], or words to that effect. Joseph said to Nibu, ''Mention me to your lord'' [Q 12:42], that is, mention to the mighty king the injustice done me and my imprisonment without cause. Nibu said, I will do it. When he, meaning the one of them who thought that he was saved, went out, he returned to what he had been in charge of, and his master was pleased with him. But Satan caused him to forget to mention to the king that which Joseph had commanded him to mention. So Joseph remained in prison for a few more years. This is according to God's saying, ''Joseph remained in prison'' [Q 12:42] because he said to the one of the prison companions who was saved, Mention me to your lord. The few years were a punishment from God.

Then the king ar-Rayan al-Walid saw a vision, and it terrified him. He knew that it was a real vision, and he did not know its interpretation. So he said to his nobles around him of the people of his kingdom, ''Indeed, I saw in a dream seven lean cows eating seven fat ones . . . up to His words . . . the interpretation of dreams'' [Q 12:43–44]. Nibu heard his question about its interpretation, and he remembered Joseph, what he explained to him and his companion, and what had happened in that regard, so he said, ''I am going to announce to you the interpretation, so send me forth,'' [Q 12:45] God, the Most High, saying, ''And He caused him to remember after a while'' [Q 12:45], that is, after a long time. So Nibu came to Joseph and said, The king has seen such-and-such, so tell him the interpretation. Joseph said about it what God, the Most High, mentioned to us in the Book, and he brought them its interpretation like the breaking of dawn. (It is said that the one who was saved said, Send me forth, because the prison was not in the city.)

Nibu left Joseph with what he had told him of the interpretation of the king's vision, went to the king, and told him what he had said. When Nibu told him, what was in his soul was like day, and the king knew that that which he had said would come about as he had said. So the king said, ''Bring him to me; but as soon as the messenger came to him, he said, Return to your lord and ask him about the case of the women who cut their hands'' [Q 12:50] and what was the case of the woman by whom I was imprisoned.

Ibn Ishaq reported on the authority of a man who got it from Abu az-Zanad, who got it from Abu Hurayrah, that the Prophet of God, may the prayers and peace of God be upon him, said, God was merciful to Joseph. He was a person of patience. If I were imprisoned, and he sent for me, I would have left quickly. Indeed, he was mild mannered and patient.

When the messenger came to the king from Joseph with the message he had sent, the king gathered the women and said, "What happened when you asked an evil act of Joseph?" [Q 12:51] Ra‘il, the wife of Atfir al-‘Aziz, said, "Now the truth is out" [Q 12:51], that is, now the truthful explanation comes forth. "I asked an evil act of him, and he is surely of the truthful" [Q 12:51], that is, what Joseph said about what I asked him is true. Joseph said, "Thus, to let him know," Atfir, my master, "that I did not betray him in secret" [Q 12:52]. I am not one to disobey him whenever he is unaware. The king said, meaning the great king of Egypt, ar-Rayan b. Al-Walid, when Joseph's innocence was explained, and he knew his trustworthiness and his intelligence, "Bring him to me that I may attach him to my person" [Q 12:54], saying, I will make him one of my loyal adherents, for no one else but me.

On the authority of Sufyan b. ‘Uqbah, who got it from Hamzah az-Zayyat, who got it from Ibn Ishaq, who got it from Abu Maysarah, Abu Kurayb said, When al-‘Aziz saw Joseph's skill, intelligence, and wit, he issued an invitation to him. He used to breakfast and dine with Joseph, and not with his servants. But when the event happened between him and the women, the wife said to him, He has become base; pass him by and let him eat with the servants. He said to him, Go and eat with the servants. Joseph said to his face, Do you loathe eating with me or are you vexed? By God, I am Joseph, the son of Jacob, the Prophet of God, the son of Isaac, the Sacrifice of God, the son of Abraham, the Friend of God.

When Joseph said, "Set me over the storehouses of the land" [Q 12:55], the king said, It is done, and according to what they say, he appointed him to Atfir's portion and removed Atfir from what he was in charge of, according to the words of God, "And we gave power to Joseph in the land" [Q 12:56]. It was mentioned to me, and God knows best, that Atfir perished that night and that the king, ar-Rayan al-Walid, married Joseph to Ra‘il, Atfir's wife. When she came to him, he said, Is this not better than what you had wanted? They allege that she said, O truthful one, do not blame me for I was a beautiful and attractive woman, as you see, and my master would not come to women. As God made you handsome and well-formed, my soul was overcome by what I saw. They allege that he found her a virgin when he took her, and she bore him two sons, Ephraim and Manasseh.

When Joseph was quietly settled in his position and had left the tribulation he was in, and the fertile years had passed during which he had commanded the people to prepare for the years he had told them about, the people from

every direction were afflicted. They came to Egypt from every country re-
questing provisions. When Joseph saw what afflicted the people, he was charitable to them, and he gave every man a camel load of food, but he would not
give one man two camel loads. He distributed fairly among the people and was
generous to them.

Among those who came to him of the people seeking food from Egypt were
his brothers. He knew them, but they were ignorant of him, because God, the
Most High, wished to achieve through Joseph what He wished. Joseph commanded that each one of the brothers be given a heavy camel load, and he said
to them, "Bring me a brother of yours from your father. Do you not see that I
fill the measure," and I have not shortweighted anyone, "and I am the best of
hosts" [Q 12:59]. I am the best host in this land. So I invite you to be my
guests. If you do not come to me with your brother from your father, then
there will be no food for you from me, and you will not come near my country. He said to the servants who were measuring the food for them, Put their
merchandise, which is the price of the food which they are buying, in their
saddlebags. So they returned to their father.

According to what some of the scholars mentioned to me, their camp was in
al-ʿArabat, in the land of Palestine, in the Jordan valley. But some say that it
was in al-Ulaj in the direction of ash-Shaghab below Hamsa in Palestine. Their
father was a desert lord who had camels and sheep. And when Joseph's brothers returned to their father, Jacob, they said to him, "O our father . . . up to
His words . . . God is a better guard and the most merciful of the merciful"
[Q 12:63–64]. When Jacob's sons who had gone to Egypt for provisions
opened their goods which they had taken from Egypt, they found the price of
the food which they had bought returned to them, so they said, "O our
father . . . up to His words . . . a camel load" [Q 12:65], in addition to the
burden of our camels.

When the children of Jacob agreed on the departure, Jacob said, "O my
sons, do not go in by one gate; go in by different gates" [Q 12:67]. He was
afraid of people's envy of them, because they belonged to one man. When the
children of Jacob entered to Joseph, they said, This is our brother whom you
commanded that we bring to you. We have come to you with him. It was
mentioned to me that he said to them, As you have done well and acted
rightly, so you will find it with me, or words to that effect. Then he said, I see
that you are men whom I wish to honor, so he called his guest-master and
said, Give each two men a separate room, honor them and treat them well as
guests. Then he said, I see this man whom you brought is without a mate, so
I will pair him with me, and his room will be with me. So he established them
as pairs of men in different rooms, put his brother up with him and received
him as a guest. When he was secluded with him, he said, I am your brother; I
am Joseph, so do not be worried about anything they have done with us in the

past, for God will ameliorate things for us. Do not tell them anything that I have told you. This is explained by God, the Mighty and the Powerful, saying, "And when they went in . . . up to His words . . . for what they did" [Q 12:69], saying to him, Do not be worried and do not grieve.

When Joseph had the camels of his brothers loaded with provisions, had settled their affairs and had supplied their measure, he put the vessel which was used to measure food—and it was a wide one—in the saddlebag of his brother Benjamin. He gave them another camel load, and gave a camel load to his brother Benjamin, in his name, as he had given to them. Then he made them delay so that, when they left and were making their way from the city, he ordered them to be overtaken and halted. "The crier cried, O you caravan, you are thieves" [Q 12:70]. According to what they say, Joseph's messengers arrived and said to them, Did we not treat you generously as guests, grant you your measure, provide you with fine lodging, treat you as we had not treated others, and take you into our houses so that an esteem developed between us, or words to that effect? They said, Oh no, what is it? He said, We have lost the king's cup, and we do not suspect anyone but you of taking it. They said, "By God, you know well that we did not come to do evil in the land . . . up to His words . . . he is the penalty for it" [Q 12:73–75]. That is, thus we do with him who steals among us. When the messenger said to them, "He who brings it shall have a camel load, and I am answerable for it" [Q 12:72], they said, We do not know it to be with us. He said, You are not going until I inspect your goods and absolve you by searching for it. So he began with their bags, bag by bag, searching them and seeing what was in them, until he came to his brother's bag, searched it, and extracted the cup from it. He took him by the neck and went with him to Joseph, God saying, "Thus did we contrive for Joseph. He could not have taken his brother according to the king's law unless God willed" [Q 12:76], that is, unjustly, but God plotted for Joseph to unite his brother with him.

When Jacob's sons saw what Joseph's brother had done, they did not doubt that he had stolen, and they said, Woe to him for what he has brought upon himself; he is to blame. "They said, If he steals, then a brother of his stole before . . . up to His words . . . We are not guardians of the unseen" [Q 12:77–81], that is, the stolen object was found in his saddlebag while we were looking; we have no knowledge of the unseen. Rubil knew in the response to his statement to his brothers that they were suspicious people with their father because of what they had done to Joseph and on account of their words, "Ask the township . . . up to His words . . . We speak the truth" [Q 12:82]. They know what we know and saw what we saw, for we are truthful even though you do not believe us.

When they reported Rubil's statement to Jacob, he was suspicious of them and thought that this was like what they had done with Joseph. He said, "Nay, you have deluded yourselves . . . up to His words . . . perhaps God will return all of them to me" [Q 12:83], that is, Joseph and Rubil, and he turned away from them. His grief became complete. He was very troubled when Joseph's brother followed him, and his grief over Joseph was stirred up. He said, "Alas, my grief for Joseph" [Q 12:84]. And when Jacob mentioned Joseph, his sons who were present at that time said, "By God, you will never cease . . . up to His words . . . I know from God that which you know not" [Q 12:85–86]. When he saw their coarseness, their rudeness, and their evil expressions, he had no doubt about them.

Ibn Hamid said on the authority of Salamah, who got it from Ibn Ishaq, who got it from Layth b. Abu Sulaym, who got it from Mujahid, I was told that Gabriel in the form of a man came to Joseph, may the prayers and peace of God be upon him, while he was in Egypt. When Joseph saw him, he knew him, came to him and said, O you good angel, pure of smell and honorably clothed before his Lord, do you have any knowledge of Jacob? He said, Yes. He said, O you angel, pure of garb before his Lord, How is he? He said, His sight has left. He said, O you pure angel, honorably garbed before his Lord, Why did his sight go? He said, Grief over you. He said, O you good angel, pure of smell, honorably garbed before his Lord, what was he given for that? He said, The reward of seventy martyrs.

While Jacob had his Lord's compassion because of his grief, Jacob said, O my sons, go to the land from which you have come "and ascertain concerning Joseph and his brother" [Q 12:87]. So they departed for Egypt, returning with a few goods which did not equal what they wanted to buy unless they were treated very kindly. They had seen what had happened with their father, the tribulations he had with his sons, and the loss of his sight, so they came to Joseph and said, "O ruler . . . up to His words . . . God will requite the charitable" [Q 12:88].

It was mentioned that when they spoke these words to him, he was overcome and broke out crying. Then he revealed to them what he had been hiding from them, saying, "Do you know what you did to Joseph and his brother in your ignorance?" [Q 12:89] He did not mean by the mention of his brother what he did to him when he took him, but the separation between him and his brother when they did to Joseph what they did. Joseph spoke to them, and "they said, Are you really Joseph? . . . up to His words . . . Come to me with all your folk" [Q 12:90–93].

When the caravan left Egypt, Jacob perceived the odor of Joseph, and he said to those sons with him, "Truly, I am conscious of the breath of Joseph, though you call me a dotard . . . up to His words . . . I shall ask forgiveness for you of my Lord" [Q 12:94–98]. Jacob traveled with his family until they stood before Joseph. When Jacob had his sons with him, they went in before Joseph. When his father, his mother, and his brothers saw him, they fell down prostrating to him, for this was the greetings for kings at that time. Joseph said "O my father, this is the interpretation of my former vision which my Lord gave in truth . . . up to His words . . . He is the Knower, the Wise" [Q 12:100]. Thus Joseph said when he saw the kindness of God and His graciousness to him and to the people of his house in His reuniting them, returning them to his father, and granting him authority and happiness. Then Joseph repented and mentioned that he did not care for the transitory things of the world. "O my Lord . . . up to His words . . . Join me to the righteous" [Q 12:101].

It was mentioned that Jacob asked forgiveness for his sons who did to Joseph what they did, and God forgave them and excused their sins. It was mentioned to me, and God knows best, that Joseph's absence from his father was eighteen years. The People of the Book allege that it was forty years or about that, and that Jacob remained seventeen years with Joseph after he came to Egypt. Then he died. According to what was mentioned to me, Joseph was buried in a coffin of marble in the Nile in the middle of the water. Some say that Joseph lived twenty-three years after the death of his father and died at the age of one hundred and twenty. In the Torah, he lived one hundred and ten. Ephraim and Manasseh were born to Joseph. Nun was born to Ephraim, and to Nun, Joshua, who was Moses' servant. Moses was born to Manasseh, and it was said that Moses, the son of Manasseh, was a prophet before Moses, the son of 'Imran. The People of the Torah allege that he is the one who sought al-Khidr.

Sources

at-Tabari, *Ta'rîkh* 371–373, 378, 392, 394, 395–396, 397, 398–399, 406–407, 413–414

at-Tabari, *Tafsîr* 13:29, 12:154, 12:156, 12:173, 12:175, 12:178, 12:180, 12:182, 12:183, 12:190–191, 12:192, 12:195, 12:196, 12:198, 12:201, 12:203, 12:204, 12:206, 12:211, 12:212, 12:213, 12:214–216, 12:217, 12:219, 12:221, 12:222, 12:224, 12:225, 12:229, 12:234, 12:235, 12:236, 12:237, 12:238, 13:4, 13:5, 13:6, 13:7, 13:8, 13:9, 13:10, 13:12, 13:13, 13:14, 13:15, 13:17, 13:20, 13:22, 13:23, 13:25, 13:29, 13:31, 13:32, 13:33, 13:36, 13:37, 13:38, 13:44, 13:45, 13:46–47, 13:49–50, 13:53, 13:54, 13:55, 13:56, 13:59, 13:60, 13:62, 13:64, 13:67, 13:68, 13:71, 13:74

ath-Tha'labi 64, 70, 81

Al-Baghdadi 3:12

Moses

The story of Moses in the *Kitâb al-Mubtadaʾ* is one of the longer and better developed narratives. Its major function is to highlight Moses' role as a precursor in the prophetic chain that leads to Muhammad, and as such his story has many features that parallel Muhammad's life. Abraham and Moses are the two prophets who most closely resemble Muhammad. Each of them had, however, a different function, and the two roles were combined in Muhammad. Abraham restored the ritual practice of God's worship around the Kaʿbah, while Moses was the recipient of revelation and law from God, matching Muhammad's receipt of the Quran. While Muslims contend that all the prophets received revelation, the distinction between the roles of Abraham and Moses with respect to Muhammad is one of major emphasis and function. Some non-Muslim scholars see the difference as primarily reflecting two periods in Muhammad's public career in which Abraham was better suited to a time of confrontation with Arabian Jews because he could be said to predate the beginnings of Judaism and Christianity.

In the *Kitâb al-Mubtadaʾ* there are quite a number of details where the life experiences of Moses and Muhammad coincide. Both were precocious infants, and both had foster mothers. Both had believing communities to protect, and both were exiled from their lands, Moses first going to Midian and then making his Hijrah to God's promised land. Muhammad saves his community through his Exodus to Medina, just as Moses saves the Jews through his flight from Egypt with the Jews. Both Moses and Muhammad receive revelation, and both see God. Moses sees God through his apocalyptic vision; Muhammad through his night journey to heaven. Both Moses and Muhammad act as military leaders of their communities, eventually restoring pure worship to God around the sacred shrine.

Moses is also linked to other prophets in the *Kitâb al-Mubtadaʾ* story. Moses escaped infanticide in a manner similar to Abraham and Jesus, and he gains a wife in the same way as Jacob. He is sexually proper like Joseph, resisting normal human temptation. From the perspective of Q 42:13, Moses, Noah, Abraham, Jesus, and Muhammad are all recipients of the same revelation and have the same task: to persuade a disbelieving people.

Even a casual examination reveals the dependence of many of the specific aspects of the story of Moses on rabbinic precursors. And, as in the other stories in the *Kitâb al-Mubtadaʾ*, we see Midrashic features that are not paralleled by any known rabbinic or Christian source. For example, the method of killing babies by canes is unknown in rabbinic texts, but it is the sort of detail that we have come to expect in the narratives we know to be derived from early Muslim preachers. On the other hand, in the *Kitâb al-Mubtada³*, advisers to Pharaoh are represented as saying that it would be unwise to kill all the Hebrews since the Egyptians benefited from them. In *Exodus Rabbah* 1.8 a similar sentiment is expressed by Pharaoh, who called the Egyptians idiots for wanting to kill the Hebrews who had saved them by Joseph's skill and planning.

The *Kitâb al-Mubtada³* mentions three different figures named Moses: Moses the son of Manasseh, Moses the son of ʿImran, and Moses the Samaritan. The first is the Moses associated with a mysterious figure in Quran 18 who is sometimes identified with al-Khidr, the "Green One" of Islamic mystical tradition. Non-Muslim scholars have identified the story of Moses in Quran 18 as a composite of several older Near Eastern stories. The oldest is the Gilgamesh epic. This epic influenced the Alexander Romance, the cycle of stories that ascribed marvelous and supernatural powers to Alexander of Macedon. The Alexander Romance circulated in most of the known ancient languages, including Hebrew, Arabic, and Ethiopic as well as Latin and Greek. We see the closest parallel to the story of Moses and his journey for the waters of life in the story of Alexander and his cook, with Moses substituted for Alexander.

The nearest extant Jewish version is the story of Elijah and Rabbi Joshua ben Levi. Because we have no legends which associate Moses with this journey/romance, some scholars have speculated that the confusion arose because the figure of Joshua ben Levi was identified with Joshua ben Nun. This identification may have resulted in a confusion of Joshua ben Levi's master, Elijah, with Joshua ben Nun's master, Moses. Musa thus represents Gilgamesh and Alexander in the first part of the Quranic story and Elijah in the second (see: "Musa," *Encyclopedia of Islam*). Another reason for the conflation of the figures of Moses and Alexander is that they are both endowed with horns, Alexander called *Dhu-l-Qarnayn,* He of the Two Horns, in Arabic, and Moses, when he returned from his conversation with God, was said to have horns (Ex. 34:30). It is highly likely that the Islamic story preserves a rabbinic precursor.

Ibn Ishaq quotes a tradition that rejects the identification of the Moses of Quran 18 with any Moses other than the biblical Moses. The genealogy of Moses the son of Manasseh is abandoned because there is no Quranic support; nowhere in the Quran is there any hint that there may be two or three different Moseses. However, the fact that Ibn Ishaq feels he has to cite a tradition in rejection of the association indicates that the problem of more than one Moses was present among the community of commentators on the Quran. And it is the very genealogy of Moses the son of Manasseh that gives us a clue to the underlying techniques and reasons for the rise of several different figures all named Moses.

In Judges 18:30 we are told that the children of Dan erected a graven image and that Jonathan ben Gershom ben Manasseh and his sons were the priests to the tribe of Dan. From 1 Kings 12:28 we know that the graven image erected in Dan was a golden calf, identified as the deity which brought Israel out of Egypt. This seems to be an indication of the survival of calf worship and hints that there is more to the story of Exodus 32 than has survived in the canonical narrative.

When we look again at the Hebrew text of Judges 18:30, we find an interesting problem. In the Massoretic representation of the oral tradition, the text gives the name Yihonatan ben Gershom ben Manasseh, Jonathan, the son of Gershom, the son of Manasseh. In the consonantal version, however, the name Manasseh is written with the Hebrew letters mem, sin/shin, and he. The nun between the mem and the sin/shin is written as a superscript letter, indicating later rabbinic interpolation. Without the nun, the name Manasseh would normally be read as Moses, making Jonathan a descendant of Moses.

With a tradition already established in rabbinic interpretation of interchanging Moses with Manasseh, and with a descendant of Manasseh already associated with idol worship, the commentators of the Moses-Alexander story had a ready-made solution for what to do with a Moses story that did not fit biblical evidence. Manasseh is of the right generation to be a contemporary of the biblical Moses, since he is the son of Joseph and Asenath, the daughter of an Egyptian priest. And there was already some confusion about the genealogy of Moses ben Amram, since Jochebed and Amram have been understood as ancestors of the tribal house into which Moses was born. The commentators, when confronted with adverse or inappropriate material ascribed to a character, created another character of the same or similar name, shifting the material to the secondary figure. This is, of course, a reversal of the usual procedure in which central figures attract material to themselves.

When the various stories of Moses were passed to Islamic scholars such as Ibn Ishaq, they were checked for accuracy against the Bible as well as against the Quran. But the Bible was losing authority by the time of the composition of the *Kitâb al-Mubtada*, so the nonbiblical story involving Moses could feature the same Moses as the biblical story. This position also strengthened the polemical position of the Quran and its commentary against the Bible by providing material that was "missing" or "deleted" from Scripture.

A second Moses is the Samaritan Moses, Moses the son of Zafar the Samaritan. I. Goldziher has already traced the origins of this etiological story

("Lâ Misâsa"), but the version in the Ibn Ishaq's narrative shows the tendency of the commentators to add further detail. The creation of another Moses allows Aaron to be less culpable of idol worship because the Samaritan Moses, after casting the dust from Gabriel's horse's hoof into the fire to make the calf, remarks that the calf is the god of Moses. Of course, he means himself, but Aaron mistakenly thinks that the Samaritan Moses meant Aaron's brother, Moses the son of ʿImran. It is implied that the Samaritan Moses received all the blame for the idol worship, because in both Islamic and rabbinic commentary God ordered the destruction of all who were involved in the false worship. Since the descendants of Aaron were destined to be the priests of Israel, some reason had to be invented to explain Aaron's salvation from the divine decree.

The third Moses is Moses the son of ʿImran. Moses the son of ʿImran in the *Kitâb al-Mubtadaʾ* is the Moses usually identified with the stories about Moses in the Quran and in antecedent Jewish and Christian literature. As with other stories in the *Kitâb al-Mubtadaʾ* the tales of Moses serve as Quranic exegesis and an explication of the office of prophet.

As in the Quran, the *Kitâb al-Mubtadaʾ* traces Moses' adventures from his infancy. As with other prophets, Ibn Ishaq appears to have followed a biblical model in choosing details to add to the narrative. As in rabbinic lore, the infant Moses presents a problem for the Egyptians when he refuses to be nursed, burning the breasts of the Egyptian women. This derives in part from a story found in *Exodus Rabbah* 1.25, in which Moses rejects the milk of the Egyptian women to preserve himself from taking in anything unclean because of his destiny as one who would speak with God. The feature of the burning appears to be a conflation of this story with a story of Moses' rescue by Gabriel. While an infant, Moses removed the crown from Pharaoh's head and placed it on his own. Pharaoh, fearing that this child might be the one predicted by his astrologers, put Moses to the test. At the urging of Jethro, Moses was given the choice of reaching for gold or a live coal. Gabriel guided his hand to the live coal, which burned him. In order to cool his hand, he thrust the hand holding the coal into his mouth, burning his lips and tongue. From this he became slow of speech (*Exodus Rabbah* 1.26). This is the usual interpretation of the Quranic statement "My brother Aaron is more eloquent than I" (Q 28:34).

In the story of choosing the nurse Ibn Ishaq mentions Zechariah by quoting Q 3:37, which raises the issue in Western scholarship of a conflation between Miriam (Arabic *Maryam*), the sister of Moses and Aaron, and Mary (Arabic *Maryam*), the mother of Jesus. Both have fathers named ʿImran, and Mary, the mother of Jesus, is called Sister of Aaron in Q 19:28. This is not explicitly spelled out in the Quran, but the consensus among Islamic commentators is that the two Marys are different and not to be conflated.

The *Kitâb al-Mubtada'* differs from the biblical story of Moses' encounter with Jethro's daughters by making them two instead of seven and by making Moses work for a term before he wins the hand of Zipporah. This appears to be a version of the story usually associated with Jacob and Laban, and from the details it appears that we have a melding of the two narratives. Zipporah's sister is called Layya, Leah, in Ibn Ishaq's version, and Moses has to work as a shepherd. This conflation could have occurred in a prior rabbinic context, for we have the tradition from Rabbi Akiba (*Pirke de Rabbi Eliezer* 36) citing a similar fortune for all who encounter maidens on first entering a land: Eliezer, Moses, and Jacob.

The legend that Moses cut his staff from the first tree planted on the earth by Adam with seeds taken from Paradise is widespread in rabbinic literature. *Pirke de Rabbi Eliezer* 40 gives a genealogy of the passing of the rod from one generation to the next, ending with Jethro, who planted it in his garden. Moses, because he was able to read the name of God inscribed on the staff, was able to extract it from the ground, winning thereby the hand of Zipporah.

The short tradition about Pharaoh's wishing to appear as a god rather than a man by not attending to his normal bodily functions is not mentioned in the rabbinic sources although it comes through Wahb b. Munabbih, a usual source for Jewish material. Whatever its origin, it shows great insight into the character of one who pretends to be greater than he is.

The tradition that the wealth of the Egyptians was turned to stone is possibly derived from observations of ancient Egyptian artifacts. The story lists a number of artifacts carved from stone that resembled objects which had once been alive. A student of ancient Egyptian culture will instantly recognize this as a description of the many objects found in tombs and burials intended for the use of the deceased in the afterlife.

The *Kitâb al-Mubtada'* has a well-developed apocalyptic vision of the heavens and the power of God. The repetitive character and formulaic elements in the story hint that this developed in the environment of the storyteller preacher, but it is not possible to ascertain whether it also had a written antecedent.

One portion of the Moses story seems to be based almost directly on the text of the book of Numbers. When God becomes angry with the Children of Israel and threatens to extirpate them, Moses argues successfully for their salvation. Nevertheless, God imposes the wandering for forty years in the wilderness. The Arabic text closely follows Numbers 14, but not so closely that we should assume that there was an Arabic translation in written form on which this was based, although that is possible. We do know that the Jews used to read the Torah in Hebrew and interpret it to the Muslims in Arabic, so it is likely that we have such an interpretation. (Note that the Arabic uses the verb *fassara*, which would be equivalent to the Hebrew *peshsher*.)

Finally, the fate of Moses' slave boy should be noted as evocative of the European legend of the Flying Dutchman. It probably derives from a sailor's yarn.

Text

In the name of God, the Merciful and the Compassionate

Ibn Hamid told us on the authority of Salamah, who got it from Muhammad b. Ishaq, who got it from al-Hasan b. ʿUmarah, who got it from al-Hakam b. ʿUtaybah, that Saʿid b. Jubayr said, I sat with Ibn ʿAbbas when some of the People of the Book were with him. Some of them said, O Abu-l-ʿAbbas: Nawf, the son of Kaʿb's wife, mentioned on the authority of Kaʿb that Moses the Prophet, the one who sought knowledge, was Moses the son of Manasseh. Ibn ʿAbbas then asked, Does Nawf say that? Saʿid said, Yes; I heard Nawf say that. He said, You heard him say it, O Saʿid? I said, Yes. Ibn ʿAbbas responded, Nawf lied!

Then Ibn ʿAbbas said, Ubayy b. Kaʿb told me on the authority of the Prophet of God, may the prayers and peace of God be upon him, that Moses, the Prophet of Israel, asked his Lord, the Blessed and Most High: Lord, If there is any one of your servants who is more knowledgeable than I, guide me to him. God said, There is one of my servants who is more knowledgeable than you. Then He described the location of this man to Moses and gave him permission to seek him out. So Moses, upon him be peace, went out with his slave boy who had a salted fish with him. Moses had been told, When this fish becomes alive, the companion you seek will be there and you will have attained your desire.

So Moses left with his slave boy and the fish which the two of them were carrying. He traveled until he grew tired and stopped at a certain rock near some water. That water was the Water of Life. Whoever drinks it lives forever, and nothing dead comes near it without attaining life.

When the two of them had made camp, the fish touched the water, became alive, and swam away into the sea. When they had gone on a little way, Moses said to his slave boy, Bring us our breakfast; fatigue has overtaken us in our journey. The youth spoke, Did you see that I forgot the fish when we rested at that rock, and that it made its way marvelously into the sea? No one but Satan could have caused me to forget to mention that before.

Ibn ʿAbbas said, So Moses went back to the rock, and there was a man wrapped in a garment. Moses greeted him and the man returned the salutation. Then the man said to Moses, Who are you? Moses replied, I am Moses, the son of ʿImran. The man said, The companion of the Children of Israel? Moses answered, Yes, I am that one. The man said, What has brought you to this land since there is work for you among your people? Moses said to him, I have come to you so that you can teach me some of the right guidance which you have been taught. The man replied, You will not be able to be patient with me. Now, he was a man who worked in secret, and he knew that Moses would not be patient. Moses said, That is not so. But the man said, "And how are you able to bear that which you cannot comprehend?" [Q 18:69] That is, you only know the externals of the honesty you see, and you do not comprehend the esoteric knowledge which I know. Moses answered, "You will find me patient, if God wills, and I will not disobey you even if I see something that offends me. He said, If you follow me, do not ask me about anything until I mention it to you" [Q 18:71]. That is, do not ask me about anything, even if you disapprove of it, until I tell you.

So the two of them departed, walking along the shore of the sea, stopping people, asking them to transport the two of them, until a new, well-made ship passed by them which was finer and more beautiful and more solid than any that had passed by. So they asked its crew to carry them, and they were given passage. When Moses and the man were settled in the ship, and it had put out to sea with them and its crew, the man took out an awl and a hammer he had. Then he went to the side of the ship and beat it with his hammer until he made a hole in it. He then took a plank and covered up the hole and sat on it, patching it.

Moses said to him, What a detestable thing to have made a hole in the ship to drown its crew. You have really done something! They took us and received us as guests in their ship, and there is not a ship like this in the sea. Why have you made a hole in it? The man said, Did I not say that you would not bear with me patiently? "He said, Do not be angry with me for what I forgot" [Q 18:74], that is, about my failure in the promise to you, "and do not be hard on me for my fault" [Q 18:74].

Then the two of them left the ship and went on until they came to the people of a village. There were some young lads playing, among whom was a young boy. There was not a finer, better, or more pure lad than he. The man took hold of him by his hand, took a stone, and hit his head until he knocked out the brains of the young boy and killed him. Moses saw the disgusting affair, and he had no patience for taking the life of a young lad who had no crime or sin against him, so he said, "Did you kill an innocent soul who has slain no one?" [Q 18:75] that is, a youngster who has killed no one. "You have done a horrible thing. He said, Did I not tell you that you would not be able to bear with me?" [Q 18:75–76] "He said, If I ask you about anything after this, do not keep company with me. You have received an excuse from me" [Q 18:77], that is, I have forgiven you in my case.

So they went on until they came to the people of a village from whom they sought food, but the villagers refused to treat them as guests. They found a wall on the point of falling down, "so he repaired it" [Q 18:78]. Moses became annoyed at what he saw him do in such an unnatural manner so that he had no forbearance and said, "If you wished, you could have taken wages for it" [Q 18:78]. That is, we asked them for food, and they did not feed us, and we asked to be guests, and they did not give us hospitality. Then you sat working without being asked, and, if you wished, you could have been given a wage.

"He said, This is the parting between you and me. I will tell you the interpretation of that which you were not able to endure. As for the ship, it belonged to poor people working on the sea. I wished to deface it because there was a king behind them taking every ship" [Q 18:79–80] (and in the variant reading of Ubayy b. Ka'b: every sound ship by illegal seizure). I only defaced it to keep him away from it, and it was saved from him when he saw the damage I had done. "As for the youth, his parents were believers, and we were afraid he would oppress them by rebellion and disbelief, so we wished that their Lord exchange him for someone better than he in purity and nearer in mercy. As for the wall, it belonged to two orphan youths in the city. A treasure was under it, belonging to them. Their father was righteous . . . up to His words . . . what you could not endure" [Q 18:81–83]. Ibn 'Abbas used to say, The treasure was nothing more than knowledge.

Ibn Hamid, who got it from Salamah, who got it from Muhammad b. Ishaq, who got it from al-Hasan b. 'Umarah, who got it from his father, who got it from 'Ikrimah, said, It was said to Ibn 'Abbas, We do not hear anything mentioned in the tradition about Moses' slave boy who had been with him. Ibn 'Abbas said, The slave boy drank from the water of eternity, and he lived forever. And God took him, put him on a ship, and sent him into the sea. It carries him on the waves until the Day of Resurrection. That was because he was not supposed to drink the water, and he drank.

On the authority of Salamah b. al-Fadl, who got it from Muhammad b. Ishaq, Ibn Hamid said, Then Levi, the son of Jacob, married Thabitah, the daughter of Mari, the son of Issachar, and she bore him Gershon, Merari, and Kohath. Kohath married Fahi, the daughter of Masin, the son of Bethuel, the son of Elias, and she bore him Izhar. Izhar married Shumith, the daughter of Batadit, the son of Barachiah, the son of Jokshan, the son of Abraham, and she bore him 'Imran and Qarun. 'Imran married Yuhayb, the daughter of Samuel, the son of Barachiah, the son of Jokshan, the son of Abraham, and she bore him Aaron and Moses, may the prayers and peace of God be upon him.

God buried Joseph and destroyed his king, ar-Rayan al-Walid. Then the Pharaohs inherited the kingdom of Egypt from the Amalekites, and God dispersed the Children of Israel. According to what was reported, Joseph was interred in a coffin of marble in the middle of the waters of the Nile. The Children of Israel remained under the power of the Pharaohs, but they kept their religion of Islam which Joseph, Jacob, Isaac, and Abraham had set for them, and they were faithful to it until the time of Moses' Pharaoh.

No Pharaoh was more haughty toward God, vile of speech, or long lived than the Pharaoh of Moses. According to what is mentioned, he was named al-Walid b. Mas'ab. There was no Pharaoh more ruthless, harder of heart, or a more evil king for the Children of Israel than he. He inflicted them with punishment and made them servants and slaves. He put them into categories for his tasks. He classified them as his builders, plowers, and sowers, and those who were not used for his labors had a head tax imposed on them. He set an evil punishment on them, as God said, but during all that they remained true to their religion, not wishing to leave it. Pharaoh even sought to marry one of their women named Asiyyah, the daughter of Mezahim, one of the best women. He lived a long time with them under his control, imposing evil punishment on them.

When God wished to liberate the Children of Israel, Moses, who had reached his majority, was given the Messengership. It was mentioned that when Moses' time came near, Pharaoh's astrologers made divinations for him, saying, Know that we have found by means of our science that one will be born from the Children of Israel whose birth will overshadow you, robbing you of your kingdom, overwhelming your authority, driving you from your land, and overturning your religion. When they said that to him, Pharaoh ordered all the young boys who were born to the Children of Israel to be killed, but he ordered the girls to be spared. He gathered all the midwives in his kingdom and said to them, Do not let a boy-child of the Children of Israel fall into your hands without killing him. Go do that! He also killed boys and ordered that pregnant women be tortured until they miscarried. On the authority of Salamah, who got it from Muhammad b. Ishaq, who got it from 'Abdullah b. Abu Najih, who got it from Mujahid, Ibn Hamid said, It was mentioned to me that Pharaoh would order canes split so they were like knives and then place them in rows one after the other. Then he would bring the pregnant women of the Children of Israel and set them over the canes. Then he would cut their feet so that a woman would give birth to her child. It would fall between her legs, and she would trample it, fearing the cut of the cane on her feet. These excesses continued until he had tortured the Children of Israel almost into extinction. Pharaoh was asked, Will you annihilate the people and cut off their progeny even though they are your property and your servants? So he commanded that the male children be killed for a year and be spared for a year. Aaron was born in the year the boys were spared, and Moses was born in the year they were killed, so Aaron was older than he by a year.

When Moses' mother bore him, she suckled him until Pharaoh commanded the killing of the boys of his year. Then she took him and did with him what God, the Most High, commanded, and placed him in a small chest and settled him down in it. Then she went to the Nile and threw him in it.

Early in the mornings Pharaoh would sit on a seat on the banks of the Nile. While he was sitting, suddenly the Nile brought a chest and discharged it. Now Asiyyah, the daughter of Mezahim, his wife, was seated at his side. He said, There is something in the river; bring it to me. So they went to it and dragged it out and brought it to him, and he opened the chest and, lo and behold, there was an infant boy in it.

God caused compassion to come over him and made him favorably disposed toward the infant boy. The One Whose Praise Is Great referred to Pharaoh when He said, "An enemy to me and an enemy to him will take him" [Q 20:39]; he is the enemy to God and to Moses. Moses' mother was gazing after him after she cast him in the river to see if she could get some sight of him, when the report came to her that Pharaoh had acquired a young boy in a chest that morning from the Nile. She recognized the description and saw that he had fallen into the hands of his enemy from whom whom she had to flee. Her heart became empty of God's promise to her about Moses; this was because the extreme difficulty caused her to forget God's pledge to her about the boy. "She said to her sister, Go and see what they are doing with him. (So the sister left) and she observed him from afar while they were unaware" [Q 28:11]. Moses needed suckling and asked for the breast, so the wet nurses gathered around him when God caused them to be compassionate. But he would take the breasts of every woman who was brought and cause them to be scorched. When a wet nurse was brought, he would take nothing from her. When his sister saw their passion and their desire for him, she said, "Shall I show you a household who will rear him for you and will be well disposed to him?"[Q 28:12], that is, because of his status among you and your desire for the happiness of the king. The meaning of His words, "Shall I show you one who will rear him" [Q 20:40] is, Shall I guide you to him who will care for him and guard him and suckle him and raise him? It is said that the meaning of "He made Zechariah her guardian" [Q 3:37] was to care for her.

When Moses' sister said what she said to them, they said, Go. So she went to his mother, told her, and brought her to them. They handed him over to her, and when she placed him in her lap, he took her breast, and they were happy at that. So God returned him to his mother to gladden her so that she would not grieve. The kindness of God came to her and to him when her son was returned to her. She got the benefits of Pharaoh and the people of his house along with the safety from being killed, which everyone else feared. It was as though they were members of the house of Pharaoh as far as safety and affluence, for Moses was on the beds of Pharaoh and his thrones.

When Moses reached his majority, God gave him wisdom and knowledge. He had a group of the Children of Israel who would listen to him, obey him, and associate with him. When he developed perspicacity and knew the truth, he saw the difference between Pharaoh and his people and the truth of religion. This made him talk and act in a hostile manner, and he censured Pharaoh's people so that they feared him and he feared them.

Moses would not enter Pharaoh's city except disguised and afraid. One day he entered at a time when the people were acting foolishly, "and he found in it two men fighting, one of his own party" [Q 28:15], a Muslim, and the other from the people of Pharaoh's religion, an unbeliever. "And the one of his own party asked him for help against his enemy" [Q 28:15]. Now Moses had been endowed with a large body and a great deal of strength, and he became angry at their enemy and fought with him. Moses struck him with his fist, and the blow killed him, but he did not intend to kill him. So he said, "This is the work of the Devil; he is clearly the one who leads astray" [Q 28:15]. When Moses killed the victim, he left and stayed in his home in Egypt while the people talked about the affair. They said, Moses killed a man, until news of that reached Pharaoh. Moses got up early one morning, and there was his companion of yesterday strangling another one of his enemies. Moses said to him, "You are clearly a hothead," yesterday one man and today another, "and when he wished to strike the one who was an enemy to them both, he said, O Moses, do you intend to kill me as you killed a person yesterday? If you intend to do it, you will be a tyrant in the land and not one who does good" [Q 28:18–19].

In the morning the council of elders of Pharaoh's people agreed to kill Moses because of what they heard about him. A man from the farthest part of the city, one who was called Simʿan, came running and said, O Moses, "the elders are taking council against you in order to kill you, so get out. I am one who gives you good advice. So he escaped from them, fearing, vigilant. He said, Lord, deliver me from the sinful folk" [Q 28:20–21].

So God paved the way to Midian, and Moses fled Egypt without provisions, sandals, riding animal, money, or bread, out of fear, keeping watch, until he came on a group of people watering in Midian, a people of cattle and sheep. "When he came to the water of Midian, he found a group of people watering, and he found two women apart from them, keeping away. He said, What is your difficulty? The two said, We cannot water (the animals) until the shepherds go away, since our father is an old man" [Q 28:23]. He is not able to water his cattle himself, so we are waiting for the people to finish so we can water. Then we will proceed. We are not able to compete with the men. "So he watered for them and then turned aside to the shade and said, My Lord, I need whatever good you will send down to me. Then one of the two women came walking to him shyly" [Q 28:24–25], placing her hand on her brow. The two women returned to their father at a time they did not normally return, and he rebuked them and asked them about it, and they told him the story. So he said to one of them, Hurry and bring him to me.

So one went to Moses shyly and said, "My father asks you to come so that he can give you payment for watering for us" [Q 28:25]. So he got up with her, according to what was mentioned to me, and said to her, Walk behind me and describe the way for me, and I will walk in front of you, because I do not look at women's buttocks.

When Moses came to their father, he told him the story of what drove him out of his country. "When he told him the story, he said, Do not fear; you have escaped a wrongdoing people" [Q 28:25]. She told her father about Moses' saying, I do not look at women's buttocks. One of them was called Safura bt. Jethro, and her sister was Sharfa, or, it is said, Layya; they were the two who were keeping away from the watering place. Safura said, "O my father, hire him, for the best one you can hire is trustworthy and strong" [Q 28:26], because of what she saw of his strength and his words to her when he said, Walk behind me, in order not to see anything loathsome of her. And that increased Jethro's desire for Moses, and he said, "I wish to marry you to one of these daughters of mine on the condition that you hire yourself to me for a period of eight pilgrimages. If you complete ten, it will be up to you, for I do not want to make it hard on you. If God will, you will find me right-eous" [Q 28:27], that is, good company and faithful to what I have said. Moses said, "That is fixed between you and me, and whichever of the two conditions I fulfill, there will be no injustice for me" [Q 28:28]. He said, Yes. "Then God will be surety over what we say" [Q 28:28]. So he performed the marriage for Moses, and Moses remained with the daughter, meeting her fa-ther's requirements and working for him as a shepherd of his flocks, and Moses never stood in need of anything from him. The wife of Moses was Safura, or her sister Sharfa, or Layya.

After Moses had fulfilled the term, he was traveling with his household when he saw a fire on the side of the mountain, so he said to his people, "Stay here; I have seen a fire. Perhaps I will bring you a report from it or a firebrand that you can warm yourselves" [Q 28:29].

Ibn Hamid reported on the authority of Salamah, who got it from Ibn Ishaq, who got it from Hakim b. Jubayr, that Saʿid b. Jubayr said, While I was pre-paring for the Pilgrimage, a Jew in Kufa said, I see that you are a man who pursues knowledge. Tell me which of the two terms Moses completed? I said, I do not know, but I am going now to the Rabbi of the Arabs, meaning Ibn ʿAbbas, and I will ask him about that. When I arrived in Mecca, I asked Ibn ʿAbbas about that and told him the words of the Jew. Ibn ʿAbbas said, Moses fulfilled the greater and better of the two of them, for when the prophet prom-ised, he did not diverge. Saʿid said, I went to Iraq, and I met the Jew and told him. He said, He is right. It was not sent down to Moses, but God knows.

Ibn Hamid, who got it from Salamah, said, When Moses fulfilled the term, he left. This is according to what Ibn Ishaq mentioned to me, and he got it from Wahb b. Munabbih the Yemenite, according to what was mentioned to him about it. With Moses were his cattle and his fire-drill, and his staff with which he would drive his cattle by day was in his hand. When it became evening, he would make fire with his fire-drill and spend the night by it, he, his people, and his cattle. When it became morning, he would breakfast with his household and his cattle, leaning on his staff, which was, as it was described to me on the authority of Wahb b. Munabbih, two-branched at its head and crooked at its end. Wahb said on the authority of one who is not to be doubted, who got it from his companions, that Ka'b al-Ahbar went to Mecca, and 'Abdullah b. 'Amr b. al-'As was there. Ka'b said, Ask him about three things, and if he answers you, then he is learned. Ask him about something from Paradise which God gave to man on earth, and ask him what was the first thing He placed on the earth, and what was the first tree planted in the earth. So 'Abdullah was asked about it, and he said, As for the first thing God gave man on the earth from Paradise, it was this black corner. As for the first thing placed on the earth, it was Barahut in the Yemen to which the chiefs of the unbelievers go, and as for the first tree which God planted on the earth, it was the boxthorn from which Moses cut his staff. When this reached Ka'b, he said, He is right; the man is learned, by God!

When the night came on which God desired to bestow His favor on Moses and initiate his prophethood and his office as spokesman, He confused the way so that Moses did not know where to turn. So he took out his fire-drill in order to strike a fire for his household to spend the night around until morning and learn the way. But God caused Moses' fire-drill to give him no spark, and it would not ignite a fire for him. He tried to strike a fire until he was exhausted. Then there was a fire, and he saw it, and said to his folk, "Wait, I see a fire. Perhaps I will bring you a brand from it or find guidance at the fire" [Q 20:10], so that you can warm yourselves and have guidance from the directions of one who knows the way which we have lost.

So Moses set off in the direction of the fire, and, lo, it was in a shrub which some of the People of the Book say was a boxthorn. When he approached it, it drew back from him. When he saw it retreat, he drew back from it, and he was filled with fear. When he wished to retreat, it approached him. Then words came from the shrub, and when he heard the voice, he listened, and God said to Moses, "Take off your sandals, for you are in the holy valley of Tuwa" [Q 20:12]. So he took them off. "Then He said, What is it in your right hand, Moses? He said, It is my staff upon which I lean and with which I beat the leaves of the trees for my cattle, and I have other uses for it" [Q 20:17–18]. "He said, Throw it down, Moses. So he threw it down, and it suddenly became a running serpent" [Q 20:20], the two branches having become its mouth, and its crooked end the comb on its back, shaking its teeth. It was as God wished it. Moses saw the thing as horrible and fled and did not pursue it. So his Lord called to him, O Moses, come near, and "Do not fear; we will return it to its former state" [Q 20:21], that is, to its shape as a staff as it was. So when Moses approached it, God said, "Take it and fear not" [Q 20:21]. Put your hand in its mouth. Moses had on a mantle of wool, and he wrapped his hand in his sleeve because he was afraid of it. He was told, Take your sleeve away from your hand. So he cast it off, and then he put his hand between its jaws. And when Moses put his hand in, he grabbed hold of the serpent, and it suddenly became his staff in his hand. His hand was between its two branches just as he had held it, and its curved part was in its place as it had been, and he was not harmed in any way.

Then it was said, "Put your hand in your breast, removing it without harm" [Q 27:12; see also Q 20:22; 28:32], that is, without leprosy. Moses, upon him be peace, was a ruddy man with a long, hooked nose, and he put his hand in his breast and then took it out, white like snow. Then he returned it to his breast and brought it out the color it had been. Then God said, "These two are proofs from your Lord to Pharaoh and his nobles, for they are an iniquitous people. He said, Lord, I killed a person among them, and I fear that they will slay me, and my brother Aaron is more eloquent than I, so send him with me as a helper to confirm me" [Q 28:32–34], that is, to explain to them about me and what I say to them because Aaron understands of me what they do not understand. He said, "We will strengthen your arm by means of your brother, and we will give you both the power so that by means of our signs they will not be able to reach you; you two and he who follows you will be victorious" [Q 28:35].

When God, the Mighty and Powerful, sent him, Moses and his brother Aaron went until he came to Pharaoh in Egypt. They stopped at Pharaoh's door and asked permission to go in to him, saying, We are messengers of the Lord of the Universe, so grant us permission to come in to this man. According to what reached us, the two remained two years, going back and forth at Pharaoh's door while he was unaware of them. No one undertook to tell Pharaoh of them until an idler he had came in to him, sporting with him, laughing at him, and saying to him, O king, there is a man at your gate who is saying marvelous things, asserting that a deity exists other than you. Pharaoh said, Make him come in. So Moses entered, his brother Aaron with him, and his staff was in his hand.

When Moses stopped in front of Pharaoh, he said, I am a messenger from the Lord of the Universe. Now Pharaoh knew him and said, "Did we not rear you among us as a child, and did you not dwell several years of your life among us and did what you did? You are among the ungrateful. He said, I did it then when I was one of those who were astray" [Q 26:18–20], that is, by mistake, not intending to do that. Then Moses approached him, rebuking him for what he had done for him, and said "This is the favor which you gave me, that you enslaved the Children of Israel" [Q 26:22]. That is, you took them as slaves, robbing their sons from their hands, forcing whom you wished into servitude and killing whom you wished, and, furthermore, I was made a member of your house.

"Pharaoh said, Who is the Lord of the Universe?" [Q 26:23] That is, he asked Moses for a description of the deity who sent Moses to him, saying, Who is this deity of yours? "He said, The Lord of the heavens and the earth and what is between them if you had sure belief. He said to those around him," of his nobles, "Do you not hear?" that is, denying what he said; he does not have a deity other than me. "He said, Your Lord and the Lord of your forefathers," who created your forefathers and created you from your ancestors. Pharaoh said, "Your messenger who has been sent to you is possessed." That is, these words are not true when he asserts that you have a deity other than me. "He said, The Lord of the East and the West and what is between them, if you only understood," that is, the Creator of the East and the West and what is between them, if you could comprehend. "He said, If you choose a deity other than me" to worship and thereby abandon my service, "I will make you one of the prisoners. He said, Even if I show you something plain," that is, something which will cause you to know by it my veracity and your falsehood, my truthfulness and your wrong? "He said, produce it, if you are truthful. So he threw down his staff, and it clearly became a serpent" [Q 26:24–32], having filled the space between the two ranks of the people of Pharaoh, opening its mouth. The crooked part had become the crest on its back. The people scattered before it while Pharaoh was on his throne, imploring his Lord. Then Moses put his hand in his bosom and took it out white as snow, and then he returned it to its former shape. And Moses put his hand in the serpent's mouth, and it became a staff in his hand, his hand between its two branches and its curved part on its bottom as it had been.

Pharaoh desired to evacuate, and, according to what they say, he remained for five or six days not seeking a place to do it, all the while wishing to evacuate as people wish. That was because he was thought not to be like the rest of mankind. I was told on the authority of Wahb b. Munabbih the Yemenite that he would go some twenty nights until he almost died, and his bowels became bound.

Pharaoh said to his nobles, "This is really a knowledgeable magician" [Q 26:34], that is, there is no magician more magical than he. Shall I kill him then in your opinion? A believer of the people of Pharaoh, a righteous servant whose name was, according to what they say, Habarak, said, "Will you kill a man who says that my Lord is God and has come to you with clear proof" [Q 40:28] with his staff and his hand? Then he frightened them with the punishment of God and warned them about what befell peoples before them and said, "Yours is the kingdom today, being foremost in the land, but who will save you from the wrath of God when it comes to us? Pharaoh said, I do not show you except what I think, and I do not guide you except on the right path" [Q 40:29]. The nobles of the people said, the authority of God having already discouraged them, "Put him off along with his brother and send into the cities summoners who will bring you every knowledgeable magician" [Q 26:36–37], that is, an abundance of magicians. Perhaps you can find among the magicians one who will bring you something like what was brought to you. Moses and Aaron had already left him when Habarak showed them what he showed them of the power of God

So Pharaoh immediately sent messengers into his kingdom, and he left no magician under his control who was not brought to him. It was mentioned, and God knows best, that he gathered fifteen thousand magicians to himself. When he had assembled them before him, he issued them his command and said to them, A magician has come to me the like of which I have never seen before. If you are able to overcome him, I will honor you and prefer you and advance you over the people of my kingdom. They said, We will have that if we overcome him? He said, Yes. They said, Make us a pledge, and we will assemble, we and he. The chief among the magicians whom Pharaoh assembled for Moses were Shabur, 'Adur, Hathat, and Musaffa, four, and they were the ones who believed when they saw what they saw of the power of God. The magicians believed together, and they said to Pharaoh, when he threatened them with death and crucifixion, "We do not choose you over what clear proofs have come to us of Him who created us. So decide what you decide" [Q 20:72].

So Pharaoh sent a message to Moses, saying, Set an appointed time between me and you in a convenient place which neither we nor you will change. He said, Your appointment is the day of adornment, a festival in which Pharaoh would go out. Let the people gather in the forenoon so that they can be present at your affair and mine [see Q 20:58–59]. Thus Pharaoh assembled the people at that gathering. Then he commanded his magicians, saying, "Come into line. He who is successful today will be the master" [Q 20:64], that is, he will be successful today who masters his companion. So fifteen thousand magicians lined up, each magician with a rope and a staff.

Moses, may the prayers and peace of God be upon him, together with his brother came out to the assembly leaning on his staff. Pharaoh was in his seat with the nobles of the people of his kingdom, while the people were thronging around him. Moses said to the magicians, when he came to them, "Woe to you. Do not make up a lie against God lest He extirpate you by a punishment; for he who slanders, fails" [Q 20:61]. And the magicians disputed among themselves, some of them saying to others in secret, "These are two magicians who intend to drive you from your land by their magic and destroy your best traditions" [Q 20:63]. Then he said, "O Moses, either you cast first or we will be the first to cast. He said, No, cast. Then their ropes and staves by their magic appeared to him as though they ran" [Q 20:65–66]. That was the first thing that dazzled the eyes of Moses and Pharaoh and the eyes of the people afterwards. Then each man among them threw the staves and ropes in his hand, and they suddenly became snakes like a mountain which filled the valley, piled one on another, "and Moses had a sensation of fear" [Q 20:67], and he said, By God, those were staves in their hands which have become snakes, and this my staff will not hinder them, or so his spirit said. But God inspired him, "Throw what is in your right hand, and it will eat up what they have made, for what they have made is a magician's artifice, and a magician will not prosper by what he obtains" [Q 20:69]. So He dispelled Moses' worries, and Moses cast the staff from his hand. It set forth against what they had thrown of their ropes and staves. It was a snake in the eyes of Pharaoh and his people, running, and it began to swallow them up, snake after snake, until only a few could be seen of what they had thrown in the valley. Then Moses took it, and, suddenly, it became a staff in his hand as it had been.

The magicians fell down prostrating, and they said, We believe in the Lord of Aaron and Moses, for this magic has conquered us. Pharaoh said to them, grieving and seeing the clear conquest, "Do you put your trust in him before I give permission; he is your chief who taught you magic. I will surely cut off your hands and feet alternately . . . up to His words . . . So decree what you will decree" [Q 20:71–72]. That is, do what seems right for you to do, for we will only terminate the life of this world over which you have authority, for you have no power after it. "We believe in our Lord that He may forgive us our sins, and the magic you made us perform; God is better and more enduring" [Q 20:73], that is, better than you in rewarding and more enduring in punishment. So the enemy of God returned vanquished and cursed. Then he insisted on remaining in unbelief and persisting in evil, and God pursued him with signs and inflicted him with famine and sent flood on him. God pursued Pharaoh with signs, and afflicted him with famine when he refused to believe after what happened to him and the magicians. He sent the flood on him, then locusts, then lice, then frogs, then blood as a succession of signs, that is, one sign following another [see Q 7:133].

God sent the flood. It was water which inundated the face of the earth and then became stagnant. The people of Pharaoh were not able to plow or do anything so that they were troubled by hunger. When that afflicted them, they said, O Moses, call upon your Lord for us; if the punishment is removed from us, we will believe in you and send the Children of Israel forth with you. So Moses called on his Lord, and He removed it from them, but they did not fulfill any of what they had said, so God sent on them the locusts. The locusts ate the trees, according to what reached me, until they were eating the iron door pins so that the houses fell in. And they said what they had said, and he called on his Lord, and He removed it from them, but they did not fulfill for him any of what they said, so God sent on them the vermin. It was mentioned to me that Moses was ordered to walk to a sandhill piled high with sand. He beat it, and lice swarmed over them until they covered their houses and food and prevented sleep and living. When this afflicted them, they said what they had said, and Moses called on his Lord, and He removed it from them, but they did not fulfill for him any of what they said, so God sent on them frogs. These filled up the houses and food and vessels so that no one could open up clothes or food or vessels without finding frogs in it, covering it. When that afflicted them, they said what they had said, and he called on his Lord, and He removed it from them, but they did not fulfill what they had promised, so God sent on them blood. The water of the people of Pharaoh became blood. They could not draw water from a well or a river or ladle from a vessel except that it became pure blood.

Muhammad b. Ka'b al-Qurazi related that a woman of the family of Pharaoh came to a woman of the Children of Israel when the thirst afflicted them. She said, Give me a drink of your water. So she ladled water for her from her jar, and she poured for her from her waterskin, and it flowed into the vessel as blood. So she said to her, put it in your mouth and then spit it in my mouth. So she took the water in her mouth, and when she spit it in her mouth, it became blood.

They remained thus for seven days. Then they said, Call on your Lord according to the covenant with you, that if the affliction is removed from us, we will believe in you and send the Children of Israel forth with you. So when the affliction was removed from them, they broke the agreement and did not fulfill anything of what they said. So God commanded Moses to depart and told him that He would save him and those with him and destroy Pharaoh and his army, Moses having already prayed for their destruction. He said, ''O Lord, you have given Pharaoh and his nobles splendor and riches in this life, our Lord, that they may go astray from your way . . . up to His words . . . Do not follow the way of those who do not know'' [Q 10:89–90]. So God transformed their wealth into date pits, as well as their slaves and food, and this was one of the signs which God showed Pharaoh.

On the authority of Yazid b. Sufyan b. Farwah al-Aslami, Muhammad b. Ka'b al-Qurazi said, 'Umar b. 'Abd al-'Aziz asked me about the nine signs which God showed Pharaoh. So I said, Flood, locusts, vermin, frogs, blood, his staff, his hand, destruction, and the sea. 'Umar said, I knew that destruction was one of them. I said, Moses called down evil on them, and Aaron corroborated, and God transformed their wealth to stones. He said, How could one think otherwise? Then he called for a leather pouch in which were things of the remains of the wealth of the people of Pharaoh that 'Abd al-'Aziz b.

Marwan had come across in Egypt when he was there. He took out an egg broken in two halves which was made of stone, and a shelled walnut of stone, and a chick-pea and a lentil. Ibn Hamid said on the authority of Salamah, who got it from Muhammad b. Ishaq, who got it from a man of the people of Syria who was in Egypt, who said, I saw a felled date palm of stone, and I saw a man whom I did not doubt was one of their slaves, and he was of stone, and God, the Mighty and the Powerful, said, "We gave Moses nine clear signs . . . up to His words . . . doomed" [Q 17:101–102], meaning damned.

Yahya b. ʿUrwah b. az-Zubayr, who got it from his father, said that God, when He ordered Moses on the Exodus with the children of Israel, commanded him to take Joseph with him to place him in the Holy Land. So Moses asked if there was anyone who knew of the place of his grave, but he did not find anyone except an old woman from the Children of Israel. She said, O prophet of God, I know its location, and if you will take me with you and not leave me in the land of Egypt, I will guide you to it. He said, I will do it. Now Moses had promised the Children of Israel that he would go with them at dawn, so he called on his Lord to change the time of dawn until he had finished with the matter of Joseph, and He did it. So the old woman went with him to show it to him in the direction of the Nile in the water. Then Moses brought out a sarcophagus of marble, and took it with him. ʿUrwah said, From that, the Jews carry their dead from every land to the Holy Land.

According to what was mentioned, Moses told the Children of Israel what God had commanded him: Borrow their goods and finery and clothes from them, for I will make them a booty for you with their destruction. So when Pharaoh called the people, one of the things he incited them with against the Children of Israel was that he said, When they go, they do not wish to go by themselves, but to take your wealth with them.

Muhammad b. Kaʿb al-Qurazi, who got it from ʿAbdullah b. Shaddad b. al-Had, said, It was mentioned to me that Pharaoh went out after Moses with seventy thousand black horses and an equal number of grays. Moses went until the sea was in front of him and there was no exit from it while Pharaoh was coming up from behind with his army. When the two appeared, the companions of Moses said, We are overtaken. He said, Nay, my Lord is with me, and He will guide me to safety, for He has promised me that, and He does not go back on his promises. According to reports, God, the Blessed and Most High, gave the inspiration to the sea: When Moses strikes you with his staff, divide for him. So the sea got ready for dividing, waiting for His command. Then God, the Mighty and the Powerful, inspired Moses: Strike the sea with your staff. So he beat the sea with it, and the power of God was in it, so it split. Each division was like a great mountain, that is, like a mountain on high ground, God saying to Moses, "Strike for them a dry path in the sea, fearing neither being overtaken nor fearing (the sea)'' [Q 20:77]. So when the sea split for him into a dry path, Moses followed it with the Children of Israel, and Pharaoh followed him with his army.

Muhammad b. Ka'b al-Qurazi, who got it from 'Abdullah b. Shaddad b. al-Had al-Laythi, said, I was told that when the Children of Israel had entered and not one of them remained, Pharaoh came on a stallion until he stopped at the shore of the sea, regarding the situation, while the stallion was afraid to step forward. Then Gabriel appeared to him on a mare in heat, and he brought her near. The stallion smelled her, and when he smelled her, he made her go forward, and the stallion went forward with Pharaoh on him. When Pharaoh's army saw that Pharaoh had entered, they entered also with Gabriel in the front of them, and they were following Pharaoh. Michael was on a horse behind the people, urging them on, saying, Catch up with your comrades, until, when Gabriel reached the other side of the sea, there was no one in front of him, and Michael stopped on the other side with no one behind him, and the sea pressed down on them. When Pharaoh saw what he saw of the power of God and His might and knew his disgrace and his defeat, he cried out that there is no deity except the One in whom the Children of Israel believe, and I am among the Muslims.

On the authority of Hakim b. Jubayr, who got it from Sa'id b. Jubayr, Ibn 'Abbas said, as-Samiri was a man of the people of Bajarma. He was from a people who worshiped cattle, and the love of the worship of cattle was in his soul at a time that Islam had already appeared among the Children of Israel. So when Aaron exercised authority over the Children of Israel after Moses had gone from them to his Lord, the Blessed and Most High, Aaron said to them, You have brought a heavy load of ornaments of the people of Pharaoh: goods and jewelry. Cleanse yourselves of it, for it is unclean. So he struck a fire and said to them, Cast what jewelry you have with you in it. They said, Yes, and began coming with what they had of that jewelry and goods and casting them in until the jewelry melted in the fire.

The Samaritan saw the prints of the horse of Gabriel and took some of the dust of the hoofprint. Then he came to the pit and said to Aaron, O prophet of God, shall I throw what is in my hand? He said, Yes, and Aaron did not think that it was anything but what goods and jewelry the others had brought. So he cast it in, and he said, Become the body of a lowing calf. It was a trial and a test. Then he said, This is your god and the god of Moses, so devote yourself to it and love it with a love that you have never loved anything before. And God, the Mighty and the Powerful, said, And he forgot, that is, he left his Islam, that is the Samaritan, ''Do they not see that it does not possess harm or help?'' [Q 20:89]

He said, The name of the Samaritan was Moses b. Zafar. He found himself in Egypt and joined the Children of Israel. When Aaron saw what happened, he said to his people, "You are being seduced . . . up to His words . . . until Moses returns to us" [Q 20:90–91]. So Aaron remained steadfast along with those of the Muslims who were not seduced. The ones who were worshiping the calf remained worshiping the calf. And Aaron was afraid that if he followed the course of those who were Muslims with him that Moses would say to him, You split the Children of Israel and did not keep my word, so he was fearful and obedient.

Moses left the Children of Israel and went to the mountain. When God, the Mighty and the Powerful, had saved the Children of Israel and destroyed their enemies, He promised them a covenant on the side of the mountain. When Moses went out of the sea with the Children of Israel, and they were in need of water, he gave his people something to drink; he was commanded to beat a stone with his staff, and twelve springs burst forth from it, a spring for each tribe which they would recognize and drink from. When God spoke to Moses, Moses desired a vision of Him, so he asked his Lord if he could look at Him, but He said to him, "You will not see me, but look at the mountain . . . up to His words . . . I am the first of the believers" [Q 7:143]. Then God said to Moses, "I have preferred you . . . up to His words . . . I will show you the abode of the iniquitous" [Q 7:144–145]. And He said to him, "What has made you hurry from your people, O Moses . . . up to His words . . . Moses returned to his people angry and sad" [Q 20:83–86]. And with him was the covenant of God on His tablets.

When Moses arrived at his people and saw their involvement with calf worship, he threw the tablets from his hand. They were, according to what has been mentioned, green chrysolite. Then he grabbed his brother by the head and the beard, saying, "What prevented you when you saw them in error from following me . . . up to His words . . . You did not wait for my word" [Q 20:92–94]. He said, O son of my mother, the people regard me as weak and almost killed me. Do not make my enemies triumph over me, and do not put me with the evildoers. So Moses desisted and said, "My Lord, forgive me and my brother and enter us into your mercy, for you are the most merciful of the merciful" [Q 7:150–151]. He approached his people and said, "Did your Lord not promise you a fair promise . . . up to His words . . . the body of the calf, lowing" [Q 20:86–87].

He went up to the Samaritan and said, "What do you have to say, O Samaritan? He said, I perceived what they did not perceive . . . up to His words . . . He embraces all things in His knowledge" [Q 20:95–98]. Then he took the tablets, God saying, "He took the tablets, and in their inscription was guidance and mercy for those who fear their Lord" [Q 7:154]. Sadaqah b. Yasar, who got it from Saʿid b. Jubayr, who got it from Ibn ʿAbbas, said, God, the Most High, had made an inscription for Moses in which was an exhortation and elaboration of everything as well as guidance and mercy.

When he threw them, God took up six of the seven parts and left the seventh, He saying, "In its inscription is guidance and mercy for those who fear their Lord" [Q 7:154]. The He commanded Moses about the calf, and he burned it to ash. The He ordered it cast into the sea. Ibn Ishaq said, I heard some of the people of knowledge saying, Rather than burn it, he filed it to dust and then scattered it on the sea, but God knows best.

Then Moses chose seventy of the very best men and said, Hurry to God and repent to Him what you have done and ask Him for repentance for him of your people whom you have left behind; fast, ablute, and cleanse your clothes. And he went up with them to Mount Sinai at the appointed time his Lord had set for him, for he would not come to Him except with his Permission and knowledge. According to what was mentioned, when the seventy had done what Moses commanded of them and he was leaving to meet his Lord, they said, Ask for us that we may hear the words of our Lord. He said, I will do it.

When Moses approached the mountain, a pillar of clouds fell on it so that it covered all the mountain, and Moses came near and entered it. He said to the people, Approach. Whenever Moses spoke with God, a bright light that no one of the Children of Adam could look at would fall on his brow, so he put a screen near him. The people approached until they entered the cloud and fell down prostrate upon hearing Him. He was talking with Moses, ordering him and admonishing him with what to do and not to do. When He finished His command, He removed the cloud from Moses, and Moses went to them. They said to Moses, "We will not believe in you until we see God out in the open" [Q 2:55]. A tremor seized them, and it was a thunderbolt, and it set their souls free, and they died all together.

Moses rose up calling his Lord, imploring Him and asking Him, "My Lord, if you had wished, you could have destroyed them before along with me" [Q 7:155]. They were foolish; he who is left behind of the Children of Israel who has done foolishness will also be destroyed, for I have chosen seventy of the very best among them. If I return to them and there is not one man with me, then who will believe me? Moses did not cease imploring his Lord and asking Him and beseeching Him until He returned their souls to them. He sought from Him repentance for the Children of Israel for their calf worship, but God said, No, not unless they are killed. It was reported that they said to Moses, We can bear the command of God. So Moses ordered him who had not been worshiping the calf to kill him who worshiped it, and they sat in open court, drew out their swords and began to kill them. Moses wept while the young men and women came up to him seeking forgiveness, and God forgave them and repented and commanded Moses that the sword be lifted from them, and He ordered Moses to travel with them to the Holy Land. He said, I have written down houses, habitations, and dwellings for you, so go to them and wage war against the enemies there. We will make you victorious over them.

So Moses went with them to the Holy Land by the command of God, the Mighty and the Powerful, until they made camp at Atlih, between Egypt and Syria, which is a land without wine or shade. Moses called on his Lord when the heat troubled them, and He shaded them with clouds. He asked for sustenance for them, and God sent down manna and quails.

Ibn Ishaq said on the authority of some of the scholars of tradition of the People of the Book that they found in the commentary on the story of Moses, when he sought from his Lord, that he said, Lord, let me look at you. When he sought the vision of God and asked that of Him and his Lord answered what He answered, Moses abluted and purified his clothes and fasted for the meeting with his Lord. When he came to Mount Sinai and God approached him in the clouds and spoke with him, he praised Him and glorified Him and magnified Him and called Him Holy with supplication and mournful tears. Then he began to extol Him and said, my Lord, how great you are, and how great is your majesty. There is nothing before you. You are the One, the Victorious. Your throne is beneath your majesty. Fire ignites from you. A canopy is placed beneath you, a canopy of fire. How great is your majesty, O my Lord, and how great your sovereignty. There is a distance of five hundred years between you and your angels. How great you are, my Lord, and how great your sovereignty in your rule. If you wished anything, you could gratify it with your hosts in heaven or those on earth and your hosts in the sea. The wind is sent from you. Nothing is seen of your creation unless you will it. You enter into whom you wish of your prophets, and they report to your servants when you desire. Not one of your angels has any power against your might nor against your throne. He cannot hear your voice.

But you have been beneficent to me, made me great with grace, made me excel with all perfection, made me great among the nations of the earth, exalted me among your angels, caused me to hear your voice, offered me your word, and given me your wisdom. If I count your blessings, I cannot reckon them. If I wish to thank you, I am unable. I appealed to you, my Lord, for great signs against Pharaoh and strong punishments. I struck the sea with the staff which was in my hand, and it split for me and him who was with me. I called on you when I crossed the sea, and you drowned your enemies and mine. I asked you for water for me and my nation, and I struck the rock with my staff which was in my hand, and from it you watered me and my community. I asked you for food for my people which no one had eaten before, and you commanded me to call on you before the rising of the sun and before sunset. My community called on you before sunrise, and you gave them manna for my sake, and you gave them quail for their evening meal near the sea. The heat bothered them, and I called on you, and you shaded them with clouds. I am not able to count or reckon your graces to me, and, if I wished to thank you, I would not be able. I come to you today longing, seeking, asking, beseeching, that you grant to me what you have forbidden others. I seek from you and I ask you, O Holder of power, might, and sovereignty, that you let me look upon you, for I would love it if I could see your face which no one of your creatures has seen.

The Lord of Might said to him, O son of 'Imran, do you not see what you say? You speak with the speech of one who is greater than the rest of creation. One cannot see me and live. There is not a place of abode in heaven for me but would become weak from the support of my greatness; nor is there a place for my abode on the earth but that it would become weak from encompassing my hosts, and I am not in one place to allow the eye to look on me.

Moses said, If I see you and I die, it is dearer to me than if I do not see you and live. The Lord of Might said to him, O son of 'Imran, you speak with the speech of one who is greater than the rest of creation. No one sees me and lives. He said, Lord, perfect your kindness on me and complete your grace toward me and finish your goodness toward me. This is what I ask you. I do not ask to see you that I die, but I wish to see you to set my heart to rest. He said to him, O son of 'Imran, no one will see me and live. Moses said, Lord, perfect your kindness on me and complete your goodness for me of this which I ask. It is not right that I see you. And I will die as a result, but that is dearer to me than life. And the Merciful of Mercifuls said to His creature, You have sought, O Moses, and I have granted your request, if you are able to look on me. So go, and take two tablets, and then look at the great stone on the top of the mountain. What is behind it and below it is narrow, not wide enough except as a place for you to sit, O son of 'Imran. Then look, and I will descend to you along with my army, great and small.

So Moses did as his Lord commanded him. He formed two tablets and then climbed with them up to the mountain and sat on the rock. When he was firmly on it, God ordered His host which was in the lowest heaven, saying, Lower your wings around the mountain. They heard what the Lord said, and they did His bidding. Then God sent bolts of lightning and darkness and mist around the mountain where Moses was, four parasangs in every direction. Then God commanded the angels of the nearest heaven to pass by Moses. They descended upon him and passed by him flying like a flock of birds, sanctification and praise gushing forth from their mouths with great voices like the sound of mighty thunder.

Moses, the son of 'Imran, upon him be peace, said, My Lord, I am rich because of this. My eyes have not seen anything like this; then sight left them from the rays of light coming from the rows of angels of the Lord.

Then God commanded the angels of the second heaven to descend on Moses. So they presented themselves to him and descended like lions with a clamor of sanctification and praise. The weak servant, the son of 'Imran, became afraid of what he saw and what he heard. Every hair on his head and skin shook. Then he said, I repent my request of you. Will anything save me from the situation I am in? And the best of the angels and their leader said to him, O Moses, be patient about what you have asked. What you have seen is only a little of much more.

Then God commanded the angels of the third heaven to descend to Moses, and they presented themselves to him. They approached like eagles with mighty roars and shaking and clamor, their mouths gushing forth praise and sanctification like the clamor of a great army or the crackling of a fire, and Moses was afraid, and his soul despaired. He thought he was ill, and he despaired of his life. The best of the angels and their leader said to him, Keep your place, O son of 'Imran, until you see what you cannot bear.

Then God commanded the angels of the fourth heaven to descend, and they presented themselves to Moses, the son of 'Imran, and approached and came down to him. Nothing that had passed by him before resembled them. Their hue was of blazing fire, and the rest of their form was like white snow. Their voices were high with praise and sanctification. None of the voices which had passed by him before approximated them. His knees knocked together and his heart palpitated. His weeping became violent, and the best of the angels and their leader said to him, O son of 'Imran, be patient about what you requested. What you have seen is only a little of much more.

Then God commanded the angels of the fifth heaven to descend, and they presented themselves to Moses. They came down to him in seven colors, and Moses was not able to follow them with his gaze. He had not seen the like of them and not heard the like of their voices. His belly was filled with fear, his grief strengthened and his weeping increased. The best of the angels and their leader said to him, O son of 'Imran, keep your place until you see what you cannot bear.

Then God ordered the angels of the sixth heaven: Descend to my servant, Moses, the son of 'Imran, who asked me to see me, and present yourselves to him. So they descended to him. In the hand of each angel was fire like a tall date palm glowing as strong as the sun. Their clothes were like blazing fire. When they praised and sanctified, the angels of all the heavens behind them answered them, saying with the strength of their voices, Praised and sanctified be the eternal Lord of Might who does not die. On the head of each angel were four faces. When Moses saw them, he raised his voice, praising them when they praised, and he was crying and saying: My Lord, remember me. Do not forget your servant. I do not know whether or not I will be toppled from where I am. If I leave, I will be burned up, and if I remain, I will die. Then the greatest of the angels and their leader said to him, Your belly is about to be filled, O son of 'Imran, and your heart taken aback and your weeping increased, but stay where you are sitting in order to look at Him, O son of 'Imran.

Now Moses' mountain was a great mountain, so God ordered that His throne be borne up. Then He said, Pass me by my servant so that he may see me, for he has seen only a little bit of much. The mountain split from the greatness of the Lord, and the light of the throne of the Merciful covered the mountain of Moses. The angels of the heavens raised their voices together. The mountain shook and crumbled along with all the trees that were on it. The weak servant, Moses, the son of 'Imran, fell down on his face, dumbfounded, without his spirit. So God sent life out of His mercy and covered him with mercy. He overturned the stone which was upon him and made it like a covering in the shape of a cupola so that Moses would not be consumed by fire. The spirit was resurrected in him like a mother gives life to the fetus at parturition. Moses got up, praising God, saying, I believe that you are my Lord. You were right that no one can see you and live. He who looks at your angels loses his heart. How great you are, my Lord, and how great your angels. You are the Lord of Lords and the God of Gods and the King of Kings. You command armies who are with you, and they obey you. You command the heaven and what is in it, and it obeys you. You do not spurn that. Nothing threatens you, and nothing stands up to you. My Lord, I repent to you. Praise be to God who has no partner. How great you are, Lord of the Universe.

God then commanded Moses to journey with the Children of Israel to the Holy Land, and He said, I have inscribed dwellings, villages, and estates for you in the heavenly book; so go to them and struggle against him who is an enemy there, for I will give you victory over them. Take twelve chiefs from your people, a chief from each tribe, who will be in charge of his people pledged to faithfulness in what they are commanded. Say to them that God says to you: "I am with you. If you observe prayer and give the zakat . . . up to His words . . . will go astray from a plain road" [Q 5:12]. So Moses took twelve chiefs from them, choosing responsible men from the tribes, those who had fidelity and responsibility. He took the best from each tribe, and a pledge was made with each man, God, the Mighty and the Powerful, saying, "God made a covenant with the Children of Israel and sent forth from them twelve chieftains" [Q 5:12]. So Moses traveled with them to the Holy Land at the command of God until they arrived at Atlih between Egypt and Syria, a land without tree or shade. Moses called on his Lord when the heat tormented them, and He shaded them with clouds. He asked for sustenance, and God sent down manna and quails.

God commanded Moses and said, Send a man from each tribe to spy out the land of Canaan which I have promised to the Children of Israel. So Moses sent all the chieftains among them. According to what the People of the Torah mentioned, these are the names of the troop which God sent from the Children of Israel to the land of Syria to spy for the Children of Israel: from the tribe of Rubil—Shamun b. Rakun; from the tribe of Simeon—Safat b. Harbi; from the tribe of Judah—Kalib b. Yuqana; from the tribe of Kadh—Mikhail b. Yusuf; from the tribe of Joseph, and it was the tribe of Ephraim—Joshua ben Nun; from the tribe of Benjamin—Falat b. Dhanun; from the tribe of Zebulon—Karabil b. Sudi; and from the tribe of Dan—Hamlail b. Hamal; and from the tribe of Asher—Sabur b. Malkil; from the tribe of Naphtali—Mahar b. Waqsi; and from the tribe of Issachar—Hulail b. Munkid. These are the names of those whom Moses sent to spy for him in the land. On that day, Joshua ben Nun was named Joshua ben Nun.

Moses sent them, saying to them, Get up before the sun, go through the mountain and see what is in the land and what people inhabit it, whether they are strong or weak, whether they are few or many. And look at the land in which they dwell, whether it is sunny or treed, and bring us some fruit of that land, and this was the first time he mentioned to them the grape.

When the offspring of their progeny grew up, meaning the progeny of those who fought the giants along with Moses and destroyed their fathers and completed the forty years of wandering, Moses traveled with them along with Joshua ben Nun and Kalab b. Yuqana. According to what they say, Maryam, the daughter of 'Imran and the sister of Moses and Aaron, was with them, and they were married. When they arrived at the land of Canaan, Balaam the magician, the son of Beor, was there. He was a man to whom God had given knowledge. The knowledge he had been given was the Great Name of God, which, according to what they say, when he called God with it, He answered, and when he asked by it, it was given.

It is related on the authority of Salim b. Abu an-Nadir that when Moses settled in the land of the tribe of Canaan in the land of Syria, Balaam was in Bali'ah, a village of the villages of al-Balqa. When Moses settled with the Children of Israel in that place, Balaam's folk came to Balaam and said, O Balaam, this Moses, the son of 'Imran, among the Children of Israel, has come to kill us or to drive us out of our land and make it permissible for the Children of Israel to dwell in it. We are your people, and we have no dwelling. You are a man whose prayers are answered. So go forth and call upon God against them. Balaam said, Woe to you; the prophet of God has with him angels and believers. How can I go and curse them when I know from God what I know? They said, We have no place to dwell, and they did not stop entreating him and struggling with him until they seduced him, and he was led from the right path.

So he rode an ass he had toward the mountain which the army of the Children of Israel had climbed, the mountain of Hisban. He only traveled a little way when his mount lay down. So he got off of it and beat it until he caused it to bleed, and it got up. He rode it and went not very far when it lay down again. So he did to it like before, and it got up, and he rode it not far until it lay down. He beat it until it gushed forth blood, so God gave it permission, and it talked to him, arguing with him.

It said, Woe to you, Balaam. Wherever you go, I see angels before me, turning me from my direction. Do you go to the prophet of God and the believers to curse them? But Balaam did not stop beating the ass, so God let it go on its way when Balaam did that. It went until it came to the top of the mountain of the Children of Israel, and Balaam began to curse them. But he could not curse them at all; God turned his tongue toward his own people. And he could not bless his people with goodness, but God turned his tongue to the Children of Israel.

His people said to him, Don't you know, O Balaam, what you are doing? You are blessing them and cursing us!

He said, I cannot help it. God had taken possession of his tongue, and he fell on his breast and said to them, This world and the next are gone from me. Nothing remains except cunning and tricks. So I will use guile and employ stratagems for you. Gather women and give them articles of sale and send them to the army to sell them. And a woman shall not keep herself from a man who wants her, for if one man commits fornication, it will be enough for you to overcome them.

So the Canaanites did that, and when the women entered the army, a Canaanite woman passed by a man of the nobility of the Children of Israel. She was named Kasbi, the daughter of Sur, who was the head of his community in Midian and the noblest of them. The man was Zimri b. Shalum, head of the tribe of Simeon, the son of Jacob, the son of Isaac, the son of Abraham. Her beauty amazed him, and he came to her and took her hand. Then he stood before Moses and said, I think you will say this is forbidden to me. Moses said, Yes, she is forbidden to you; do not approach her. He said, By God, I will not obey you in this. Then he entered his cupola with her and fell on her. So God sent a plague among the children of Israel.

Phinehas, the son of Eleazar, the son of Aaron, was a follower of the command of Moses. He was a man who had been endowed with a large body and great strength. He had been absent when Zimri b. Shalum did what he did, so he came while the plague was advancing through the Children of Israel, and he was told the story. He took his spear, which was entirely of iron, and entered the cupola while they were having sexual intercourse and strung them on his spear. Then he went out with them raised up to heaven, having taken his spear with his arm and supported it on his elbow and his hips and rested the spear on his beard, for he was the firstborn of Eleazar. He did this saying, O God, thus we do with him who disobeys you, and the plague was lifted. Moses counted those Children of Israel who perished in the plague when

Zimri took the woman until Phinehas killed him, and found that seventy thousand perished. But a few say it was twenty thousand in one hour of the day. From this the Children of Israel would give Phinehas, the son of Eleazar, the son of Aaron, the front of the breast and the forearm and the jawbone of every sacrifice which they sacrificed, because of his supporting the spear on his hip and taking it with his forearm and propping it up with his head, and they give the firstborn of all their animals and themselves, because he was the firstborn of Eleazar.

As for Balaam, the son of Beor, God sent down to Muhammad, may the prayers and peace of God be upon him, saying, "Recite to them the account of him to whom we gave signs, but he abandoned them," meaning Balaam, the son of Beor, "and followed Satan . . . up to His words . . . Perhaps they will give thought" [Q 7:175–176], meaning the Children of Israel. This means, I have come to the Children of Israel with a message which was hidden to make them realize that Balaam only came as a prophet to whom a report from heaven had been given.

Then Moses sent Joshua, the son of Nun, to Jericho with the Children of Israel. He entered the city with them, killed the giants who were there, and attacked whom he attacked. On the day Joshua attacked them, some remained, and the dark of night settled on them. Joshua feared that night would cloak the giants, and they would overcome him. So he commanded the sun to stand still and called on God to bar its movement. And the Mighty and the Powerful did that until Joshua rooted them out. Then Moses entered with the Children of Israel and remained there as long as God wished him to remain.

Some of the men of knowledge of the First Book told me that when the Children of Israel disobeyed their prophet and were about to do the same with Caleb and Joshua, commanding them to enter the city of the giants, and when the Children of Israel said to them what they said, the might of God appeared in clouds of fire with a sign for each of the Children of Israel. God said to Moses, How long will this tribe disobey, and how long will they not believe in all my signs which I have given them? I will strike them with death, destroy them, and I will give you a tribe stronger and greater than they. Moses said, The people of Egypt from whom you took this tribe by your might and told to dwell in this land will hear, for they have heard that you are God among this tribe. If you kill this tribe to a man, all of them, then the people who hear your name will say that you killed this tribe because you were unable to bring them into the land which you created for them, so you killed them in the wilderness. But lift your hands and let the power of your reward be great, just as you have spoken. I have said to them that your patience is long-suffering and your mercy is great and that you forgive sins. Nor do you efface, but you preserve for the fathers and the sons to the third and fourth generations. So, O

Lord, forgive the sins of this tribe according to the greatness of your majesty and mercy as you forgave them from the time you led them out of the land of Egypt until now.

God, great be His praise, said to Moses, may the prayers and peace of God be upon him, I have forgiven them because of your words, but indeed I am God, and all the earth is filled with my glory. Because the people who have seen my glory and my signs which I gave in the land of Egypt and in the wilderness have tempted me ten times and have not obeyed me, they will not see the land which I created for their fathers. He who angers me will not see it. As for my servant Caleb, whose spirit was with me and who followed me, I will lead him into the land to which he went, and his offspring will see it. Now the Amalekites and the Canaanites dwell in the mountains. Set out early in the morning and travel in the wilderness on the road they are guarding.

God, the Mighty and the Powerful, spoke to Moses and Aaron, saying to them, How long will this congregation, a congregation of evil, whisper against me; for I have heard the whispering of the Children of Israel. I will surely do as I have said to you: I will let the corpses of those of you aged twenty and above lie in this wilderness, because you whispered against me. You will not enter the land which I pledged to you nor settle in it, any of you, except Caleb and Joshua, and your burdens shall, as you said, be the booty. As for your children who this day do not know the difference between good and evil, they shall enter the land, for I am with them and will allow them the land which I wished for them. Your carcasses will lie in this wilderness, and you will wander in this wilderness according to the reckoning of the days which you spied out the land, forty days, a year in place of each day. You will become thoroughly acquainted with your sins for forty years, and you will know that you whispered. Indeed I am God, and I will do this to the congregation of the Children of Israel who were promised that they would wander in the wilderness and die therein. As for the troop whom Moses had sent to spy out the land and then who sowed discord among the congregation and spread evil among them, all of them died all at once. But of those who went to spy out the land, only Joshua and Caleb remained alive.

When Moses, upon him be peace, said all this to the Children of Israel, the tribe was greatly distressed. They rose early and went up to the top of the mountain and said, We will go up to the land which God spoke of, for we have sinned. And Moses said to them, Why do you go against the word of God? Your act will not benefit you. Do not go up. God is not with you. You will be struck down in front of your enemies, because the Amalekites and the Canaanites are before you. Do not go to war, because you are turned from God, and God is not with you. But they continued to climb the mountain. And the ark which held the covenant of God did not leave the camp, nor did Moses, out of wisdom, until the Amalekites and the Canaanites came down to the wall. They burned the Children of Israel, hounded them and killed them. And God, mighty is His praise, caused the Children of Israel to wander in the wilderness for forty years because of their sins, until he who participated in the rebellion against God was destroyed. When the young of the offspring were grown and their fathers destroyed, the forty years of wandering had ended. According to what they say, Moses, Joshua, and Caleb had gone with them; Maryam, the daughter of 'Imran, the sister of Moses and Aaron, who was kin to them, and Joshua, the son of Nun, all went into Jericho with the Children of Israel. And Moses remained as long as God wished him to remain. Then God took him, and no creature knows his grave.

God caused Moses to die, and no one knows his grave. The Bosom Friend of God hated death and found it distressing. Although Moses hated it, God, the Most High, wished him to love death and to cause him to hate life, so He turned over the office of prophet to Joshua, the son of Nun, and God would come and go to Joshua. Moses would say to Joshua, O prophet of God, what did God tell you? And Joshua, the son of Nun, would say to him, O prophet of God, was I not your companion for a great many years, and did I ask you about anything that God told you until you were ready to say it? Joshua said that to him, but he did not mention anything else to him. So when Moses heard that, he hated life and loved death.

The Bosom Friend of God, according to what Wahb b. Munabbih mentioned, used to seek shelter in a booth and would eat and drink from a hollowed-out stone. When he wished to drink after he had eaten, he would sip as a beast sips from that stone, humbling himself to God, when God honored him with His word. Wahb said, It was mentioned to me that when the command for his death came, the Bosom Friend of God went out one day from his booth for a certain need without the knowledge of any of God's creatures, and he passed by a troop of angels digging a grave. He knew them and approached them until he stood by them. And behold, they were digging a grave more beautiful, green, splendid, and opulent than he had ever seen. He said to them, O angels of God, for whom do you dig this grave? They said, We dig it for a noble servant of his Lord. Moses said, When this servant of God is brought by the command of his Lord to his grave, he will have a dwelling, a couch, and an entrance hall the like of which I have never seen. The angels said to him, O friend of God, do you wish to have this? He said, I would. They said, Enter, lie down in it and face your Lord. Then breathe easier than you have ever breathed. So he went down and lay down in it and faced his Lord and expired. God took his spirit, and the angels raised their voices over him.

The Bosom Friend of God shunned the things of this life, seeking what was with God.

Sources

at-Tabari, *Ta'rikh* 424–428, 442–443, 444–445, 445–446, 461–462, 464–467, 471–474, 483–484, 485–486, 486–487, 487–488, 492–495, 495–496, 508–512, 503–504, 504–505

at-Tabari, *Tafsîr.* 15:273, 15:279–281, 16:2, 16:7, 20:105, 1:280, 1:270–271, 16:161, 20:32, 20:36–37, 20:39, 20:41, 16:163, 20:43, 20:45–46, 20:49, 20:51, 20:52, 20:54, 20:57, 20:61, 20:64–65, 20:66, 20:68, 9:21, 16:142, 16:143, 16:156, 16:157, 16:158, 20:73, 20:74, 16:179, 16:184, 16:185, 16:186, 16:187, 16:188, 16:189, 16:190, 19:71, 16:186, 15:171, 9:35, 1:275, 19:80, 1:276, 1:280, 1:282, 16:195, 16:201, 16:203, 16:205, 1:327, 1:367, 1:368, 9:64, 1:287, 1:291, 9:72, 9:76, 9:125–126, 6:183–184

ath-Tha'labi 83, 119

Al-Baghdadi 2:117, 2:134, 2:146

Ezekiel

In this short tale of Ezekiel the usual occasion verse, Q 2:259, is missing from Ibn Ishaq's version, and the story is glossed to Q 2:243. This verse is not usually related to Ezekiel and is regarded by some Muslim commentators as referring to the Exodus. The reference to Ezekiel's mother's age is reminiscent of the story of Sarah bearing Isaac in her old age. The major point of the story of Ezekiel, who is not named in the Quran, is that God has the power to bring to life those who had died. Muhammad's detractors regularly dispute him on that point, and the Ezekiel narrative offers corroboration of the Quranic message, thus fulfilling one of the major functions of the Kitâb al-Mubtada': to offer "proofs of prophethood."

Text
In the name of God, the Merciful and the Compassionate

Wahb b. Munabbih said that Caleb, the son of Yuqana, died after Joshua. Then Ezekiel, the son of Buzi, succeeded him among the Children of Israel. Ezekiel, the son of Buzi, was called Son of an Old Woman because his mother asked God for a son after she had grown old and had become barren. So God gave him to her, and for that reason he was called Son of an Old Woman. Ezekiel was the one who prayed for the people whom God mentioned to Muhammad in the Book, as it reached us: "Do not look at those who went forth from their houses . . . up to His words . . . But most of mankind does not give thanks" [Q 2:243].

It was said that according to the history of the Children of Israel, some of them fled as a precaution against death from a certain epidemic of plague or sickness which was afflicting the people. They had been faithful until they settled in a plateau area of the country. God said the them, Die, and they all died together. The people of that country made an enclosure around them to keep out the wild beasts and left them in it. That was because they were too numerous to cover up. Time and ages passed over them until they became decaying bones.

Ezekiel, the son of Buzi, passed by them, stopped and marveled at their condition. Compassion for them filled him, and he was asked, Do you wish God to resurrect them? He said, Yes. He was told, Call them and say, O you decaying bones which have dried and rotted, let each bone return to its companion. So he called them with those words, and he looked at the bones jumping to take hold of one another. Then he was told, Say, O you flesh and sinew and skin, cover the bones, by permission of your Lord. He said those words, and looked at them, and the flesh took hold of the bones, then the muscle and skin and hair, until they were creatures without souls. Then Ezekiel prayed for life for them. He was covered over by something from heaven which distressed him, and he fainted from it. Then he recovered, and the people were seated, saying, Praise be to God, for God had given them life.

Sources

at-Tabari, *Ta'rîkh* 535–536, 539–540
at-Tabari, *Tafsîr* 2:587–588
Al-Bagdadi 4:24

Elijah

This short tale of the important prophet Elijah follows the biblical and rabbinic sources, citing Q 37:123–128 as the occasion verse: "And Elijah was one of the messengers, when he said to his people, Will you not fear God? Do you call on Baal and forsake the best of Creators, Allah, your Lord and the Lord of your forefathers? But they regarded him as a liar, so they will surely be brought forth, except for the redeemed servants of God." The other Quranic reference to Elijah is Q 6:86, where Elijah is mentioned in a list along with Zechariah, John, and Jesus. The Arabic form of the prophet's name, Ilyas (Elias), indicates that the name came into Arabic ultimately through Greek.

The story of Elijah addresses the question of the benefits of worshiping God. Elijah's king saw no difference between himself and his pagen neighbors and so turned to the worship of Baal, whom some said was only a woman whom they worshiped. God then gave Elijah the power to withhold rain from his people, which leads to a contest between God and the idols, reminiscent of the contests mentioned in the stories of Abraham, Salih, and at the occasion of the introduction of Judaism in southern Arabia. Even the clear proof brought by Elijah fails to persuade his people to repent and worship God.

In the mold of the prophet warner Elijah encountered rejection, persecution, and disappointment even when he presented incontrovertible evidence that he was right. Muhammad's experience with the Meccans parallels Elijah's troubles. Muhammad was regarded as a liar, was persecuted, and was forced to flee from his people's anger.

Elijah's translation to heaven follows the well-established rabbinic traditions that Elijah never "tasted death" [cf. *Genesis Rabbah* 21.5]. There is no hint in this version of the traditions about Elijah that he was thought to be the prefiguration of the Messiah. Even though he is said to have been made into an angel, he remains distinctly human throughout the story, and it is the humanity of the prophets which is emphasized in Islam. Elijah's association with food appears to be a reflection of the belief among some Jews that Elijah as a spiritual figure visits each home during Passover and partakes of the ritual meal.

Text

In the name of God, the Merciful and the Compassionate

Then God, the Mighty and the Powerful, caused Ezekiel to die, and misfortune oppressed the Children of Israel. They forgot what God had pledged to them, so they set up idols and worshiped them instead of God. As a result, God sent them Elijah, the son of Yasin, the son of Phinehas, the son of Eliezar, the son of Aaron, the son of 'Imran, as a prophet. After Moses, prophets were only sent among the Children of Israel for the restoration of what they had forgotten of the Torah.

Elijah accompanied a king of Israel who was called Ahab. Ahab's wife's name was Jezebel. Ahab would heed Elijah and believe him, and Elijah would take care of Ahab's affairs. The rest of the Children of Israel had taken an idol they called Baal, which they worshiped instead of God. It was reported that some of the scholars said that Baal was nothing but a woman which they would worship instead of God. About this, God said to Muhammad, may the prayers and peace of God be upon him, "Elijah was one of the ones sent when he said to his people . . . up to His words . . . and the Lord of your forefathers" [Q 37:123–126]. So Elijah began to invite the Children of Israel to God, the Mighty and the Powerful, but they would not listen to anything from him, only what came from that king.

Each of the various kings in Syria had a district which he controlled. The king whose affairs Elijah controlled and who regarded Elijah as someone guided, said one day, O Elijah, by God, it is my opinion that you pray to the Lord in vain. By God, I do not see so-and-so, who is a king of the Children of Israel and who has worshiped idols instead of God, living any different way than we in what they eat, drink, and enjoy of their possessions. Their belief does not diminish their earthly possessions which you assert are vanities. And I do not see that we have superior benefits to them.

They assert, and God knows best, that Elijah's hair stood up on his head and skin, and he said, All belongs to God and to Him is the return [cf. Q 2:46 et passim]. Then Elijah abandoned his king and left him, and that king worshiped idols and performed as his peers did. Elijah said, O God, the Children of Israel refuse to give you anything but ungratefulness, and they worship something other than you, so change your blessings for them.

It was mentioned that the following inspiration came to Elijah: We have placed the matter of their sustenance in your hand and under your power. You can be the one to issue the command about that. Elijah said, O God, withhold rain from them. So it was withheld from them for three years until the livestock, the beasts, the vermin, and the trees were destroyed, and the people suffered terribly.

According to what they say, when Elijah prayed for that for the Children of Israel, he kept out of sight out of fear of them, and wherever he was, he was given sustenance. So when they found the smell of bread in a house or an apartment, they said, Elijah has entered this place, and they would seek him out, and the people of that place would suffer evil from them. Then one night he sought accommodations with a woman of the Children of Israel who had a son called Elisha, the son of Akhtub, who had an impairment. She gave him shelter and lightened his burden, so Elijah prayed for her son, and the infirmity which he had was cured. Elisha followed Elijah, trusted in him, believed in him, stuck close to him, and would go with him wherever he would go. Elijah was an old man, and Elisha was a young lad.

They allege, and God knows best, that God inspired Elijah: Because of the sins of the Children of Israel, you have, by withholding rain from them, destroyed many creatures whose destruction I did not want, such as cattle, beasts, birds, vermin, and trees, who did not rebel as did the Children of Israel. Elijah said, O Lord, let me be the one who urges them on and be the one to come to them with the relief from the tribulation which has afflicted them. Perhaps they will return and abandon their worship of other than you. Elijah was told, Yes. So he came to the Children of Israel and said to them, You are destroyed by pains, and the cattle, the beasts, the birds, the vermin, and the trees are destroyed by your sins. You are engaged in vanity and delusion. If you wish to know that God is displeased with you for what you are doing and that to which I invite you is the truth, then bring out your idols which you worship and assert are better than that to which I invite you. If they answer you, then it will be as you said, and if they do not answer, you will know that you are engaged in folly. You will desist, and I will pray to God, and he will relieve you of the trials you suffer.

They said, You have acted justly. So they brought out their idols, and they prayed to them, but they did not bring themselves near to God because of their misdeeds with which He was displeased. The idols did not answer them, and the people were not delivered from their tribulation, so that they knew that they were in error and vanity. Then they said to Elijah, O Elijah, we are destroyed, so pray to God for us. Elijah prayed for deliverance for them from what they were suffering and that they be given water. Then by the permission of God a cloud came out like a shield along the edge of the sea while they were watching. The cloud rushed at them, and it got dark. Then God sent rain, and it gave them aid. Their country lived, and they were delivered from their trials.

But they did not desist from evil or return to God, and they remained more wicked than they were before. When Elijah saw their ingratitude, he prayed to his Lord to cause him to die and take him from them. It was said to him, according to what they assert, On a certain a day, go to a certain a place where something will come to you; ride it, and do not be afraid. So Elijah went out with Elisha, the son of Akhtub, to the location mentioned to him in the place which he was commanded, and a horse of fire appeared and stopped in front of him. He jumped on it, and it left with him. Elisha called to him, O Elijah, O Elijah, what do you command me? And that was the last they knew of him. God wrapped Elijah in feathers and clothed him with fire and removed his need for food and drink, and he flew among the angels, and he was half man, half angel, half earthly, half heavenly.

Sources

at-Tabari, *Ta'rîkh* 540–544
at-Tabari, *Tafsîr* 23:91, 23:92, 23:93
ath-Tha'labi 141
Al-Maqdisi 3:99
Al-Baghdadi 2:31

Elisha and Successors

Elisha is mentioned twice in the Quran, each time in a list of God's messengers. The point of this section is not, however, to tell Elisha's story but to lay out a genealogy of sin and redemption. An important notion in Islam is that human history is a succession of periods of sin followed by periods of redemption and restoration through the agency of a messenger from God. This process culminates in the final messenger, Muhammad, the Seal of the Prophets. The Quran does not lay out a chronology or a genealogy in a historical manner. Ibn Ishaq's scheme for the *Kitâb al-Mubtada'* in general and for this section is to present an overview of that historical process. One could also speculate that the genealogies and historical plans presented in the *Kitâb al-Mubtada'* serve as a corrective to what Muslims would have perceived as distortions in the Torah. Muslims believe that the Torah, while still God's word, was corrupted over time and needs the corrective of the Quran.

An interesting detail is the magical associations with the rock, presumably to be identified with the Eben Shtiya, the Foundation Stone in Jerusalem in the Dome of the Rock. The pressing of oil and grain on the rock is reminiscent of a pre- and early Islamic Jewish cult associated with the rock which has been identified by David Halperin.

Text
In the name of God, the Merciful and the Compassionate

According to Wahb b. Munabbih, Elisha came as a prophet to the Children of Israel after Elijah. Elisha remained among the Children of Israel as long as God wished, and then God caused him to die.

Successors followed, and sins became enormous among the Children of Israel. They had the ark, which was passed form noble to noble as an inheritance in which was the Shechinah and the rest of what the families of Moses and Aaron had left. Whenever an enemy would meet them, they would bring out the ark, advance with it, and God would destroy that enemy. According to Wahb b. Munabbih on the authority of some of the scholars of the Children of Israel, the Shechinah was the head of a dead cat. When it cried out in the ark with the cry of a cat, they were sure of victory, and triumph would come to them.

Then a king called Eli came to power among them. God had given the Children of Israel a blessing for their mountain called Aelia that an enemy would not come against them and that they would not have need of anything else. According to what they mention, one of them could gather dirt on the rock and press grain on it, and God would extract for him what he and his dependents would eat for a year. Another one of them might have an olive tree, and he could press from it what he and dependents would eat for a year.

When their misdeeds became enormous, and they abandoned the covenant with God, their enemy descended on them. They went out against them, taking out the ark as they used to take it out. Then they advanced with it, but they were fought against until the ark was plundered from their hands. Their king, Eli, came, announced that the ark had been taken and plundered, and his neck bent, and he died of grief.

Their affairs became confused, and their enemies descended and trod on them until their sons and daughters were afflicted. They remained in disarray and confusion, persisting in error and sin, and God would set over them him who would take His vengeance against them. They would return to repentance for a time, and God would save them from him who would oppress them with evil. This went on until God sent them Saul as a king and returned the ark of the covenant to them.

The length of time between the death of Joshua, the son of Nun (part of which was the period of the Judges and part of which was when they were conquered and ruled over by outsiders), and the establishment of a king among them and the return of prophecy by Samuel, the son of Bali, was four hundred and sixty years. According to what is said, the first of those who ruled over the Children of Israel was a man of the lineage of Lot called Cushan. He conquered and subdued them for eight years. Then a younger brother of Caleb, called Othniel, the son of Kenaz, saved them from him, and he lasted forty years.

Then a king called Eglon was given power over them, and he ruled eighteen years. Then, according to what is said, they were saved from him by a man from the tribe of Benjamin called Ehud, the son of Gera, the wither-handed Yemenite, and he lasted eighty years. Then a king of the Canaanites called Jabin conquered them and ruled twenty years. Then a woman prophet called Deborah saved them, and according to what is said, their affairs were managed for her by a man called Barak for forty years. Then a people of the offspring of Lot whose home was on the borders of the Hijaz conquered them and ruled them seven years. Then a man of Naphtali, the son of Jacob, who was called Gideon, the son of Joash, saved them, and he oversaw their affairs for forty years. Then, after Gideon, his son, Abimelech, the son of Gideon, managed their affairs three years. Then, after Abimelech, Tola, the son of Puah, the son of the maternal uncle (and, it is said, the paternal uncle), of Abimelech managed their affairs for twenty-three years. After Tola their affairs were managed by a man of the Children of Israel called Jair for twenty-two years. Then the

Children of Ammon ruled over them for eighteen yeas, and they were a people of the Philistines. Then a man from among them called Jephthah arose and ruled for six years. Then, after him, they were ruled by Jashun, a man of the Children of Israel, for seven years. Then after him for ten years was Elon, and then after him, Kirun, and some call him 'Akrun, for eight years. Then the people of Palestine conquered them and ruled over them for forty years. Then Samson commanded them, according to what is said, for ten years. Then after that Eli the Priest managed them, and in his days the people of Gaza and Ashkelon took the ark. When forty years had passed, Samuel was sent as a prophet, and Samuel took charge of their affairs for ten years. Then, when he humiliated them for their rebellion against their Lord, they asked Samuel that a king be sent to them so that they could struggle in the way of God, and Samuel said to them what God said in the Book [see Q 2:246ff.].

Sources

at-Tabari, *Ta'rikh* 544–547
at-Tabari, *Tafsîr* 2:596–597

Samuel b. Bali

In the story of Samuel and other summaries of the history of the Jewish people, the national elements are suppressed when compared to the biblical versions. Instead,the ethical and moral elements are emphasized. In particular, we are once again reminded with Samuel that adherence to God's word through a prophet will bring reward, while disobedience will bring destruction. Since we know that more material was available to the early Muslim collectors, we can assume that the material included represents a choice reflecting Ibn Ishaq's vision of the prophetic mission.

A mark of Samuel's prophethood is his ability to locate lost animals. Through God, prophets are able to see the unseen and know the unknown. Muhammad, for example, on his Night Journey to Jerusalem passed by a caravan and is reported to have been able to help the drivers recover a camel that had bolted. Making Saul king when he was not a member of one of the royal or prophetic tribes is also a reminder that Muhammad did not come from the expected upper class of Meccan leadership.

Text
In the name of God, the Merciful and the Compassionate

The affairs of the Children of Israel became confused, and their enemies descended and trod on them until their sons and daughters were afflicted. There was a prophet among them called Samuel, whom God had sent to the Children of Israel and from whom they would accept nothing. He is the one whom God mentioned to his prophet Muhammad: "Do you not see the nobles of the Children of Israel after Moses when they said to their prophet, Send us a king so that we can fight in the way of God . . . up to His words . . . We have been driven from our dwellings along with our children" [Q 2:246]. God said, "And when fighting was prescribed for them, they turned away, all but a few of them . . . up to His words . . . In that is a sign for you if you are believers" [Q 2:246–248].

Wahb b. Munabbih said that when the trials came down on the Children of Israel, and their country was conquered, they spoke to their prophet, Samuel, the son of Bali, saying, Send us a king so that we can fight in the way of God. This was because the prophets were in charge of the kings of the Children of Israel and in charge of obedience to them. The king would be easy on the crowd, and the prophet would correct his affairs for him and give him reports

154

from his Lord. Now when the Children of Israel would go along with this, their affairs would prosper. But when their kings rebelled and abandoned the advice of their prophets, their affairs went awry.

When the crowd followed their king in error, abandoning the orders of the prophet, some calling him a liar and not accepting anything from him, and some fighting them, their tribulation continued until they said to the prophet, Send us a king so that we can fight in the way of God. He said to them, You do not have the fidelity, truthfulness, or desire for the struggle. They said, We are the spoils of the struggle and have little property. If we are to be kept from our land, no one will tread on it. No enemy will come against us in our land, but if it does come about, there will be no recourse but to resist, and we will obey our Lord in the struggle against our enemy, and we will guard our sons, women, and offspring.

When the nobles of the Children of Israel said that to Samuel, the son of Bali, he asked God to send them a king. God said to him, Look at the horn in your house which contains oil. When a man comes to you and the oil in the horn bubbles, he is the king of Israel. Anoint his head with it, and make him king over them, and inform him about what has come to him. So Samuel waited for that man to come to him.

Now Saul was a tanner who worked with leather. He was of the tribe of Benjamin, the son of Jacob, and the tribe of Benjamin was a tribe which did not have a prophet or a king in it. Saul had gone out along with a boy he had, seeking an animal which he had lost, when two of them passed the house of the prophet, upon him be peace. The servant boy said to Saul, You should go in to this prophet, and we will ask him about our animal so that he can guide us and bless us. Saul said, There is no harm in what you say, so the two of them entered to him. While the two of them were with him mentioning the state of their animal and asking him to pray for them, the oil in the horn began to boil. The prophet, upon him be peace, got up and took hold of Saul and said to him, Bend your head down. So he bent it down, and Samuel anointed him with the oil. Then Samuel said to Saul, You are the king of the Children of Israel whom God commanded me to make king over them. The name of Saul in Syriac is Shaul b. Qays b. Abyal b. Sarar b. Yuhrab b. Afiyyah b. Ayis b. Binyamin b. Ya'qub b. Ishaq b. Ibrahim.

Samuel sat with Saul, and the people said, Saul a king? The mighty ones of the Children of Israel came to their prophet and said to him, What is the reason that Saul is made king over us since he is not of a prophetic or kingly house? It is known that prophethood and royalty are among the Levites and Judah. Samuel said to them, "Indeed, God has chosen him over you and increased him in wisdom and stature" [Q 2:247]. The sign of his sovereignty and his right to rule before God is that the ark will come to you. The Shechinah and the rest of what the families of Moses and Aaron left will be returned to you. It is the thing with which you defeated those of your enemies who met you, and you appeared before them with it. They said, If the ark comes to us, then we are satisfied and at peace.

The enemy who had taken the ark was below the mountain, Mount Aelia, in the area between them and Egypt. They were idolaters, and among them was Goliath. Goliath was a man endowed with a large body, great strength and power in war, which was well known among the people. When the ark had been captured, it had been placed in a Philistine village called Jordan. They had put the ark in a sanctuary in which were their idols. When the prophet, may the prayers and peace of God be upon him, promised the Children of Israel that the ark would come to them, the idols in their sanctuary fell on their heads. Then God sent mice to the people of that village, a mouse per man, and in the morning they were dead, their bellies having been eaten out from behind. The Philistines said, You know, by God, that the affliction that has come on you is what has afflicted nations before you. We have only known this affliction since this ark has been among us, resulting in what you have seen among your idols, causing them to be upside down each morning, a thing that does not happen unless the ark is with them. So get it out from among you.

They got a cart and suspended the ark between two bulls and beat them on their sides. An angel led the two bulls away, and whenever the ark passed by anything on the earth, it said, Holy, Holy, Holy. Nothing frightened them except the ark on a cart being pulled by two bulls until it stopped in front of the Children of Israel. They magnified and praised God, and they strove in war, putting their confidence in Saul.

When Saul set out with the army, they said, This water will not be enough for us, so pray to God to make a river run for us. Saul said to them, "God will try you by a river" [Q 2:249]. It is said that the river which Saul told them that God would try them by is a river between Jordan and Palestine. God said, "He who drinks of it is not of me except him who takes it in the hollow of his hand, so they drank from it, all but a few of them" [Q 2:249]. According to what they allege, he who followed in drinking what was forbidden was not satisfied, and he who did not taste except as ordered, with the hollow of his hand, was rewarded and satisfied. "When he had crossed . . . up to His words . . . And David killed Goliath" [Q 2:249–251].

Source

at-Tabari, *Tafsîr* 2:597, 2:601–602, 2:608–609, 2:618, 2:621

David

The heroic figure of David is portrayed as a very human prophet in the *Kitâb al-Mubtada*. His piety, his ability to recite the psalms, his bravery, all combine to make him larger than life, but he sins twice. The first is a near sin when he wishes to kill Saul so that he can take over the kingship, and the second is when he lusts after Uriah's wife. In the first God turns him away from the desire to kill Saul, a view consistent with the notion in Islam that prophets are rightly guided. In the second David is not turned away by God but allowed to sin, even to the point of killing Uriah and taking his wife. Only when the angels present his case clearly before him does he realize his error. He weeps until plants grow, a sign that he is once again in harmony with nature. And he prostrates until he shows the mark of prayer. Many pious Muslims have such a mark on their foreheads resulting from prostrating in daily prayer.

The story of David reflects many features of rabbinic sources in its anecdotal detail, such as his election and the encounter with Goliath, where the pebbles speak to him as the three patriarchs [*Midrash Shemuel* 21.108]. The story of David's sexual passion and his repentance is popular in Haggadic literature, as is the detail of his punishment by leprosy (Ginzberg, *Legends* 6:266). The use of angels instead of the prophet Nathan to tell the story of the litigants shows a nice narrative sense, particularly the graphic detail of the angels falling down on David, fighting. David is usually represented in rabbinic literature as having been allowed to sin to show the world how to repent by weeping copiously (*Apocalypse of Sedrach* 14). Proper and improper music derive from David, who is also a metallurgist, because, while he chants the proper music of the psalms, the devils imitate his sound by the construction of musical instruments. This view is reminiscent of the dichotomy between instrumental music and *musica mundana* in the Neoplatonic tradition.

Text
In the name of God, the Merciful and the Compassionate

Wahb b. Munabbih said, David, upon him be peace, was a short, yellow, partly bald man, pure of heart and clean. David the prophet had four brothers who were with their father when he was an old man. The four brothers had gone out with Saul, and their father had remained behind. David remained with him among his father's flocks, tending them for him, for he was the youngest. His father called him when the people had gathered around in a crowd, and said to him, O my son, we have prepared provisions for your brothers to strengthen them against their enemies, so take these to them, and when you give these to them, return quickly to me.

David said, I will do it, and he left with what he was to carry to his brothers. He had his pouch with him in which he carried stones and also his sling with which he would throw stones to protect his flock. So when he left his father, he passed by a stone, and it said, O David, take me and put me in your pouch so that you can kill Goliath with me, for I am the stone of Jacob. So he took it and put it in his pouch and walked on. While he was walking, he suddenly passed by another stone, and it said, David, take me and put me in your pouch so that you can kill Goliath with me, for I am the stone of Isaac. So he took it and put it in his pouch and went on. And while he was walking, he passed by another stone, and it said, O David, take me and put me in your pouch so that you can kill Goliath with me, for I am the stone of Abraham. So he took it and put it in his pouch. Then he went on with what he had until he came to the people of the army. He gave his brothers what was sent to them, and he heard what was known around the army about Goliath, his huge size and the people's fear of him. He said to them, By God, you are distressed by this enemy in a way I do not understand. By God, if I see him, I will kill him. Take me to the king.

So David was brought to king Saul, and he said, O King, I see that you are distressed by this enemy. By God, if I see him, I will kill him. Saul said, Tell me of your powers to do that and how you have tested yourself. David said, A lion attacked a sheep of my flock, and I overtook it, grabbed it by its head, severed its jaws from it, and took the sheep from its mouth. So bring me a coat of armor to put on me. A suit of armor was brought, he put it over his neck, and it was as though it were made for him. Saul and those who were with him of the Children of Israel were amazed, and Saul said, by God, perhaps God will destroy Goliath by him.

When it was morning, they returned to Goliath. When he met the people, David said, Show me Goliath. So they showed Goliath to him wearing a cuirass, on a horse. When David saw him, the three stones began to jump around in his pouch, each one saying. Take me. So he took one of them, put it in his sling, and killed him with it. He flung it, and it struck between the eyes of Goliath and branded him, and he fell off his animal, and David killed him. Then Goliath's army was defeated. The people said, David killed Goliath, and Saul is deposed. The people went over to David, so that Saul is not heard from, except that the People of the Book allege that he, when he saw the departure of the people from him to David, worried that David would assassinate him, and he desired David's death. But God turned that away from him and from David, and Saul knew his sin and repented it to God.

When the Children of Israel agreed on David, God sent the psalms down to him and taught him the working of iron, softening it for him. He commanded the mountains and the birds to sing praises with him when he sang praises, and according to what they say, God did not give any one of His creatures a voice like his. When David would read psalms, the wild beasts would come near enough so that he could take them by their necks, and they would be silent in order to hear his voice. The devils made flutes, lutes, and cymbals according to the various qualities of his voice. He was assiduous in the tireless pursuit of worship, and he remained among the Children of Israel, judging them wisely by the command of God, as a prophet and a vicar. He was vigorous in prophethood, given to much weeping. Then the temptation of that woman happened.

David had a tower to which he would go alone to recite psalms and to pray when he would pray. Below it was a garden which belonged to a man of the Children of Israel. That man had a wife with whom David was smitten. When David entered his tower one day, he said, Do not let anyone come in to my tower today until night, and do not bother me with anything you need until evening. Then he entered his tower and recited his psalms, reading them aloud.

The tower had a window which was above the garden. While David was sitting, reciting his psalms, a dove of gold entered suddenly and stopped on the window. David raised his head, saw it, and was amazed. Then he remembered that he had said that he would not be disturbed by anything that entered to him, so he lowered his head and commenced his psalms. The dove got down from the window to test and try him and fell in front of him. David reached out for it with his hand, and it withdrew a little bit. He followed it, and it got up on the window. He reached for it in the window, and it went down to the garden. He followed it with his eyes to where it landed, and behold, there was a woman, sitting, bathing herself, extremely good-looking and beautiful.

They allege that when she saw him, she let down her hair and hid her body from him. But his heart was captured. He returned to his psalms and his court, but she caused his heart to be unable to stop thinking about her. The temptation persisted until he became jealous of her husband. According to what the People of the Book assert, he ordered his army commander to march her husband to destruction, and he was destroyed as David wished.

Now David already had ninety-nine wives, and when her husband was struck down, David proposed to her and married her. Then when he was in his tower, God sent him to angels bringing a dispute, beating on one another. David was startled at the two of them falling on his head in his tower and said, What brings the two of you in to me? They said, Do not fear. We have not come suspiciously with evil intent but as "two litigants, one of whom has wronged the other" [Q 38:23]. We have come to you so that you can judge between us, "so judge us in truth; be not unjust, and guide us on the right way" [Q 28:23]. That is, bring us to the truth, and do not diverge to something else.

The angel that was taking the part of Uriah, the son of Hananiah, the husband of the woman, said, "This brother of mine," that is in my debt, "has ninety-nine ewes, and I have one ewe. And he said, Entrust it to me" [Q 38:24]. That is, hand it over to me. Then he overpowered me by entreaty and conquered me with speech, for he was stronger than me and more powerful. So I gave my ewe to his ewes, and that left me with nothing.

David became angry and looked at the litigant, who did not speak, and said, If what he has told me is true, I should strike you between the eyes with an ax. Then David listened, and he knew that he was the one intended because of what he had done with Uriah's wife. So he fell down, prostrating, repenting, and weeping. He prostrated forty mornings, fasting, not eating or drinking, until his tears caused plants to grow under his face and until the prostrations made a scar on his face.

God forgave him and accepted repentance from him. They allege that he said, O Lord, you have forgiven what I have brought about in the case of the woman, but what about the blood of the wrongfully killed one? According to the People of the Book, he was told, O David, As for your Lord, He has not oppressed you with his blood, but He will ask him about you, and you will be relieved of it. So when He showed David the mark of sin on the inside of the palm of his right hand, he went out to the people that they might see the mark of sin on his hand.

Sources

at-Tabari, *Taʾrîkh* 559, 562–563
at-Tabari, *Tafsîr* 2:626, 2:626–627, 23:143, 23:149–150

Solomon

The story of Solomon has captured the imagination of numerous writers and commentators, and Muslim exegetes are no exception. Solomon's wisdom, his judgment, his ability to communicate with animals, his encounters with the Queen of Sheba, and his encounters with Jinn and devils have made fascinating reading. Jews and Christians often regarded him as one of the two believing *cosmocrators,* rulers of the world, the other being Alexander the Great. In rabbinic sources Solomon is also a magician and the source for the world's magic.

For Muslims, Solomon is a prophet first and a wise ruler second. The Quran emphatically denies that he is a magician. Magic, it is said, was revealed to two Babylonian angels, Harut and Marut, as a temptation for mankind [Q 2:102]. Solomon's prophetic activity is in the public sphere, in his role as the wise judge and community leader. The one example cited by Ibn Ishaq shows Solomon besting his father in judging a case because he was inspired by God. Solomon resists the temptations of worldly wealth to invite the Queen of Sheba to monotheism. He also oversees the marriage of the Queen of Sheba, reminding her that women in Islam must marry.

Solomon's humanity is stressed through the story of his fall from God's favor because of his wife's worship of an idol representing her dead father. By a trick, the Devil was able to impersonate Solomon for forty days, the same period of repentance that his father, David, endured. After that the world was restored to its proper order, and Solomon regained his throne. A subtheme that runs through several of the stories in the *Kitâb al-Mubtada᾽* is that women are potential sources of trouble and evil.

Ibn Ishaq presents Solomon as a model ruler, wise, judicious, not tempted by normal human passions and desires, and repentant when he errs. Indeed, this theme is present in a number of stories of prophets who are princes as well as prophets. Not only does this model inform our understanding of Muhammad's role as leader of the Muslim community, but it also points up another function of the *Kitâb al-Mubtada᾽*. Ibn Ishaq served as the court tutor for the caliph al-Mansur's son and heir, al-Mahdi, and the *Kitâb al-Mubtada᾽* appears to have been one of the texts for the young prince's instruction. David, Solomon, Alexander the Great, and Muhammad were all paradigms for proper public conduct as well as for personal and private action.

In considering the relationship between Ibn Ishaq's version of the Solomon story and antecedent examples, it is clear that it is fruitless to seek an ur-story that would cover all the themes found in the Quran. Such a search leads to a misunderstanding and distortion of the Quranic milieu. It is possible to find, however, parallels in antecedent literature to many of the details and particular aspects of the story.

Solomon's judgment and his competition with his father, David, point to the differences between the messages of the Psalms and Proverbs, and his wisdom and judgment are frequently mentioned in rabbinic sources. Mentioned also is Solomon's ability to talk with animals, trees, birds, and indeed, all of nature. His gift of speech with nature derives from 1 Kings 4:33 [Heb. 5:13] and is already a tradition so well established that it is argued against in *Numbers Rabbah* 19.

Solomon's encounter with the Queen of Sheba is one of the most popular stories of Solomon. In later Islamic versions more details are added than are included by Ibn Ishaq until the story becomes an enjoyable entertainment romance. In the Islamic tradition the queen is called Bilqis, which is thought by some to come from the Hebrew *pilegesh,* meaning concubine. If so, it would argue for a Jewish precursor. That argument is further strengthened by the description of Asaf b. Barakhya, who is able to conjure God by means of the ineffable Name.

The story of Solomon's fall from the throne, with the clever end of finding his sealring in the belly of a fish and his ultimate triumph over the demon, also has a basis in Jewish sources. *Numbers Rabbah* 11:3 associates this with the Ashmodai legend in which the demon cast Solomon from his throne because of his sins. According to the older views that regarded the book of Ecclesiastes as having been written by Solomon, that book was supposed to have been written during Solomon's exile from his throne.

Text

In the name of God, the Merciful and the Compassionate

Then Solomon, the son of David, took charge of the affairs of the Children of Israel after his father, David. According to what is alleged, Solomon was white, stout, pure, hairy, and wore white clothes. During his reign, after he reached his majority, his father used to ask him about matters of governance. He and his father, David, were involved with the judgment about the flocks which strayed in the fields, which God told about in His Book, giving their story.

God said, "And David and Solomon, when they gave judgment about the field when the flock of the people strayed therein, and we were witnesses to their judgment, and we caused Solomon to understand, and to each of them we gave judgment and knowledge" [Q 21:78–79]. Ibn Bashshar, commenting on

Gods words, "when the flock of the people strayed in it," said on the authority of ʿAbd ar-Rahman, who got it from Sufyan, who got it from Ibn Ishaq, who got it from Murrah; The fields were green, and the flocks wandered in them at night. They brought the case to David, and he judged the case of the flocks against the owners of the fields, so they went to Solomon and mentioned that to him. He said, No, the flock will pay; the owners of the fields will take them, and these animals will stay in their fields. When all becomes as it was, they will return them. And it was revealed, "And we caused Solomon to understand."

Az-Zuhri related on the authority of Harram b. Muhayyisah b. Masʿud that a she-camel belonging to al-Bara b. ʿAzib ran into a wall of some of the Ansar and destroyed it. This was sent to the Messenger of God, may the prayers and peace of God be upon him, and he said, When the flock of the people strayed, and he judged against al-Bara for what the she-camel destroyed. He said about he owners of cattle, cattle are watched by night, and about the owners of walls, walls are guarded in the day. I was told that someone heard al-Hasan saying that this was the judgment of Solomon, and that God did not berate David for his judgment.

Solomon was a man who went on raids, and whenever he would hear of a king, he would go to him and conquer him. According to what they allege, when he decided to go on a raid, he would call up his army. Then he would chop a piece of wood, prepare a plank, and then put the people, the animals, and the instruments of war on it, so that a gale of wind would carry them where he wished by his command. The wind would go under the plank and lift it up in order that he could command the wind as it was carrying it. It would carry him a month's journey in an evening and a month's journey in a morning wherever he wished to go, God, the Mighty and the Powerful, saying, "So we made the wind subservient to him, going fair wherever he commanded" [Q 38:37], that is, wherever he wished. And God said, "And to Solomon we gave the wind so that a morning's course was a month's journey and an evening course was a month's journey" [Q 34:12]. It was mentioned to me that there was a house in the direction of the Tigris in which was a book which some of the companions of Solomon had written, either men or Jinn, saying: We lodged here and did not build, but found a building. We breakfasted in Istakhr. We were told, We are going from there, if God wills, and will spend the night in Syria. According to what reached me, the wind took his army by air wherever he wished, passing over cultivated fields without touching them.

Wahb b. Munabbih said, Whenever Solomon, the son of David, would go out of his apartment to his court, the birds would circle around his head, and the Jinn and the men would stand until he sat on his throne. So one time he went out in the morning to his court at which he would sit, and he inspected the birds. According to what they say, one of each kind of bird would come to him for guard duty. He looked and saw that one of each kind of bird was present except the hoopoe, so he said, "Why do I not see the hoopoe, or is he among the absent?" [Q 27:20]. That is, is my sight mistaken, or is he absent and not here? "I will punish him with a severe punishment" [Q 27:21]. Yazid b. Ruman said that the punishment with which he would punish the birds was to pluck out their wings. Wahb b. Munabbih, commenting on "or he will bring me a clear excuse" [Q 27:21], said, That is, a pass excusing him from his absence.

"He was not gone long," and then the hoopoe came. Solomon said to him, What has kept you from your guard duty? "He said, I have comprehended something that you have not, and I come to you from Sheba with a sure report" [Q 27:22], that is, I have become aware of a ruler which has not reached you. "I found a woman ruling them, and she has been given some of everything, and she has a great throne . . . up to His words . . . if you are among the liars" [Q 27:23–27]. Solomon, the son of David, with the aid of the hoopoe, wrote, In the name of God, the Merciful and the Compassionate. From Solomon, the son of David, to Bilqis, the daughter of Dhu Sharh, and her people: Now then, Do not rise up against me, and come to me in submission. Then Solomon said, "Go with this letter of mine and throw it down to them. Then turn away from them and see what they answer" [Q 27:28].

The hoopoe took the letter in his talon and went away with it until he came to Bilqis. She had a window in her apartment so that when the sun rose, she could look at it and prostrate to it. The hoopoe came to the window and blocked it with his wings so that the sun rose and she did not know it. Then he threw the letter through the window, and it fell on her where she was. She took it and said "O you nobles, a letter has been thrown to me. It is from Solomon, and it says, In the name of God, the Merciful and the Compassionate, Do not rise up against me, and come to me in submission. She said, O you nobles, give me a legal opinion about my affair, for I do not decide an affair unless you are witnesses. They said, We are the possessors of great might and power. The command is yours, so consider what you will command. She said, When kings enter a town, they lay waste to it and make base the honor of the people, and thus will they do. I am going to send presents to them and see what the messengers return" [Q 27:29–35].

Bilqis was an intelligent, well-educated woman of the palace who only ruled according to what had been passed down among her people, so that she was governed by it. She governed in such a way that it gave her strength. According to what they say, her religion and the religion of her people was Manichaeanism. When she read the letter, she understood that it was a letter unlike the other royal letters before, so she undertook to talk to the people of the Yemen, saying to them, "O you nobles, I have been given a letter . . . up to His words . . . what the messengers return" [Q 27:29–35]. Then she said,

A letter has come to me the like of which has not come from any king before. If he is a prophet, then there is no recourse for us against him, but if the man is a king who is competing with us in numbers, then he is not stronger or greater in numbers than us. So she prepared gifts of the sort given to kings to entice them. Then she said, If he is a king, he will accept the gifts and desire property. But if he is a prophet, he has no need of the things of this world, and he will not want them, but will want instead that we enter his religion with him and that we follow his command.

When the gifts were brought to Solomon, among which were maid servants and manservants, Arabian steeds, and things of this world, he said to the messengers who came to him, "Do you seek to assist me with wealth; what God has given me is better than what He has given you. It is you who rejoice in your gifts" [Q 27:36]. I do not need your gifts, for my perspective is not your perspective. So return to her with what you brought from her. "We will come to them with an army which they cannot resist, and we will drive them out in shame, and they will be abased" [Q 27:37], or she will come to me as a Muslim, she and her people.

When the messengers returned to Bilqis with what Solomon said, she said, By God, I knew that this was not a king and that we have no recourse against him. We will not be able to compete with him in numbers. So she sent the message: I am coming out to you with the kings of my people so that I can see what your command is and what you invite me to of your religion. Then she called for her royal throne upon which she would sit, which was of gold inlaid with sapphire, chrysolite, and pearls. It was put inside seven rooms one inside the other. Then locked the doors. Whenever a woman served her, six hundred women would accompany her. She said to one of the ones whom she left with her authority, Guard the throne of my kingdom that is entrusted to you. Do not let anyone of the worshipers of God come to it, and do not show it to anyone until I come to you. Then she set out for Solomon with twelve thousand chieftains of the kings of the Yemen, under the power of each chief being many thousands.

Solomon sent for the Jinn, and they came to him, traveling all day and night until all the Jinn and men under his control approached. He said, "O chiefs, which of you will bring me her throne before they come to me as Muslims?" [Q 27:38] An ʿifrit of the Jinn whose name was Kuzan said, "I will bring it to you before you can rise from your place" [Q 27:39], meaning, I will bring it to you before you can get up from this seat of yours. According to what was mentioned, Solomon was sitting in judgment among the people, and the Jinn said, I will bring it to you before you get up from your judgment seat on which you are sitting for adjudication among the people. And it was mentioned that he used to sit until mid-day. "I am strong and trustworthy for such a task" [Q 27:39]. They allege that Solomon, the son of David, said, I desire it faster than that, so Asaf b. Barakhya, who was a righteous person who knew the great Name by which, when God was called, He would answer, and when asked, give, said, "I will bring it to you before your gaze returns to you" [Q 27:40]. Your glance will not end until it will stand before you. He said, I wish that. They mention that Asaf b. Barakhya performed ablutions and then prostrated twice. Then he said, O prophet of God, extend your gaze to its limit. So Solomon looked in the direction of the Yemen, and Asaf prayed. The throne burst forth from the place it was and sprung up before Solomon. When Solomon saw it sitting before him, "He said, This is of the bounty of my Lord to test me as to whether I give thanks or am ungrateful. He who gives thanks is only giving thanks for his own soul, and he who is ungrateful; my Lord is independent, bountiful" [Q 27:40]. He said, "Disguise her throne for her so that we can see if she is rightly guided or one of those who is not rightly guided" [Q 27:41], that is, whether she has intelligence or is one of those who have no sense. So it was done to see if she would know it or not know it.

When Bilqis came to Solomon and talked with him, he brought out her throne for her and then said, "Is this your throne? She said, It is as though it were. We were given the knowledge before her, and we were Muslims. All that she worshiped instead of God hindered her, and she was of the unbelievers" [Q 27:42–43].

Solomon called for a lake, and the devils made it for him out of glass as though it were pure water. Then he made water flow under it, put his throne on it and sat on it, while the birds and the men gathered around him. Then he said to her, "Enter the hall" [Q 27:44], to show her a rule greater than her rule and show her a power greater than her power. "When she saw it, she thought it was a pool and uncovered her calves" [Q 27:44], not doubting that it was water into which she was wading. It was said to her, Enter the hall made of smooth glass. When she came to Solomon, he invited her to the worship of God and censured her for her worship of the sun to the exclusion of God. She spoke with the speech of the Manichaean, and Solomon fell down, prostrating and magnifying God. When she spoke, the people were prostrating with him; so she fell on her hands when she saw Solomon do what he did. When Solomon raised his head, he said, Woe to you for what you said, and she forgot what she said and replied, "My Lord, I have wronged myself and I submit along with Solomon to God, the Lord of the Universe" [Q 27:44]. So she became a Muslim, and her submission was beautiful.

It is alleged that when she converted to Islam, and Solomon finished with her, he said to her, Choose a man from among your people that I may marry you to him. She said, Shall the likes of me, O prophet of God, marry a man, considering my power and rule among my people? He said, Yes, there is no other way in Islam, and it is not necessary for you to make unlawful what God makes lawful for you. She said, Marry me, if there is no escape, to Dhu Batᶜ, the king of Hamadan. So he married him to her. Then he returned her to the Yemen and gave her husband, Dhu Bat^c, power over the Yemen. Then he called Zawba^cah, the commander of the Jinn of the Yemen, and said, Do for Dhu Bat^c what he asks you to do for his people. So he worked for Dhu Bat^c in the Yemen, doing what he wanted for him whose rule continued until Solomon, the son of David, may the prayers and peace of God be upon him, died.

When time passed, and the Jinn learned of the death of Solomon, one of them traveled into Tihamah so that, when he was in the middle of the Yemen, he screamed at the top of his voice, O you company of Jinn, the king, Solomon, has died, so rise up. The devils set up two great stones and wrote on them an inscription in South Arabian script: We built Sulhin in seventy-seven years, and we built by the sweat of our hands Sarwah, Marah, Baynun, Hind, Hunayd with seven cisterns in the entrance, and Talthum with an entrance hall. If it were not for the cry in Tihamah, we would still be under his command.

According to Ibn Hamid, on the authority of Salamah, who got it from Ibn Ishaq, who got it from some scholars, Wahb b. Munabbih said, Solomon heard of a city on an island called Sidon in which was a king who had great power and to whom there was no access by sea. God had given Solomon such power that he was not held back by anything on land or sea. Whenever he rode anywhere, he would ride on the wind. So he set out for this city with the wind carrying him over the surface of the water, until he came down in it with his army of Jinn and men. He killed its king and took what was in the city as war spoils. He acquired the king's daughter, who was more beautiful and graceful than he had ever seen. He chose her for himself and invited her to Islam, but she became a Muslim with aversion and little confidence. He loved her with a love with which he had not loved any other woman and became enchanted with her.

While she lived with Solomon, her sorrow would not leave nor would her tears cease. When he saw what was going on with her, he was grieved and troubled at what he saw. He said, What is this grief which does not leave and the tears which will not cease? She said, I remember my father, his kingdom, what was in it, and what happened to him, and it grieves me. He said, God has changed kings for you. He is greater in power and might than he was. Your guidance in Islam is better than all of that. She said, That may be so, but when I think of him, what you see of my grief strikes me. If you would only command the devils to fashion a likeness of my father in the house in which I am, so that I could see it morning and evening, then I would hope that my grief would go away, and it would console some of what I find in my soul. So Solomon ordered the devils, saying, Make an image of her father for her in her house so that she will not in any way deny that it is he. So they made a likeness for her so that it was as if she looked upon her father himself, except that there was no breath in him. When they made it for her, she approached it, wrapped it, put a shirt on it, and covered it with the likeness of the clothes he used to wear, so that it had his former appearance. Then when Solomon had gone out of her house, she would run to it with her girls to prostrate before it. And they would prostrate to it just as she used to do during his reign. For forty days she would go every evening that way without Solomon's knowing anything about it.

The situation reached Asaf b. Barakhya, who was righteous, and who was never turned away from Solomon's door at any hour he wished to enter for anything whether Solomon was present or absent. So Asaf came to Solomon and said, O prophet of God, I am growing old; my bones are fragile; my life is coming to an end, and my departure draws near. I would like to set up an assembly before I die in which I will mention some of the prophets of God who have passed, praise them, and teach the people some of what they do not know about their affairs. He said, Do it. So Asaf gathered the people to him and gave them a sermon. He mentioned those prophets of God who had gone before, and he praised each prophet for what he had done. He mentioned how God had graced him, until he came, at the end, to Solomon. He mentioned him and said, How gracious you were in your youth; how pious you were in your youth; and how well you judged affairs in your youth; and how well you put off in your youth what was hateful.

Then he left, and Solomon found himself alone, filled with anger. When Solomon entered his house, he sent for him and said, O Asaf, you mentioned the past prophets of God, and you extolled their virtues in all of their times and under every condition of their lives. But when you mentioned me, you began to praise my virtues in my youth, but you were silent on the rest of my affairs in my old age. Why did you not tell of the rest of my affairs?

Asaf said, Other than God has been worshiped for forty days because of the love of a woman. Solomon said, In my house? He said, In your house. Solomon said, We belong to God, and to God we return. I know that you only speak about something that has reached you. Then Solomon returned to his house, broke that idol, and punished the woman and her daughters. Then he called for ritually pure garments, which were brought to him. These were the clothes that were only spun by the firstborn, only woven by the firstborn, only washed by the firstborn, and were not touched by a menstruating woman. He put them on and then went out in the desert alone, called for ashes, and spread them out. Then he repented to God while he sat on those ashes. He rubbed them on his clothes, humbling himself to God and beseeching Him, crying and praying and seeking forgiveness for what was in his house and saying, according to what was mentioned to me, and God knows best, O Lord, why is there the trial among the house of David that they worship other than you, and the worship of other than you resides in their houses and their inhabitants? He did not cease doing this for a whole day until evening, weeping to God, beseeching Him, and seeking His forgiveness. Then he returned to his house.

The mother of his child was called al-Aminah. When he would enter his bathroom or wish sexual intercourse with any woman, he would place his seal with al-Aminah until he was purified, because he could not touch the seal except when he was ritually pure. His authority was in the seal. So he gave it to her one day as he was wont to give it, and then he entered his bathroom. The Devil, the lord of the sea, whose name was Sakhra, came to her in the exact image of Solomon. He said, My seal, O Aminah. So she gave it over to him, and he placed it on his hand. Then he went out, sat on Solomon's throne, and the birds, the Jinn, and the men gathered around him. Solomon came out to al-Aminah with his appearance changed for all who saw him, and said, O Aminah, my seal. She said, Who are you? He said, I am Solomon, the son of David. She said, You lie; you are not Solomon, the son of David, because Solomon has come and taken his seal, and he is the one sitting on his throne in rule.

Solomon knew that his sin had caught up with him. He left, stopping at the houses of the Children of Israel, saying, I am Solomon, the son of David. They threw dirt on him and took him prisoner, saying, Look at this lunatic, at what he is saying. He asserts that he is Solomon, the son of David. When Solomon saw that, he went to the sea and would carry two serpents for the fishermen to the market,and he was given two fish each day. When it was evening, he would sell the first of his fish for bread and would roast the other and eat it. He remained like that for forty days, the length of time that the idol had been worshiped in his house.

Now Asaf and the mighty Children of Israel disapproved of the judgment of the Enemy of God, the Devil, in those forty days. Asaf said, O you assembly of the Children of Israel, do you see the controversy in the judgment of the son of David? They said, Yes. He said, Delay him so that I may go in to his women and ask them if they disapprove of him in his private affairs as we disapprove of him in the public affairs of the people. So he went in to the women and said, Woe to you, do you disapprove of the affairs of the son of David as we disapprove? They said, He will not leave a woman of us alone during menstruation, and he will not wash off a major impurity. He said, We belong to God, and to God we return. Indeed, this is a clear trial. Then he went out to the Children of Israel and said that what was in private was worse than that which was in public.

When the forty days had passed, the Devil flew from his seat. Then he passed by the sea and threw the seal into it, and a fish swallowed it. Some of the fishermen saw it and took it. Solomon had worked for him for the whole day, and when it was evening, he gave him his two fish, and he gave him the fish which had taken the seal. Then Solomon left with his two fish and sold for bread the one which did not have the seal in its belly. Then he turned to the other fish, split it open to roast it, and came across his seal in its inside. He took it, put it on his hand, and fell down prostrating to God. The birds and the Jinn gathered around him, the people approached him, and he knew that that which had happened had been because of the event in his house. He returned to his rule and proclaimed his repentance of his sin and called for the devils and said, Bring Sakhra to me. So the devils sought him until they captured him. Then they brought Solomon a bottle of stone he had, and he put Sakhra in it. Then he blocked it up with a stone, made it firm with iron and lead, and then commanded that it be thrown into the sea.

On the authority of Salamah, who got it from Ibn Ishaq, Ibn Hamid said, When the death of Solomon, the son of David, upon him be peace, was known, the devils gathered and wrote various kinds of magic: He who wishes to get such–and–such, should do such–and–such. They made various kinds of spells, and they placed them in a book. Then they sealed it with the figure of the seal of Solomon. They wrote on its title: This is what Asaf b. Barakhya, the pious, wrote for the king, Solomon, son of David, of the Treasure of the Treasures of Knowledge. Then they buried it under his throne. The Children of Israel brought it out after that, when what happened happened. When they found it, they said, Solomon, the son of David, was none other than this. So magic spread among the people, and they taught it and learned it, and there is not more of it among any but the Jews. When the Messenger of God, may the prayers and peace of God be upon him, mentioned what was sent down to him from God about Solomon and counted Solomon among the messengers, a Jew from Medina said, Are you not amazed at Muhammad, may the prayers and peace of God be upon him, that he asserts that Solomon, the son of David, was a prophet? By God, he was none other than a magician. So God, the Mighty and the Powerful, sent down about their speech against Muhammad, may the prayers and peace of God be upon him, "They follow that which the devils falsely ascribed against King Solomon. Solomon did not disbelieve, but he devils disbelieved" [Q 2:102].

When King Solomon fell away from the group of Jinn and men and followed carnal desires, and after God returned Solomon to his kingdom, He established the people in the religion as they had been. Then Solomon published their books and buried them under his throne. Solomon died, and the Jinn and men made the books public after the death of Solomon. They said, This is a book from God sent down to Solomon which he kept secret from us. So they took it and made it a religion. So God sent down, "When there comes to them a messenger from God confirming that which they have, a party of those who have been given the Scripture fling the Scripture behind their backs as if they knew it not and follow that which the devils related" [Q 2:101–102].

Sources

at-Tabari, *Taʾrikh* 572–573, 585–586, 586–591
at-Tabari, *Tafsîr* 19:144, 17:55, 17:52–54, 17:55–56, 22:69, 19:144–145, 19:146, 19:147, 19:152, 19:156, 19:157–158, 19:159–160, 19:162, 19:163, 19:164–165, 19:166, 19:167, 19:168, 1:446, 1:451

Sheba

This appears to be a purely Arabian legend about the destruction of a people whose remains were visible to the travelers in the area of the Yemen. It glosses the verses in the Quran which refer to Sheba, but it also links several of the Arabian tribes to prophetic history. In particular, the tribes of the B. Aus and the B. Khazraj are mentioned. Those were the two tribes who are reported to have originated in the south, migrated to Medina and become the Helpers, the Arabs who welcomed Muhammad and his followers to Medina after the Hijrah. Ibn Ishaq, himself raised in the city of Medina, was accused by some critics of including such remarks to aggrandize the history of his home city at the expense of Mecca.

While there does not seem to be a rabbinic parallel to mice causing the destruction of the dam, Josephus (*Antiquities* 10. 1.4) speaks of a tradition, evidently from Herodotus, that mice destroyed the Assyrians under Sennacherib and mice were sent against the Philistines (Ginzberg, *Legends* 6:263). As we know from the story of Noah and from rabbinic literature, mice are often associated with evil. In some Jewish accounts they broke the prohibition against reproduction while riding on the ark.

Text
In the name of God, the Merciful and the Compassionate

"There was indeed a sign for Sheba . . . up to His words . . . Do we ever punish except the ungrateful?" [Q 34:15–17]. Ibn Hamid related on the authority of Salamah, who got it from Ibn Ishaq, that Wahb b. Munabbih the Yemenite said, God sent thirteen prophets to Sheba, and they were denied. "So we sent on them the flood of Iram" [Q 34:16], the Most High saying, So when they turned away from the truth of the prophets we pierced their dam which was used to block the floods.

Sheba had a dam which had been built to last forever. It was a thing which would turn the floods back so that their property would not drown. According to what they allege, the people had a prognostication that their dam could be destroyed only by a mouse. So they would put a cat by every hole between two rocks.

According to what was reported, when the time came for what God intended of the flood, a red mouse came to one of the cats and assaulted it until it got by it, entered into the hole which was near it, burrowed into the dam and excavated in it until it had weakened it to the flood while the people were unaware. When the flood came, it found a fissure and went in it until it tore out the dam. The flood inundated the property and carried it along, and nothing remained except what God mentioned.

When the people dispersed, they surrendered to the prognostications of ʿAmran b. ʿAmir. They allege that ʿAmran b. ʿAmir, the paternal uncle of the people, was a seer and that he saw in his omens that his people would split apart and dispersed. So he said to them, I know that you will split apart. Whoever among you is distressed by distance, a strong camel, and a new pack, let him get hold of a drinking cup or a watered land. Wadiʿah b. ʿAmr and those of you who are with him who are distressed by cities and barrenness, let him take the land of Shann. ʿAwf b. ʿAmr, those called Bariq and those of you who wish to live for a time and put off safety, let him take al-Arzin. The Aws and the Khazraj (who are the two tribes of the Helpers), and he who wants wine, fermentation, gold, silk, rule and command, let him take Kutha and Busra. Ghassan, the sons of Jafnah, are the kings of Syria and those with them in ʿal-Iraq. Ibn Ishaq said, I heard some of the scholars say that Tarifah, the wife of ʿAmran b. ʿAmir, who was a seeress, said that, and that she was the one who saw that in her prognostications. God knows which is so.

Source

at-Tabari, *Tafsîr* 22:78, 22:80, 22:86

Isaiah

The story of Isaiah and King Hezekiah glosses a Quaranic theme that is central to the Islamic view of history: God sends revelation to mankind through prophets. When God's word is followed, all goes well, but when there is disobedience, then all suffer. The Quran regards this as a recurrent theme in the history of the world until the culmination of the process with Muhammad. Muhammad is the last of the prophets, the end of that phase of the historical process. After Muhammad and the advent of Islam we are, according to the Islamic view, in a new historical age.

The prophecies of Isaiah had been important to both Judaism and Christianity. Rabbinic Jews often interpreted the ninth chapter of the book of Isaiah as foretelling the advent of the Messiah, without always agreeing who that might be or when the event would occur. Christians have generally assumed that this passage referred to Jesus as the Messiah. In the *Kitâb al-Mubtadaʾ* we are told that Isaiah was the one who announced the advent of Jesus and Muhammad. Muhammad is not a messiah in the Jewish sense, nor is he the son of God as is Jesus for Christians. He is the initiator of the new historical era, and, according to some, will be present at the eschaton. By linking Muhammad with the prophecies of Isaiah, the *Kitâb al-Mubtadaʾ* invokes in the minds of Jews, Christians, and those Muslims familiar with the prophecies of Isaiah resonances with the older understandings that Isaiah was foretelling a messiah. This text helps redefine the interpretative tradition and promotes an Islamic claim to the prophetic line that had started with Judaism, had been claimed by Christians, and was now to serve Islamic ends.

Themes associated with the Temple in Jerusalem in this story of Isaiah recur later in the biography of Muhammad where Abraha's unsuccessful siege of Mecca is described in terms applied to Sennacherib in the Bible and the Talmud. This has the effect of making Mecca the new Jerusalem and Islam the new messianic religion (see Newby, "Abraha and Sennacherib"). Circumambulation of the Temple for repentance is later transferred to the Kaʿbah after the advent of Islam. Finally, Isaiah's martyrdom in the tree follows traditions found in the Jerusalem Talmud.

174

Isaiah

175

Text

In the name of God, the Merciful and the Compassionate

Included in what God sent down to Moses about the deeds of the Children of Israel was: "We decreed for the Children of Israel in Scripture, You will act corruptly on the earth two times . . . up to His words . . . And we have made Hell as an enclosure for the ungrateful" [Q 17:4–8]. That passage refers to the Children of Israel, who committed misdeeds and sins. During that period God overlooked their actions, had compassion on them, and was kindly toward them. There was already a report from Moses to them in what God had revealed to Moses.

The first thing God sent down to them about these events was that they had a king named Hezekiah. When a king ruled over them, God would send a prophet to strengthen him and guide him, the prophet being between the king and God. He would talk to him about their affairs, not sending books to them, but telling about their being commanded to follow the Torah and the laws that were in it, and their being prohibited from sin, and he would invite them to return to what obedience they had abandoned. When this king ruled, God sent Isaiah, the son of Amoz, along with him. That was before the sending of Zechariah, John, and Jesus. Isaiah was the one who announced the glad tidings of Jesus and Muhammad. This king ruled the Children of Israel and Jerusalem for a time, and, when his rule ended, misdeeds arose among them.

Isaiah was with him when God sent over them Sennacherib, the king of Babylon, with whom were six hundred thousand troops. He came forced march until he made camp around Jerusalem. The king was ill with ulcerating sores on his legs, and the prophet Isaiah came to him and said, O king of the Children of Israel, Sennacherib, the king of Babylon, has made camp around you, he and his army of six hundred thousand troops. The people are afraid and terrified of them. This greatly afflicted the king, and he said, O prophet of God, does an inspiration come to you from God in which He informs us what God will do with us and with Sennacherib and his army? The prophet, upon him be peace, said to him, There does not come to me a more recent inspiration of your situation.

While they were thus occupied, God inspired the prophet Isaiah: Go to the king of the Children of Israel and command him to make a will and appoint as successor over his kingdom whom he wills of the people of his house. So the prophet Isaiah came to the king of the Children of Israel, Hezekiah, and said to him, Your Lord has inspired me to command you to make a will and choose a successor whom you will of your house over your kingdom, for you will die.

When Isaiah said that to Hezekiah, he approached the prayer niche and prayed and glorified and beseeched and wept. He was weeping and beseeching God with a pure heart and trust in God and patience and righteousness and right belief in God: O God, Lord of Lords, and God of Gods, Holy of Holies, O Merciful, O Compassionate of the compassionate, the Benevolent who never rests nor sleeps, remember me for my knowledge and my deeds and the goodness of my judgments over the Children of Israel. All of that was from you, for you know the secrets of my soul, and my public behavior belongs to you. The Merciful One answered him, for he was a righteous servant.

God inspired Isaiah that he should tell Hezekiah, the king, that his Lord had answered him, accepted prayers from him, and granted mercy to him, and that He had seen his weeping and had changed His decree for fifteen years and had saved him from his enemy, Sennacherib, the king of Babylon, and his army. So Isaiah, the prophet, came to that king and told him of that, and when he said that, the pain left him and the evil and the grief were removed from him, and he fell down prostrating. He said, O my God and God of my fathers, I prostrate to you and sing your praises and honor you and glorify you. You are the one who gives the rule to whom you will and takes it from whom you will. You make strong whom you will and debase whom you will, Knower of the unseen and the seen. You are the First and the Last, the Manifest and the Hidden. You grant mercy and answer the requests of those in distress. You are the One who answered my prayers and was compassionate toward my entreaties. When he raised his head, God inspired Isaiah that he should say to the king, Hezekiah, that he should ask a servant of his for a fig, that he should bring fig juice and put it on his ulcerating sores, and he would be healed, and when he would get up in the morning, he would be free. He did that, and he was cured.

The king said to Isaiah, the prophet, Ask your Lord to give us knowledge of what he is going to do with our enemy. God said to Isaiah, the prophet, Say to him that I have spared you from your enemy and saved you from him. They will wake up dead, all of them except Sennacherib and five of his scribes. So when they got up in the morning, a crier came to them, announcing to them at the gate of the city, O king of the Children of Israel, God has spared you from your enemy.

He went out, and Sennacherib and those with him had been destroyed. When the king went out to search for Sennacherib, he did not find him among the dead. The king looked for him and came upon him in a cave with five of his scribes, one of whom was Nebuchadnezzar. So they put them in a group and brought them to the king of the Children of Israel. When he saw them, he fell down prostrating from sunrise to late afternoon. Then he said to Sennacherib, What is your opinion of what our Lord did with you? Did he not kill you by His might and power while we and you were ignorant? Sennacherib said to him, The report of your Lord, His assistance toward you and His mercy which He bestowed on you had come to me before I left my country, but I have not been given right guidance, so I have only been afflicted by a paucity of wit. If I had only heard or understood, I would not have raided you. But misfortune has overcome me and those with me.

The king of the Children of Israel said, Praise be to God, the Lord of Might, who spares us from you however He wills. Our Lord has not allowed you and those with you to remain alive out of mercy for you, but He has allowed you and those with you to remain because of the evil you have, that misfortune increase in this world and punishment in the next, and so that you tell those you left behind what you have experienced of the deeds of our Lord, and that you warn those after you. Were it not for that, you would not be left alive. Your blood and the blood of those with you is less significant with God than the blood of a flea, if you were to kill it.

Then the king of the Children of Israel called for the commander of the guard. He flung them down on their necks as a group and made them circumambulate the Temple for seventy days like cattle. Each day he would give them two pieces of barley bread for each man to eat. Sennacherib said to the king of the Children of Israel, Being killed is better than what you do to us, so do what you have ordered. So the king ordered them to the prison of death. But God inspired Isaiah, the prophet, that he should say to the king of the Children of Israel that he should send Sennacherib and those with him to warn those left behind them and that he should treat them generously and take them until they reached their country. So the prophet Isaiah apprised the king of that, and he did it. Sennacherib and those with him went out until they reached Babylon. When they came, Sennacherib assembled the people and told them what God had done with his army. His seers and magicians said to him, O king of Babylon, we told you the account of their Lord and the story of their prophet and the inspiration of God to their prophet, but you did not follow us. It is a religious community against which no one is able to go. The affair of Sennacherib was as they feared, but God spared them as a warning and an admonition. After that, Sennacherib remained seventy years, and then he died.

When Sennacherib died, he was succeeded by Nebuchadnezzar, his grandson, doing what his grandfather did and judging according to his judgments. He remained seventeen years, and then God took the king of the Children of Israel, Hezekiah. The situation of the Children of Israel was thrown into confusion, and they struggled for rule until some killed others for it while their prophet Isaiah was among them. They did not submit to him nor accept anything from him. When they did this, according to what was said, God said to Isaiah: Rise up among the people; cause your tongue to give expression. So when the prophet got up, God caused his tongue to speak with inspiration, and he said, O Heavens, listen to me, and, O Earth, hearken to me. God wishes that there be told the state of the Children of Israel whom He has increased by His grace, whom He has chosen for Himself, on whom He has bestowed His kindness, whom he has preferred over His servants and selected for honors. They are like the lost sheep who have no shepherd. He gives shelter to their stray, He gathers their errant and restores their broken ones. Woe to this sinful community and woe to those sinning people who do not know from whence destruction comes to them. The camel knows its home and returns to it, and the ass remembers the fodder which satisfied its hunger and goes back to it. The bull remembers the meadow which fattened it and returns to it. These people do not know from whence destruction comes to them, and yet they have hearts and minds and are neither cattle nor asses.

I coin a parable for them in order that they might hear it. Say to them, What is your view of a land which was destroyed, with no life in it, and it had a lord, wise and strong, and he came to it with buildings. He hated that his land was destroyed while he was strong or, it is said, wasted while he was wise. So he surrounded it with a wall and set up castles in it and caused a river to spring forth in it and planted rows of olives, pomegranates, dates, grapes, and all manner of fruit, and entrusted it and gave it to the protection of a custodian who was perspicacious and eager for guardianship, strong and trustworthy. The time of pollination drew near, and he looked forward expectantly to it. And when it bore fruit, the fruit came up destroyed.

They said, The land is evil. We think that he should destroy its wall and its castles and bury the river and seize the guardian and destroy its orchards until it becomes as it was in the first place, a dead ruin with no life in it. God said to them, The wall is my protection and the castle is my law, and the river is my Scripture. The guardian is my prophet, and the orchard is the people, and the destroyed fruit is their evil deeds. I have decided on the judgment for them.

They will come near me with the sacrifice of cattle and sheep, but the meat will not reach me, and I will not eat it. They pray that they can come near with piety and abstinence from the sacrificing of themselves which I have forbidden, but their hands are dyed with it and their garments are covered with their blood. They set up houses for me as places of prostration, and they purify their insides, but their hearts and bodies are unclean, and they soil them. They ornament the houses and places of prostration with images of me, and they waste their intellects and their reason, and they corrupt them. What need have I for the setting up of houses? I do not dwell in them. What need have I for the adornment of places of worship? I do not enter them. It is only commanded that I be mentioned and praised in them. They are only a place for him who wishes to pray in them.

They say, If God is able to bring us together in amity, then let Him do so. So take two dry sticks and bring them to the middle of where they are, and say to the two sticks, God commands you two become one stick. So when he said that to them, they moved together and became one. God said, Say to them, I am able to unite two dry sticks and combine them; so how is it that I am not able to unite you if I wish, or how is it that I am not able to instruct your hearts? I am the one who formed them. They say, We fasted, but our fast was not reported, and we prayed, but our prayer was not recorded, and we gave charity, but our charity was not inscribed. We have prayed with the soft voice of the dove, and we wept like the howl of the wolf, and with all that, we are not heard, nor does He answer us.

God said, Ask them what prevents me from answering them. Do I not cause the hearer to hear and the seer to see, and bring near the answerer and give mercy to the compassionate? Is my wealth diminished? How could it be, while my two hands are outstretched with good? I disburse as I will, and the keys of the treasury are with me. No one opens it or locks it but me. Is it not the case that my mercy encompasses all things, and the merciful show compassion by their grace; or is it the case that niggardliness overtakes me? Do I not honor the noble? Am I not the opener of good things? I bestow on him who gives and honor him who is asked. Were these people to look at themselves with the wisdom with which I have enlightened their hearts, then they would discard and sell all of the things of this world. They would then know with certainty that they themselves are the worst of enemies. How should I know their fasts while they are wearing falsehood and strengthening themselves with forbidden food? How should I shed light on their prayer while their hearts incline to one who fights against me and opposes me and denies my prohibitions? Or, how do they show charity with me while they are giving as alms money other than their own, rewarding people with ill-gotten gains? Or, how am I to answer their prayer while it is a speech of their tongues, and the deeds for it are distant, for I only answer tender requests, and I hear the speech of the weak and the poor? If they were merciful to the poor and brought near the weak and shared with the ill-treated and aided the tyrannized and dealt fairly with the absent and were kind to the widow and the orphan and the poor and gave all their due, then if it were necessary that I speak to a man, then I would have spoken to them, and I would have given light to their sight and hearing to their ears and wisdom to their hearts, and I would have supported their foundations and strengthened their hands and legs and fixed their tongues and intellects. But when they heard my speech, and my messages reached them as transcribed speech and transmitted tradition, published as you write magic and prognostication, they alleged that they, if they wished, could bring forth accounts like it. If they are informed of the supernatural, let them be informed, and for all of them it will be hidden, and they will know that I am the Knower of the secrets of the heavens and the earth and the Knower of what is manifest and what is secret. I decided on the day I created the heavens and the earth a decree which I made firm myself, and I made the time of death from which there is no escape. If they are truthful in what they purport to pass off as the supernatural secrets, let them tell you until I implement it, at whatever time. If they are able to bring what they wish, let them write the like of the wisdom which I have devised, if they are truthful. I decreed on the day I created the heavens and the earth that I would put prophecy in action and that I would allow a king custody and might among the lowly, and power over the weak and riches among the poor and abundance amidst little and cities in the desert and forests in the waste and papyrus in the depressions and knowledge among the ignorant and wisdom among the illiterate. So ask them at what time this was and who was old enough to exist and who helped and who aided?

If they know, I will send an illiterate prophet who is neither blind among the blind nor in error among those in error nor crude nor harsh nor clamorous in the markets nor lewd and obscene. I will guide him to every courtesy and will present him to every noble creature. I will make the Shechinah his garment and righteousness his hair and piety his heart and wisdom his intellect and righteousness and fidelity his nature and forgiveness and knowledge his disposition and honesty his life and truth his path and right guidance his lead and Islam his religion. Ahmad is his name. I will guide by him the errant and inform by him the ignorant and raise by him the unknown and make known by him the unknown and make abundant by him the ones with few and make rich by him the poor and unite by him the factions and tame by him the hearts and make the scattered love and establish a religious community which will be the best community which I have set forth to mankind, which will lead by knowledge and prohibit the hateful, being monotheistic, trusting and pure toward me, praying to me, standing, sitting, inclining, and prostrating, fighting in my way in ranks and rows. They will go out from their homes and their property for my favor, mumbling God is Great, God is One, praised, glorified and magnified is God, to me in their mosques and places of assembly and their beds and their places of abode, saying, God is great, God is praised, God is holy, in their markets purifying their faces to me and their limbs, and tying their clothes in the middle while sacrificing and siring, fearing at night, lions in the day. That is my grace given to whom I will, and I am the possessor of exceeding grace.

When Isaiah finished prophesying to them, they became enemies and sought to kill him. So he fled from them, and a tree took him, split itself, and he entered it. The Devil made him known and took the fringes of his clothes and showed them to them. They took a saw and sawed until they cut it and him in two. On the authority of some of the scholars, it is reported that Zechariah died and was not killed, and the one killed was Isaiah, and that Nebuchadnezzar was the one who ruled over the Children of Israel in the first period after the killing of Isaiah.

Sources

at-Tabari, *Taʾrikh* 638–645
at-Tabari, *Tafsîr* 15:22–27
ath-Thaʿlabi 182ff.
Al-Baghdadi 3:152–153

Al-Khidr

The figure of al-Khidr is not mentioned in the Quran by name but is prominent in post-Quranic commentaries. Sometimes he is identified with the companion of Moses who seeks the waters of eternal life, sometimes he is identified with Elijah, sometimes he is equated with Jeremiah, and sometimes he is without certain identification with a figure known from the biblical past. Al-Khidr is usually associated with fertility and fecundity, as indicated by his color and the story that he sat on a white skin which turned green. Muslim commentators usually identify the skin as the earth and the green as plants. For Muslim mystics al-Khidr is an important saint, ever-living and usually in occultation.

The story of al-Khidr in the *Kitâb al-Mubtada* focuses chiefly on the identification of al-Khidr with Jeremiah. This suits Ibn Ishaq's purposes of fitting the chief characters of his book into the Judeo-Christian scheme. We are told that Jeremiah was chosen by God before he was formed in his mother's belly, purified before he was born, and made a prophet while still a child. This notion of the election of a prophet fits Ibn Ishaq's general notion of how individuals are chosen for the office and, in particular, parallels his presentation of the process of Muhammad's election.

Jeremiah/al-Khidr is represented as weak and sinful without God's intervention. This is another characteristic of the Muslim prophet, whose humanity is overcome only through divine guidance. Jeremiah was sent to the descendants of past prophets who had become rich, powerful, immoral, and deceitful. Yet they claimed to be closer to God than anyone else. This is another reminder of Muhammad's encounter with the Jews of Arabia, who are represented as claiming special privilege in spite of their behaviors.

The story of the angel who came to Jeremiah as a litigant is reminiscent of the story in the *Kitâb al-Mubtada* of the angels who litigate in front of David. The larger frame of the Jeremiah/al-Khidr story is set as a historical gloss on the repeated sin-repentance cycle that is Ibn Ishaq's characterization of Jewish history. The story of Jeremiah's vision of the restored bones is reminiscent of Ezekiel's vision of restoration. Finally, it is implied that Jeremiah did not die because he is the "one who is seen in the open fields and in the cities." In rabbinic literature Jeremiah is one of the ones, along with Moses, Ezra, Baruch, and Enoch, who are assumed into heaven without having died.

182

Text
In the name of God, the Merciful and the Compassionate

Ibn Hamid, who got it from Salamah, who got it from Ibn Ishaq, said, According to what reached me, after the Children of Israel killed Isaiah, God appointed Manasseh, the son of Amus, as a successor over the Children of Israel, and He sent al-Khidr as a prophet. The Prophet of God, may the prayers and peace of God be upon him, used to say that al-Khidr was called Green because he sat on a white pelt, and when he got up from it, it was green.

According to what Wahb b. Munabbih used to assert on the authority of the Children of Israel, the name of al-Khidr meant Jeremiah, the son of Hilkiah. He was of the tribe of Aaron, the son of ʿAmran. Muhammad b. Sahl b. ʿAskar and Muhammad b. ʿAbd al-Malik b. Zanjawiyyah both reported on the authority of Ismail b. ʿAbd al-Karim, who got it from Ibn ʿAbd as-Samad b. Muʿaqqil, who got it from Wahb b. Munabbih, and Ibn Hamid reported on the authority of Salamah, who got it from Ibn Ishaq, who got it on the authority of one who is not to be doubted, who got it from Wahb b. Munabbih the Yemenite (and the wording of the tradition is that of Ibn Hamid), that Wahb used to say, God, the Blessed and Most High, said to Jeremiah when He sent him as a prophet to the Children of Israel, O Jeremiah, from the time I created you and chose you and before I formed you in the belly of your mother, I sanctified you. Before I caused you to go out from the belly of your mother, I purified you. Before you reached the ability to run, I made you a prophet, and before you reached your majority, I chose you, and I have concealed you for a great affair. So God sent Jeremiah to the king of the Children of Israel in order to strengthen him, guide him, and bring him reports from God concerning what was between him and God.

Then things became oppressive for the Children of Israel. They fomented rebellion, made the forbidden licit, and forgot what God, the Most High, did for them, and how He saved them from their enemy, Sennacherib, and from his army. So God inspired Jeremiah by saying, You should come to your people of the Children of Israel and relate to them what I command you. Remind them of my kindness to them and let them know of their deeds. Jeremiah said, But I am weak if you do not strengthen me, and feeble if you do not fortify me, and sinful if you do not bolster me, impotent if you do not aid me, and base if you do not empower me.

God, the Blessed and Most High, said, Do you not know that all affairs originate from my will and that all hearts and tongues are in my hand? I turn them as I will, and they obey me. I am God of whom there is none like me. The heavens and the earth and what is in them exist by my word. I spoke to the sea and it understood my voice. I commanded it, and it understood my command. I set limits for it in the lowlands, and it did not exceed my limits. It brings waves like mountains until, when they reach my limits, I clothe them with the humility of my obedience, fearing and confessing my command. I am with you, and with me there, nothing will reach you. I have sent you to a great people of my creation to bring them my message and to demand recompense from them like the wage of one who follows you, which shall not be lessened from their recompense. If you curtail it, then on you will be the burden of one who rides blind. Their burden shall not be lessened. Go to your people and say, God reminds you of the righteousness of your fathers, and that is what brings Him to ask your repentance, O you group of sons. Ask them how their fathers found the consequence of obedience to me and how they found the consequence of rebellion against me. Do they know of anyone before them who obeyed me and was made wretched by obedience to me, or disobeyed me and was made happy by rebellion against me? Even the beasts remember their homes and return to them, and these people have grazed in the meadows of destruction. As for their rabbis and monks, they took my servants as chattel in order to make them worship other than me. They instructed them with other than my Book until they made them ignorant of my command and caused them to forget the mention of me and beguiled them from me. As for the princes and leaders, they are reckless with my kindness and feel safe from my cunning. They reject my Scripture, forget my covenant, and change my law. My servants found them guilty of an obedience which was not appropriate except toward me. They would follow them in disobedience and go with them in innovations which they would invent in my religion, insolence toward me, and heedlessness and slander against me and against my messengers. Praise be my glory, exalted my place, and great my situation.

Is it proper for a man that he obey by rebellion against me, and is it necessary for me that, if I create servants, I give them lords other than me? As for their readers and wise men, they devote themselves in the mosques, and they adorn themselves with buildings belonging to other than me for seeking this world through religion. They regard themselves as wise without knowledge and regard themselves as knowledgeable without deeds. As for the children of the prophets, they are rich, powerful, immoral, given to false talk, and they seek help from me like the assistance given their fathers and the honor which I bestowed on them. They assert that there is no one who is closer to me than they for that purpose, without truth, reflection, or meditation. They do not remember how their fathers were patient with me and how they were diligent in my affairs when they could make no change and how they sacrificed themselves and their blood. They were patient and truthful until my affairs became strong and my religion became manifest. I have been patient with these people that perhaps they would respond. I have been long-suffering to them and forgiven them that perhaps they would return. I have given much and stretched out the time so that perhaps they would remember. I forgave in every way, sending rain on them from heaven and making the earth bring forth vegetation for them, clothing them with good health and causing them to vanquish the enemy. But they only grew more oppressive and distant from me. I swear by my might that I will send a trial on them in which the gentle will be dismayed and the man of judgment will be led into error by judgment and the wise by wisdom. Then I will give my power over them to a harsh, wild tyrant whom I will garb in awe. I will pluck kindness and mercy and tenderness from his breast, and blackness will follow him like the black of the dead of night. He will have armies like the blacking out of clouds, mounts like smoke, as though the sound of the banners were like flocks of vultures, and his cavalry like eagles.

Then God inspired Jeremiah, I will destroy the Children of Israel by means of Japheth, and Japheth was the people of Babylon, and they were the descendants of Japheth, the son of Noah. When Jeremiah heard the revelation of his Lord, he cried out and wept and tore his clothes and sprinkled ashes on his head and said, Cursed be the day in which I was born and the day I received the Torah. Of the most evil of my days is the day in which I was born. I was not left alive beyond the other prophets except for the evil He does to me. If He wished me good, He would not have left me as the last of the prophets of the Children of Israel. On my account misery and destruction will befall them.

When God heard the entreaties of al-Khidr, his weeping and how he spoke, He called him: O Jeremiah, does what I inspire grieve you? He said, Yes, O Lord. Destroy me before I see among the Children of Israel what I will not be able to conceal. God said, By my might, I will not destroy the Temple and the Children of Israel until the command comes from you for that. So Jeremiah rejoiced at that when his Lord spoke to him, and he repented and said, No, by Him who sent Moses and the prophets with truth, I will not command my Lord in the destruction of the Children of Israel, ever!

Then he came to the king of the Children of Israel and told him what God had revealed to him. He rejoiced and was glad and said, If our Lord punishes us, then it will be for the many sins which we have done against ourselves, and if He forgives us, then it will be by His power. After this revelation, they remained three years not doing anything other than disobedience and evil. That was when their destruction came and revelation diminished, when they made no mention of the afterlife and were taken by the world and its affairs.

Their king said to them, O Children of Israel, cease what you are doing before the adversity of God touches you and before He sends on you a people who have no mercy for you. Your Lord is near for repentance with outstretched hands for good, merciful to him who repents to God. But they refused to leave off anything they were doing, so God put in the heart of Nebuchadnezzar, the son of Sennacherib, the son of Darius, the son of Nimrod, the son of Falikh, the son of ʿAbir, the son of Nimrod the companion of Abraham, that which he debated about with his Lord, that he go to the Temple and do in it what his grandfather wished to do. So he set out with six hundred thousand banner-carrying units making for the people of Jerusalem.

When he set out, the report came to the king of the Children of Israel: Nebuchadnezzar had come, he and his army, seeking you. So the king sent for Jeremiah, and he came to him, and he said, O Jeremiah, where is what you alleged to us that your Lord revealed to you that He would destroy the people of Jerusalem until the order came from you to do it? Jeremiah said to the king, My Lord does not go back on a promise, and I am certain of that.

When the appointed time came and the end of their kingdom drew near, and God had decided on their destruction, God sent an angel from Himself and He said to it, Go to Jeremiah and seek a legal judgment from him, and order him about giving the judgment. So the angel went to Jeremiah after he had made himself into the form of a man of the Children of Israel. Jeremiah said to him, Who are you? He said, A man from the Children of Israel. I seek legal opinion from you about some of my affairs.

So Jeremiah gave him permission, and the angel said to him, O prophet of God, I have to you to seek a legal opinion about my kin. I came into a relationship with them according to what God commanded me. I gave them nothing but good, and I did not refrain from generosity, but my generosity produced nothing but annoyance for me. So give me a legal opinion, O prophet of God.

He said, Do good according to what is between you and God and bestow what God has commanded you and rejoice in goodness. So he left him and remained away for a few days and then came to him in the form of the one who had come to him and sat in front of him. Jeremiah said to him, Who are you? He said, I am the man who came to you and sought a legal opinion in the case of my family. The prophet of God said to him, Did their character not come out for you, and did you not see from them that which you love? He said, O prophet of God, by that which sent you with the truth, I do not know of a generosity which anyone of the people has brought to his kin except that I have brought it to them and more than that. The prophet said, Return to your people and do good to them. Ask God who reconciles His righteous servants that He ameliorate the matter between you and that He unite you in amity and avert disharmony.

So the angel got up and remained away from him for a few days. Nebuchadnezzar and his army had camped around Jerusalem, and with him were his people like locusts. The Children of Israel were very afraid of them, and that troubled the king of the Children of Israel. So he called Jeremiah and said, O prophet of God, where is your promise of God? He said, I am confident in my Lord. Then the angel approached Jeremiah while he was sitting on the wall of

Jerusalem, laughing and rejoicing in the victory of his Lord which He had promised him, and he sat before him. Jeremiah said to him, Who are you? He said, I am the one who came to you about the case of my family two times. The prophet said to him, Is it not time that they stop what they are doing? The angel said to him, O prophet of God, everything has happened to me because of them. Before today I have been patient even though I know that the result will be disharmony. But when I came to them today, I saw them doing what would not please God, and that which God, the Mighty and the Powerful, would not love. The prophet of God said to him, What did you see them doing? He said, O prophet of God, I saw them doing something which would greatly anger God. If they had only been doing the like of what they had been doing before today, my anger would have been patient toward them, and I would have asked indulgence for them. But I became angry today for God and for you, and I came to you to tell you their story. I ask you by God who sent you in truth that you pray to your Lord that He destroy them.

Jeremiah said, O Possessor of the Heavens and the Earth, if they act accordingly to truth and correctness, then leave them alone. But if they have incurred your anger and have done that which you do not find pleasing, then destroy them. The words had not come out of Jeremiah's mouth when God sent a thunderbolt from heaven against Jerusalem. The place and sacrifice ignited and its even gates fell down. When Jeremiah saw that, he screamed and rent his clothes and poured ashes on his head and said, O King of the Heavens and the Earth, in your hand is the sovereignty over all things. You are the most merciful and the merciful. Where is the promise you pledged to me? And it was announced to Jeremiah, They were not afflicted by what they were afflicted with except by your legal judgment which you rendered to our messenger. The prophet, may the prayers and peace of God be upon him, knew for certain that it was his legal judgment which he rendered three times, and that that had been a messenger from his Lord.

Then Jeremiah flew until he was with the wild animals. Nebuchadnezzar and his army entered Jerusalem and trampled Syria and killed the Children of Israel until they were annihilated and Jerusalem was ruined. Then he commanded his army to have each man fill a shield with dirt and then throw it on Jerusalem. So they threw dirt on it until they had filled it up. Then he left, returning to the land of Babylon, and he took with him the prisoners of the Children of Israel. He ordered all who were in Jerusalem to come together. So young and old of the Children of Israel gathered to him, and he chose from them seventy thousand young men. When the booty was brought out for his army and he wished to divide it among them, the kings who were with him said, O king, you can have all that booty. Divide among us these youths which you have chosen from the Children of Israel. He did that, and each man got four youths. Among the youths were Daniel, Hananiyah, Azariah, and

Mishael, and seven thousand of the house of David, and eleven thousand of the tribe of Joseph, the son of Jacob, and his brother Benjamin, and eight thousand of the tribe of Asher, the son of Jacob, and fourteen thousand from the tribe of Zebulon, the son of Jacob, and Naphthali, the son of Jacob, and four thousand from the tribe of Judah, the son of Jacob, and four thousand from the tribe of Reuben and Levi, the two sons of Jacob, and the rest of the Children of Israel.

Nebuchadnezzar divided them into three groups. A third he settled in Syria, a third he took prisoner, and a third he killed. He took the implements of Jerusalem, and he took the seventy thousand youths to Babylon. This incident was the first that God sent down on the Children of Israel for their sins and transgressions. When Nebuchadnezzar was about to return to Babylon with those who were with him of the prisoners of the Children of Israel, Jeremiah came on an ass he had, with the squeezings of grapes in a wineskin and a basket of figs, until he came to the city of Jerusalem. When he stopped on it and saw the destruction, doubt entered him, and he said, "How shall God revive this after its death? So God caused him to die for a hundred years and then revived him" [Q 2:259]. His ass and his grape juice and his basket of figs were with him when God caused him to die. And his ass died with him. God blinded all eyes from him, and no one saw him.

Then God, the Most High, said to him, "How long have you tarried? He said, I have tarried a day or so. He said, Nay, you have tarried a hundred years. Just look at your food and drink, which have rotted, and look at your ass. In order that we make you a sign for mankind, look at the bones, how we arrange them and cover them with flesh" [Q 2:259]. So he looked at his ass, and one joined to another, its nerve and sinew having died. Then in the manner of before, He encased it in flesh until it was whole and then caused the breath of life to go in it, and it stood up and brayed. He looked at the grape juice and his figs and they were suddenly as they had been when he put them down, not rotten. When he saw what he saw of the power of God, he said, I know that God is powerful over all things. Then God made Jeremiah prosper after that, and he is the one who is seen in the open fields and in the cities.

Sources

at-Tabari, *Taʾrikh* 415–416, 658–670
at-Tabari, *Tafsîr* 3:32–34, 15:36–40
ath-Thaʿlabi 83, 185, 126
Al-Baghdad: 3:155

Daniel, Hananiah, Azariah, Mishael and Ezra

This historical section includes brief stories of Daniel, Ezra, and the three youths, Hananiah, Azariah, and Mishael, who in the Bible are saved from death in a fiery furnace. The opening theme of the story involves Nebuchadnezzar's dream, which Daniel successfully identifies and interprets. This theme is repeated later at the opening of the *Kitâb al-Mab'ath* section of Ibn Ishaq's biography of Muhammad. Rabi' b. Nasr has a dream similar to that of Nebuchadnezzar, which is interpreted in a similar manner. It should be noted that in Arabic, Nebuchadnezzar's name, Bukht Nasr, is similar to Rabi' b. Nasr. Both dreams predict the demise of kingdoms and the eventual judgment of God, and when the dream is used in the *Kitâb al-Mab'ath,* it links the Arabs, Muhammad, and Islam with the biblical prophecy.

The *Kitâb al-Mubtadaᵓ* informs us that Hananiah, Azariah, and Mishael were spared death, but we are not told in what manner they were threatened or how they escaped. For those familiar with the Bible, the three youths are associated with deliverance from the fiery furnace. The motif of deliverance from fire is found in stories about Abraham, but is not mentioned here. Nebuchadnezzar's death by a gnat boring into his brain is paralleled in rabbinic literature by the story of the lowly gnat with a one-day lifespan killing the emperor Titus.

Ezra's restoration of the Torah is depicted as the means for the restoration of the Jews to God's favor. Again, as part of the theme of sin/punishment/repentance/restoration, proper conduct gives way to a falling away. This time Ezra is called the son of God by the Jews, as explicated in Q 9:30. Ezra, regarded in Jewish legend as one of those assumed into heaven alive, stripped of his humanity and changed into Metatron, was the leader of the Bene Elohim, the Sons of God (see Newby, *History of the Jews of Arabia*).

Text
In the name of God, the Merciful and the Compassionate
Nebuchadnezzar remained in power as long as God wished him to remain. Then he saw a vision, and while he was amazed at what he saw, something happened to him, and it caused him to forget what he had seen. He called Daniel, Hananiah, Azariah, and Mishael, who were offspring of the prophets,

and said to them, Tell me about the vision which I saw, but something happened to me and caused me to forget it. It amazed me.

They said, Tell us about it, and we will tell you its interpretation. He said, I do not remember it, but if you do not tell me, I will cut you off at the shoulders. So they went out from him, called on God, sought help from Him and asked Him to tell them about it. He caused them to know that which they asked of Him, and they went to the king and said to him, You saw a statue. He said, You are right. They said, Its feet and ankles were of clay. Its calves and thighs were of brass; its belly was of silver, and its breast was of gold, and its head and neck were of iron. He said, You are right. They said, while you were looking at it, amazed, God sent a thunderbolt on it from heaven and it shattered it. That is what caused you to forget it. He said, You are right, but what is its interpretation?

They said, Its interpretation is that you saw the power of kings. Some are softer than others; some are more beautiful than others, and some are stronger than others. The first king of clay was the weakest and the softest. Then above him was brass, and he was more generous and stronger. Then above the brass was the silver, and it was more generous than that and more beautiful. Then above the silver was the gold, and it was more beautiful than the silver, and superior. The iron is your sovereignty, and it is the strongest of the kings and the most mighty of all before it. The thunderbolt which you saw God send down on it from heaven and shatter it was a prophet that God sent from heaven. He will shatter that altogether, and the command will become his.

Then the people of Babylon said to Nebuchadnezzar, Do you see these young men of the Children of Israel that we asked you to give us, and you did? Well, by God, our women reject us since they are with us, and we have seen our women cling to them and turn their faces away to them. So get them out from our midst or kill them. He said, Your situation with them has always been that one can kill one under his control, so let him do it. So they took them out, and when the Children of Israel came close to being killed, they sought God and said, O our Lord, we are afflicted with a trial for a sin not of our doing. So God in His mercy commiserated with them and promised them that He would bring them to life after they were killed. So they were killed, except those that Nebuchadnezzar spared. Of those who were spared were Daniel, Hananiah, Azariah, and Mishael.

God, the Blessed and the Exalted, when He wished the destruction of Nebuchadnezzar, sent him out. He said to those he controlled of the Children of Israel, Do you see this house which I have destroyed and these people whom I killed? Who are they, and what is this house? They said, This is the house of God and the supreme place of worship. These people were the offspring of the prophets, but they sinned and transgressed and rebelled. You were given power over them because of their sins. Their Lord is the Lord of the heavens and the earth, and the Lord of all creatures whom He honored and spared and made strong. But when they did what they did, God destroyed them and gave others power over them.

Nebuchadnezzar said, Tell me what will take me up to the highest heaven so that I can go up there and kill who is there and take the rule of it, for I am finished with the earth and those in it. They said, You cannot do that, for no creature can do that. He said, You will do it, or I will kill the rest of you. So they cried to God and sought Him, and God sent a gnat from His might to show Nebuchadnezzar his weakness and that he was lowly. It entered his nostril and then sunk into his brain until it tormented his brain. He did not sit down or rest but his head would pound. When he knew death, he said to the highborn of the people, When I die, crack open my skull and look to see what killed me. So when he died, they cracked open his skull, and they found a lowly gnat in his brain, that God might show the servants His power and might.

God saved those of the Children of Israel under Nebuchadnezzar's control, was merciful to them, and returned them to Syria and to the Temple mount. They built there, became fat and multiplied until they were as handsome as before. They allege, and God knows best, that God brought to life those dead who had been killed. Then they, when they entered Syria, did not have the promise of God. The Torah had been captured from them, burned, and destroyed. Now Ezra had been one of the prisoners in Babylon, and he returned to Syria, weeping night and day. He went out from the people and isolated himself from them. While he was out in the midst of the valleys and desert, weeping, and while he was in grief over the Torah and crying for it, suddenly a man appeared, while he was sitting, and said, O Ezra, what causes you to cry? He said, I cry over the Book of God and His covenant which was in our midst. Our sins reached a climax and our Lord became angry, so that He gave our enemy power over us. He killed our men and destroyed our country and burned the Book of God which was in our midst and without which the world and the afterlife are not possible. Over what should I weep if not that? He said, Do you wish it to be returned to you? He said, Is that possible? He said, Yes; go back and fast and purify your clothes and then your meeting will be at this place in the morning.

Ezra returned and fasted and purified his clothes and then made for the place of his appointment and sat there. That man came with a vessel in which was water, for he was an angel whom God had sent, and he gave him something to drink from that vessel, and the Torah was replicated in his breast. He returned to the Children of Israel and gave them the Torah and taught them the positive and negative precepts and the laws, the religious duties and ordinances, and they loved it with a love like they never loved anything else. The Torah remained in their midst, and their affairs were improved by it. Ezra remained among them, observing according to God's truth. Then things happened until they said about Ezra, He is the son of God. So God returned to them and sent a prophet among them as He had done with them before to firm up their affairs and teach and command them in the observance of the Torah and what is in it.

Sources

at-Tabari, *Taʾrîkh* 667–670.
ath-Thaʿlabi 188.

Alexander

The Quran [Q 18:84ff.] tells the story of an individual named Dhu-l-Quarnayn, the Two-Horned One. Post-Quranic Muslim commentators have offered a number of identifications for the one with two horns, including the fourth caliph, Ali; the South Arabian king Tubbaᶜ al-Akran; Marzaban, the great-great grandson of Japheth; and Alexander the Great, to name a few. The most frequent identification in Sunni Muslim circles, particularly among those who made some use of Jewish and Christian material, was that Dhu-l-Qarnayn was Alexander the Great.

Western scholars have also generally favored the identification of the Two-Horned One in the Quran with Alexander the Great of the Alexander Romance. Alexander of Macedon's extensive conquests were exceeded after his death by the spread of a romance literature that portrayed him as one of the pious *cosmocrators*. The romance has appeared in most of the languages around the Mediterranean, including Hebrew for the Jewish versions and Syriac for one of the Christian versions. Throughout all the legends Alexander is regarded as superhuman. For some non-Muslim scholars Alexander Dhu-l-Qarnayn's identification and story derive from Syriac sources, while for others the issue of the two horns identifies the figure with portraits of Alexander the Great as Jupiter-Ammon incarnate, a motif found on coins.

Ibn Ishaq in the *Kitâb al-Mubtadaʾ*, while offering the geneology which traces Dhu-l-Qarnayn to Japheth through Yunan, seems to prefer the identification as Alexander. He is presented to us as a messenger who went to the limits of the earth to bring the whole of the world to the proper worship of God. By means of an eloquent prayer, we are shown that even the great Alexander relied on God for his powers and strengths. And God promised to open his breast to give him the powers of a divinely commissioned messenger. This parallels Muhammad's experience when two heavenly creatures open up Muhammad.

When Alexander was given all the mental and physical powers to realize God's plans for him, he set out to bring the world to submission. When there was resistance, we are told that he used darkness and confusion until the resisters submitted; he did not destroy them but brought them to God. When they had adopted proper worship, Alexander recruited his army from them and moved on to the next group. This represents the notion of the Muslim community in early Islam, where the newly submitted population joined the expanding Muslim force to conquer the next territory.

During his travels Alexander is said to have walled up Gog and Magog, who will be loosed at the eschaton and, led by the antimessiah, ad-Dajjal, will lay waste to the earth. When their destruction is complete, only the pious Muslims will remain. In later geographical lore, such as Yaqut's *Dictionary of Countries,* this theme is expanded into an elaborate romance.

In the *Kitâb al-Mubtada³,* Alexander is depicted as coming across a perfect community, and we are given a description of a Muslim utopia. Everyone acts according to proper ethical and religious ideas and, as a consequence, lives in peace, harmony, and without disease. This description abstracts the ideals for the Muslim community and provides a model for proper behavior. Since the function of the *Kitâb al-Mubtada³* was as a textbook for the prince al-Mahdi, Alexander can be seen as the ideal ruler and the community he encounters as the ideal state.

Text
In the name of God, the Merciful and the Compassionate

Some of the non-Arab People of Scripture who had converted to Islam and had inherited some knowledge about Dhu-l-Qarnayn said that Dhu-l-Qarnayn was an Egyptian whose name was Marzaban b. Mardabah al-Yunani, of the offspring of Yunan, the son of Japheth, the son of Noah. Thawr b. Yazid reported from Khalid b. Maʿdan al-Kalaʿi, who was a man who had told the people that if the Messenger of God were to be asked about Dhu-l-Qarnayn, he would say, He was a king who traversed the earth from bottom to top. Khalid said, ʿUmar b. al-Khattab heard a man saying, O Dhu-l-Qarnayn, ʿUmar said, O God, be forgiving. What gives you the right to name the names of the prophets so that you will eventually name the names of the angels? If the Messenger of God, may the prayers and peace of God be upon him, said that, then it is right for him but wrong for those who follow him.

Ibn Ishaq said, I was told on the authority of one whom I do not doubt, who got it from Wahb b. Munabbih the Yemenite, who had knowledge of the first events, that he used to say that Dhu-l-Qarnayn was a man of Rome who was the son of an old woman who had no other sons than him and that his name was Alexander. He was named Dhu-l-Qarnayn because the two sides of his head were of brass. When he matured and became a righteous servant, God, the mighty and the Powerful, said to him, O Dhu-l-Qarnayn, I am sending you to the peoples of the earth. They are people with different languages, and comprise all the communities of the earth. There are two communities between which is the whole length of the earth, and two communities between which is the whole width of the earth. The communities in the middle of them are the Jinn, men, Gog, and Magog. As for the two communities between whom is the length of the earth, there is a community at the setting place of the sun called Nasik. The one at the rising place of the sun is called Mansik. And as for the two between whom is the width of the earth, there is a community in the southern quarter of the earth called Hawil and another in the northern quarter of the earth called Tawil.

When God said that, Dhu-l-Qarnayn said, O my God, you chose me for a great task. No one is able to do it save you. So tell me about these countries to which you are sending me: with what strength do I exceed them and with what group do I outnumber them, and with what plot do I outwit them and with what patience do I endure them, and with what language do I talk to them and with what hearing do I perceive their speech, and how can I be able to understand their language, and with what sight do I see through them, and with what proof do I argue with them, and with what heart do I understand them, and with what judgment do I decide their affairs, and with what equity do I treat them without discrimination, and with what good grace am I enduring of them, and with what knowledge do I make certain of their affairs, and with what hand do I attack them, and with what foot do I trample them, and with what ability do I litigate with them, and with what army do I fight them, and with what kindness do I treat them? There is not in me, O my God, anything that I have mentioned which will stand up to them or have power over them or encompass them. You are the Lord of Mercy who does not commission a soul except to do that which it is able to accomplish, and does not cause it to meet with grief or oppressiveness. Nay, you show mercy and are compassionate.

God the Mighty and the Powerful, said, I will make you able to encompass what I have imposed on you, for I will lay open your breast so that it will be wide enough for everything. I will open your understanding so that it will comprehend everything, and I will spread your tongue so that you will speak everything. I will open your hearing so that you will hear all things. I will extend your sight so that you can perceive everything. I will settle your affairs for you so that you can bring everything to perfection, and I will count everything so that you will not leave anything behind. I will make you remember so that nothing escapes you, and I will strengthen your heart so that nothing will frighten you. I will make light and darkness subservient to you, and I will make the two of them as armies of your armies, the light to guide in front of you and the darkness to conceal behind you. I will increase your understanding so that nothing will terrify you, and I will spread everything before you so that you will be able to attack everything. I will increase your force so that you can destroy everything, and I will garb you in awe so that nothing will desire you.

When that was said to him, he departed, guiding his course toward the community which was at the setting of the sun. When he reached them, he found them to be so many that no one but God could count them and with a strength and force which could not be overcome except by God, possessing diverse languages, passions, and hearts. When he saw that, he vied with them by means of darkness, put three armies around them, surrounded them in every place, and held them back until he had gathered them in one place. Then he placed light over them and called them to the worship of God and to His service. There were those who believed in Him and those who turned away. So Dhu-l-Qarnayn made for those who turned from Him and caused darkness to come over them. It entered their mouths and their noses and their ears and their bellies. It entered into their apartments and their houses. It covered from above and below and from every side of them. They surged in it and became confused. When they became apprehensive that they would be destroyed, they cried out to him with one voice, so he uncovered the darkness from them and took them by force, and they responded to his invitation.

He recruited a great community from the people of the Maghrib and made them one army. Then he departed with them, leading them, the darkness urging them on from behind and guarding around them, and the light in front of them leading and guiding them, while he was traveling in the direction of the land of the south, for he was making for the southern quarter of the earth which was called Hawil.

God made his hand, his heart, his perspicacity, his intellect, his sight, and his counsel useful for him. He did not make an error when he sought advice, and when he did an act, he was adroit. So he departed, leading these people who were following him. When he came to a sea or a ford, he would build ships from small boards, like sandals, and put them all together at once. Then he would put on them all of those people and those armies who were with him. When he had crossed the rivers and the seas, he would take them apart. Then he would give a board to each person, so that carrying them was no burden. He continued this tirelessly until he came to Hawil, and he did there what he had done in Nasik.

When he had finished, he passed over the face of the earth to the right until he came to Mansik at the rising of the sun. He acted therein and recruited an army from it as he had done with the other two communities before it. Then he turned the direction of the north, making for Tawil, which was the community which was opposite Hawil. They were opposite because they had the width of the earth between them. When he reached it, he behaved in it and recruited from it as he had done before. When he had finished with it, he set out for the nations who were in the middle of the earth, the Jinn, the rest of mankind, and Gog and Magog.

When he was on one of the roads which lie in the remote regions of the Turk in the direction of the east, a community of righteous said to him, O Dhu-l-Qarnayn, there are between these two mountains creatures of the creatures of God. Many of them resemble people, but they are like beasts, eating grass and ravishing beasts and wild animals like lions. They eat the vermin of the earth, all of them, from the snake to the scorpion and anything of God's creatures which has life on the earth. God does not have a creature that increases as they do nor multiplies as they do nor grows as abundantly as they do. According to what we see of their increase and multiplication, if they have the time, there is no doubt that they will fill up the earth, displacing its people from it, vanquishing it and spoiling it. A year has not passed for us since we have been living near them that we have not dreaded them and expected that the main group of them would overtake us from between these two mountains. "Shall we pay you a tribute so that you will make a barrier between us and them? He said, What my Lord has established me with is better, so help me with strength, and I will make a dam between you and them" [Q 18:95–96]. Prepare boulders and iron and copper for me while I go into their country and find out about their knowledge and measure between their two mountains.

Then he went off in their direction until he came to them and was in the midst of their country. He found them all one size, their males and their females, one of them reaching the height of about half a medium-sized man. They had claws in place of fingernails on our hands, and molar and canine teeth like the molars and canines of a lion, palates like the palates of a camel in strength which you could hear move when they ate like the movement of the cud of a camel in strength which you could hear move when they ate like the movement of the cud of a camel or like the gnawing of an old stallion or a strong horse. They were covered with hair on their bodies which covered them up and guarded them from heat and cold. Each one of them had two great ears, one of them hairy on its outside and inside, and the other one fuzzy on its outside and inside. The ears were wide enough that when they dress with them, they were wrapped with one of them and the other is spread out. They spent their winter in one of them and their summer in the other. There was not one of them, male or female, but knew the appointed time in which he will die at the end of that year. That is because their males do not die until a thousand children come from their loins. The female will not die until a thousand children come from her womb. When that happens, they are certain of death.

They are given a [great sea creature called a] Tinnin as sustenance in the spring which they pray for when it is time as we pray for rain in its time. One is thrown up at them each year. They eat it for the whole year until another like it the next year. It is sufficient for them for their numbers and their increase. They are rained on, made fertile, and live long and grow fat. The evidence of it is seen on them, the women becoming abundant, and the men grow lustful. But when it fails them, they grow thin and become barren, and the men abstain from intercourse. The females change and immediately separate from them. They call each other with the cries of pigeons and howl with the howling of dogs. They have sexual intercourse wherever they meet, like beasts.

When Dhu-l-Qarnayn saw that, he departed for the area between the two mountain peaks in the remote land of the Turk near the rising of the sun. He found the distance between them to be a hundred parasangs. When he started construction, he dug a hole for himself until he reached water. He made its width fifty parasangs and filled it with boulders and coated it with molten copper. Then he cast over it so that it became like the root of a mountain under the earth. Then he raised it up and topped it with pieces of iron and molten copper and made its transoms of brass, so that it became like an elegant cloak from the yellow of the copper and the red and black of the iron. When he had finished with it and made it strong, he set out toward the community of men and Jinn.

While he was traveling, he arrived at a righteous community which was rightly guided by the truth and was acting justly by it. He found a community just, provident, dividing with equality, judging with justice, being kind and merciful, and one condition and one speech, their natures similar, their ways straight, and their hearts friendly and the courses of life beautiful. Their graves were at the doors of their houses, and there were no doors on their houses. They did not have commanders over them, nor were there judges nor riches nor kings nor nobles. They did not differ or disagree or contend or intrigue or fight or suffer from drought or become annoyed. They were not afflicted with plagues which afflict mankind. They were longer-lived than men, and among them are no poor or impoverished or base or coarse people.

Now when Dhu-l-Qarnayn saw their condition, he marveled at it and said, Tell me, O people, your story. I have surveyed the whole world, land and sea, east and west, its light and its dark, and I have not found your like. So tell me your story.

They said, Very well, ask us about what you wish. He said, Tell me for what reason the graves of your dead are at the doors of your houses. They said, We deliberately do that so that we will not forget death, and its memory will not go out of our hearts. He said, What is the reason that your houses have no doors? They said, There is no one who is suspicious among us, nor is there anyone among us except those who are trustworthy. He said, Why do you have no commanders over you? They said, We do not act in an unjust manner. He said, Why do you not have judges? They said, We do not litigate. He said, Why do you not have rich? They said, We do not seek abundance. He said, Why do you not have kings? They said, We do not seek to be admired. He said, Why do you not fight and disagree? They said, Because of the kindness of our hearts and the peace between us. He said, Why do you not insult and fight each other? They said, Because we conquer our individual natures with resolve, and rule our souls with proper gentleness. He said, What is the reason that your speech is one and your way straight and even? They said, Because we do not lie or dupe or slander one another. he said, Tell me from where you get your hearts to be the same and deal justly with your course of life. They said, Our breasts are healthy, and so because of that, rancor and envy depart from our hearts. He said, Why do you have no poor or impoverished? They said, Because we divide equally. He said, Why do you have no base or crude? They said, Because of humility and self-effacement. He said, What makes you live longer than mankind? They said, Because we obey the truth and judge with justice. He said, Why do you not suffer lack of rain? They said, Because we are not heedless of seeking forgiveness. He said, Why do you not become annoyed? They said, Because we subject our souls to misfortune and want and desire and are free from it. He said, Why do not plagus afflict you as they afflict other people? They said, We trust in no other than God, and we do not deal with astrology. He said, Tell me, is this what you found your fathers doing? They said, Yes, we found our fathers acting mercifully toward the poor and sharing their worldly goods with their impoverished and forgiving the one who had sinned and acting well toward him who was grieved and being kind to one who was rough to them and seeking forgiveness to one who abused them and treating them with mercy and acting in a trustworthy manner, guarding the times of prayer, discharging their obligations, and believing in their promises and not loathing their equals and not rejecting their relatives. So God treated them justly for that and guarded them while they were alive and, in truth, He guarded them in the legacy.

ʿAsim b. ʿUmar b. Qatadah al-Ansari, later az-Zafari, reported on the authority of Muhammad b. Labid, the brother of the B. ʿAbd al-Ashal, who got it from Abu Saʿid al-Khudari: I heard the Messenger of God, may the prayers and peace of God be upon him, say, Gog and Magog will break open and come forth against the people as God said. They will procreate from all sides and will cover the earth, and the Muslims will retreat from them to their cities and their castles. They will seize their cattle and drink the water of the earth until some of them will pass by the river and drink what is in it so that they leave it dry. After that, one will pass by that river and say, There used to be water here. No one will remain among mankind without retreating to a castle or a city. Someone will say, We have finished with these people of the earth; the people of heaven remain. Then one of them will brandish his spear, throw it at heaven, and it will return to him covered with blood because of the trial and rebellion.

While they are about his, God will send worms in their necks like borers, which will go into their necks, and they will be dead in the morning without a sound being heard from them. Then the Muslims will say, Is there not a man who will take the risk to see what the enemy is doing? So a man of them will give himself up to it, having decided that he was already dead. He will go out and find them dead, one on top of the other. So he will call out, O you company of Muslims, rejoice. For God has saved you from your enemies. They will come out from their cities and fortresses, and their cattle will walk freely around them, and there will be no guard except their flesh, and their udders will become as full as they ever have been from an abundance of herbage.

Source

at-Tabari, *Tafsîr* 16:9, 16:17–21

Zechariah and John

This section is another of the history sections the main focus of which is to portray the corruption of the Jews and the persecution of the prophets. Because the perspective of the world in the *Kitâb al-Mubtadaʾ* is so centered on what we would call biblical history, the main actors are Jews and the secondary actors, such as Babylonians and Egyptians, are introduced as instruments of God's retribution. It is probably anachronistic to read this material as anti-Jewish or anti-Semitic. It rather portrays what Jewish prophets and preachers themselves have said about the corruption and sin of the Jews at various times in history.

The conflation of the Haggadic elements associated with Zechariah, the prophet and high priest in the time of King Joash, and Zechariah, the father of John the Baptist, is evident here. (For references to this conflation in Jewish and Christian literature, see Ginzberg, *Legends* 6:396.) It is impossible to tell whether this story came to Muslim sources from a Jewish or Christian antecedent. The identification of the king of Babylon and the Enemy of God as Herod (Arabic *haradus*) is of Jewish origin, as he is listed as a descendant of Haman in the commentaries on the book of Esther.

Text
In the name of God, the Merciful and the Compassionate

The Children of Israel lived after their return from the land of Babylon to Jerusalem doing evil. God had returned them and sent messengers among them. A group of the messengers were regarded as liars, and a group of them were killed, until the last of those sent among them as prophets were Zechariah, John the son of Zechariah, and Jesus the son of Mary. They were of the family of David, upon him be peace. God said, "Mention the mercy of his Lord to His servant Zechariah when he cried to his Lord a cry in secret . . . up to His words . . . Glorify your Lord at the break of day and at evening" [Q 19:2–11].

Ibn Ishaq said on the authority of one who is not to be doubted, who got it from Wahb b. Munabbih the Yemenite, God took hold of his tongue without ill and made it so that he could not speak. His speech with his people was by signs for a period of three days, which God had set as a mark of the belief in His promise. This person was John, the son of Zechariah, the son of Adi, the son of Muslim, the son of Righteous, the son of Blessed, the son of Sha-

201

fatiyyah, the son of Fahur, the son of Shalum, the son of Yahufashat, the son of Asa, the son of Abiyya, the son of Rehoboam, the son of Solomon, the son of David. ʿUmar b. ʿAbdullah b. ʿUrwah reported on the authority of ʿAbdullah b. az-Zubayr that he said, talking about the killing of John, the son of Zechariah, John was not killed except because of a prostitute of the Children of Israel.

There was a king among them, and John, the son of Zechariah, was under the authority of that king. Now the daughter of that king desired her father, and she said, Would that I could marry my father so that his power would come to me rather than to another woman. So she said to him, O my father, marry me, and she invited him to herself. He said, O my daughter, John, the son of Zechariah, will not permit that to us. So she said, Who is John, the son of Zechariah, to me? Who restricts me or prevents me from marrying my father so that I can take over his kingdom and possessions rather than another woman? So she called for athletes and plotted with them for the reward of killing John, the son of Zechariah. She said, Go to the king and contend until you are finished, and he will judge you. Say, The blood of John, the son of Zechariah, and do not accept anything other than it.

The name of the king was Rawad, and the name of the daughter was Baghiyy. The king among them, when he spoke and lied or when he promised and went back on his word, would be dethroned and would be replaced by someone else. So when they contended and his marvel at them increased, he said, Ask me to give you something. They said, We ask you for the blood of John, the son of Zechariah. He said, Woe on you; ask me for something else. They said, We ask you for nothing other than it.

So he feared for his kingdom because his going back would allow him to be dethroned; so he sent for John, the son of Zechariah, while he was sitting in his place of prayer, praying. They sacrificed him in a basin and cut off his head. A man carried it in his hands, and the blood was carried in a basin. He went up carrying his head until he stopped before the king with it, while the head was saying, in the hands that were carrying it, It is not permitted to you.

A man of the Children of Israel said, O you king, would that you would give me this blood. He said, What will you do with it? He said, I will cleanse the earth with it. So he put the head in the blood, locked it up, and the blood boiled with the head until it came out under the door of the house in which it was. When the man saw that, it became detestable to him, and he took it out and put it in a deserted place in the land. It continued to boil, and mischief grew among them. Of them was one who said, He established his place among the sacrificed and did not change.

When God raised up Jesus from their midst, may the prayers and peace of God be upon him, and they killed John, the son of Zechariah, may the prayers and peace of God be upon him, some people saying that they killed Zechariah,

God sent them a king from Babylon called Herod. He traveled to them with the people of Babylon until he came to Syria. When he appeared to them, he commanded a chieftain of the heads of his army called Nebuzaradan, the commander of the elephants, and said to him, I have sworn to my god that if I appeared in the midst of the people of Jerusalem, I would kill them until their blood flowed in a stream in the midst of my army, except that I find no one to kill. So he ordered him to slaughter them up to that point.

Nebuzaradan entered Jerusalem and stood up among a group of people who were sacrificing their sacrifices, and found blood boiling there, so he asked them, saying, O Children of Israel, what is the cause of this blood which boils? Tell me its account and do not conceal anything from me about its situation. They said, This is the blood of a sacrifice of ours which we offered but which was not accepted from us, and because of that, it boils as you see. Indeed, we have sacrificed for eight hundred years sacrifices which have been accepted, all except this sacrifice. He said, You have not told me a truthful account. They said to him, Would that it were for us as in former times and be accepted from us, but sovereignty and prophethood and inspiration have been cut off from us, and for that reason it has not been accepted from us.

So Nebuzaradan slaughtered seven hundred and seventy souls cutting off their heads for that blood, but that did not calm it down. So he called for seven hundred of their youths and slaughtered them for the blood, but it did not calm down. He ordered seven thousand of their sons and wives and slaughtered them for the blood, but it did not calm down. When Nebuzaradan saw that the blood did not calm down, he said to them, O Children of Israel, woe to you. Tell me the truth. Endure the command of your Lord. You have ruled the land for a long time, doing in it what you will. Before long the breath of fire will kill every man and woman. So when they saw the effort and strength of the killing, they told him the true story and said, This blood is of a prophet of ours who forbade us many things that were loathsome to God. Would that we had obeyed him in them, for he would have guided us right. He was telling us about you, but we did not believe him, so we killed him, and this is his blood.

Nebuzaradan said to them, What was his name? They said, John, the son of Zechariah. He said, Now you have told me the truth. For a like amount your Lord has taken revenge of you. So when Nebuzaradan saw that they had told him the truth, he fell down prostrate and said to those around him, Lock the gates of the city and send out anyone who is of the army of Herod here, and let go free the Children of Israel. Then he said, O John, the son of Zechariah, my Lord and your Lord knows what has happened to your people on your account and how many were killed of them on your account. So calm down with the permission of God before no one remains among your people.

So the blood of John calmed down with the permission of God, and Nebuzaradan lifted the killing from them. He said, I believe in what the Children of Israel believe, and I testify to His truth, and I am certain that there is no Lord other than Him. If there is another with Him, he will not prosper, and if there is a partner with Him, it will not seize the heavens and the earth, and if He has a son, he will not prosper. So may He be blessed and sanctified and praised and magnified and glorified, the King of Kings, who rules the seven heavens in knowledge and justice and glory and might, who spread out the earth and cast out the unshakable mountains which do not move. Thus it is necessary that my Lord be and that His sovereignty be.

Then it was inspired to the heads of the heads of the rest of the prophets that Nebuzaradan was a righteous leader. Nebuzaradan said to the children of Israel, The enemy of God, Herod, commanded that I kill you until your blood flows in the middle of his army, and I will do it because I am unable to resist him. They said to him, Do what you were commanded to do by him. So he ordered them to dig trenches and called for their horses and mules and asses and cows and sheep and camels, and he sacrificed them until the blood flowed in the army. He called for the killed who had been killed before that, and they cast them on what he had killed of their cattle until they were atop them, and Herod would not think but that that which was in the trench was of the Children of Israel.

When the blood reached his army, he sent to Nebuzaradan: Raise the siege for them, for their blood has reached me, and I have taken revenge for what they did. Then he went away from them to the land of Babylon, and the Children of Israel were destroyed, or nearly. It was this last event which God sent down about the Children of Israel, God, the Most High, saying to His prophet, Muhammad, may the prayers and peace of God be upon him, "We decreed for the Children of Israel . . . up to His words . . . We have appointed Hell as a prison for the unbelievers" [Q 17:4–8]. The first occurrence was Nebuchadnezzar and his army. Then God returned the attack on them, and the last occurrence was Herod and his army, and it was the greatest of the two events in which was the destruction of the city and the killing of their men and boys and offspring and women, God saying, "And they will lay waste what they conquered with an utter waste" [Q 17:17].

Sources

at-Tabari, *Taʾrikh* 719–730
at-Tabari, *Tafsîr* 3:248, 15:40, 16:58, 16:52, 15:40–42, 17:4–8
ath-Thaʿlabi 190, 207

The Family of ʿImran
and Jesus the Son of Mary

The Quranic view of Jesus is that he was a mortal and a prophet whose message the Jews rejected. He is called the Messiah, but that means only that he is a messenger from God [Q 4:171]. He brought the Gospel, apparently regarded as one book [Q 57:27], which was the confirmation of what had been revealed to Moses [Q 61:7]. The most prominent aspect of Jesus' life is his conception and birth, found in Q 19:1–34, although Q 5:110 gives a short precis of his life, the details of which are elaborated in this passage of the *Kitâb al-Mubtadaʾ*.

Ibn Ishaq seems to have two main points to make in the story of Jesus. The first is historical: to account for the origin of Christianity and place Jesus in the line of prophets. The second is to stress Jesus' humanity against claims that he is the son of God. Ibn Ishaq opens the story with a genealogy for Jesus that places him in the Davidic line, but no eschatological overtones are attached. He then presents an interesting version of the immaculate conception of Mary, which accounts for her lack of sin because her mother sought God's protection for her and her offspring. In this notion man's propensity for sin is ascribed to an attack by the Devil each time a child is born.

The *Kitâb al-Mubtadaʾ* glosses the story of Jesus' birth as found in chapter 19 of the Quran. In this version Jesus is able to speak as an infant and proclaim God's power. This is consistent with the concept of prophethood found in Ibn Ishaq's writings. Jesus, like the other prophets, was elected and chosen by God from before his birth to be a prophet, and the power of such selection and inspiration manifests itself even when the prophet is in infancy. Muhammad, it will be remembered, caused such blessings among the tribe of his foster mother that drought and poverty were eliminated.

The main events of Jesus' early life are presented as glosses to the sparse Quranic verses, and Western scholars have identified most of the themes as paralleled in the pseudepigraphic Infancy Gospels. Little is mentioned in Ibn Ishaq's account of Jesus' middle career, except to note that Jesus was the vehicle for God's giving the Gospel as another manifestation of the same revelation from heaven. Instead, we are told about the events surrounding the crucifixion. Ibn Ishaq, following the Quran [A 4:157], denies that Jesus was killed. Instead, a companion named Sergius is said to have been designated as a stand-in. Ibn Ishaq does present a report that Jesus was taken up to heaven alive, stripped of his humanity, and made into an angel. Such a view of Jesus' assumption into heaven makes him similar to Enoch and the others who were taken to heaven alive.

Several important and controversial Christian doctrines are dealt with in this narrative, and it is interesting to see how some early Muslim exegetes treat them. The first is the doctrine of the immaculate conception. Mary is freed from sin by her mother's prophylactic prayer, which covers Jesus as well, not allowing the Devil to implant sin into either Mary or Jesus. By implication the story also deals with the doctrine of original sin. As for the virgin birth, it is accepted in a straightforward manner, acknowledging God's ability to create life with or without human agency, which He did, after all, with Adam.

One major controversy which had rocked the Christian church in the fifth century was the definition of the nature(s) of Jesus: were they one, two, combined, separate, etc. The *Kitâb al-Mubtada'* presents an interesting argument for Jesus having two natures, one heavenly and one earthly. He possessed the heavenly one after God assumed him into heaven and removed part of his human attributes. This parallels some Arabian Jewish notions and is reminiscent of the translation of Elijah. Finally, the tradition of finding Jesus' grave near Medina in Arabia connects Jesus with Arabia and reemphasizes his humanity.

Text
In the name of God, the Merciful and the Compassionate

God said, "When the wife of ʿImran said, My Lord, I have vowed to you that what is in my belly is consecrated, so accept it from me, for you are the Hearer, the Knower" [Q 3:35]. The wife of ʿImran was the mother of Mary, the daughter of ʿImran, the mother of Jesus, the son of Mary, may the prayers of God be upon him. According to what was mentioned to us, her name was Hannah, the daughter of Faqudh, the son of Qutayl. Her spouse was ʿImran, the son of Yashaham, the son of Amun, the son of Manasha, the son of Hezekiah, the son of Ahriq, the son of Yuwaym, the son of ʿAzaraya, the son of Amusiya, the son of Yaush, the son of Ahrihu, the son of Yazim, the son of Yahufashat, the son of Ashabaraban, the son of Rehoboam, the son of Solomon, the son of David, the son of Jesse.

According to what reached us, the reason that Hannah, the daughter of Faqudh, the wife of ʿImran vowed that which God mentioned in this verse was that Zechariah and ʿImran married two sisters. The mother of John was married to Zechariah and the mother of Mary was married to ʿImran. ʿImran died while the mother of Mary was carrying Mary, she being a fetus in her belly. According to what they say, a child had been withheld from her until she grew old. Now they were of the house of God, great be His praise, and while she was in the shade of a tree, she looked at a bird feeding a child it had, and she was moved to want a child, so she prayed to God to give her a child. She bore

Mary, and 'Imran was killed. When she knew that a fetus was in her belly, she pledged it to God for the worship of God. She made it a hermit in the church so that it would make no use of the matters of this world. Yazid b. 'Abdullah b. Qusayt reported from Abu Hurayrah that the Messenger of God, may the prayers and peace of God be upon him, said. There is not a person born but the Devil attacks him, and thus gets easy access to desire, except with respect to Mary, the daughter of 'Imran. When Hannah bore her, she said, Lord, I place her in your refuge and her offspring also from the accursed Devil. So a veil was drawn around her, and the Devil attacked that.

Zechariah provided for Mary after the death of her mother. She was sent to her aunt, the mother of John, until she reached majority and then was put in the church because of the vow her mother had sworn. She grew and matured. Then the Children of Israel reached a crisis while she was in that state until Zechariah was weak from supporting her, so he went to the Children of Israel and said, O Children of Israel, do you know, by God, that I have become weak from the support of the daughter of 'Imran?

They said, We strived, but what happened to you this year happened to us. So they all pushed her away, and they could not see a way out of supporting her, so they began to cast lots. The lot for her support was drawn by a man of the Children of Israel, a carpenter, who was called George. Mary knew from his face the enormity of the burden on him, and she would say to him, O George, think well of God, for God will provide for us. So George began to provide for her where she was, and every day he would bring her what would be useful to her from his earnings. When he would bring it in to her while she was in the church, God would increase it and cause it to grow. Zechariah came to her and saw the surplus of provisions which was not possible for George to have brought to her, and said, O Mary, what is this? She said, It is from God. God provides for whom He wills without reckoning.

Mary was secluded in the church with a youth whose name was Joseph. His mother and his father had placed him in by a vow, so the two of them were in the church together. When Mary had depleted her water and Joseph's water, the two of them would take their water pitchers, go to the desert in which was water which they found sweet, would fill their jugs, and then return to the church. The angels approached Mary and said, "O Mary, God has chosen you and purified you and preferred you over the women of the world" [Q 3:42].

When Zechariah heard that, he said, There is something going on with the daughter of 'Imran. One who is not to be doubted reported on the authority of Wahb b. Munabbih that she found Gabriel with her, whom God had made like a well-proportioned man, and "she said, I seek refuge with the Merciful from you, if you are God fearing" [Q 19:18]. It did not seem to her that he was anything but a man of the children of Adam. "He said, I am a messenger from your Lord in order to give you a pure son. She said, How can there be a son to me when no man has touched me, and I have not been unchaste? He said, Thus said your Lord, It is easy for me; we will make him a sign to mankind and a mercy from us. It is a matter decided'' [Q 19:19–21]. That is, God had already decided on that, and there is no escape. When Gabriel said that— meaning when Gabriel said, "Thus said your Lord; it is easy for me"—she yielded to the will of God, and he breathed into her bosom and then departed from her.

When it came time for Mary to give birth and she found what women know about labor pains, she went out of the city west of Jerusalem to a village called Bethlehem some six miles from Jerusalem until the time for birth overtook her. The labor pains drove her to the base of a palm tree which had a manger for cattle under it, with a river of water, and she gave birth there. And Jesus "cried out from beneath her, Do not grieve, for your Lord has put a river beneath you. So shake the trunk of the palm toward you, and you will cause ripe fruit to fall on you. So eat and drink and be consoled. And if you see any mortal, say, I have vowed to the Merciful to fast, and I may not speak to any mortal today'' [Q 19:24–26], for I will satisfy you in speech.

God caused Mary to forget the distress of her trial and the fear of people by what she had heard from the angels announcing the glad tidings of Jesus, until Jesus spoke with her, and the confirmation of what God had promised her came to her. Then she brought him to her people. "They said, O Mary, you come with an amazing thing" [Q 19:27], that is, an abomination without kin. "O sister of Aaron, your father was not an evil man, and your mother was not a whore. So she pointed at him, and they said, How are we to talk with one who is still a young boy in the cradle?" [Q 19:28–29] But Jesus answered them for her and said to them, "I am the servant of God; He has given me Scripture and made me a prophet and made me blessed wherever I am and has commanded me to pray and to give alms as long as I am alive. He made me dutiful toward the one who bore me and did not make me arrogant and mis- chievous. Peace be on me the day I was born and the day I die and the day I will be sent forth alive" [Q 19:30–33]. In the versions of his story of himself, he had no father, and he would die and then be sent forth alive, God, the Mighty and Exalted, saying, "Thus is Jesus, the son of Mary; this is a true statement about which they doubt" [Q 19:34].

According to what they assert, when Jesus reached about nine or ten years, his mother enrolled him in an elementary school. He was with a man of the school who taught him as he taught the young boys. Now the man would not start to teach anything of what he taught the boys except Jesus would know it before he taught it to him. The man would say, Are you not amazed at the son of this widow? I scarcely begin to teach him anything, but I find that he knows it from me. Jesus, may the prayers of God be upon him, was sitting one day with the youths of the school, and he picked up some clay. Then he said, I will make a bird for you of this clay. They said, Are you able to do that? He said, Yes, with the permission of my Lord. Then he shaped it until he formed it into a bird. Then he breathed into it and said, Be a bird with the permission of God, and it flew out of his palms. The boys left with that and mentioned it to their teacher, and they spread it around among the people. Jesus grew up, and the Children of Israel were uneasy about him. When his mother feared for him, she took him on an ass she had and left, fleeing with him.

The name of the king of the Children of Israel who ordered Jesus killed was a man from among them called David. According to what was mentioned to me, when they decided on that, not one of the servants of the servants of God found his death to be hateful. Jesus was not distressed, and he did not call on God in his adversity until he said, according to what they allege, O God, I am turning away this cup from one of your creatures, so turn it away from me, and he was lashed so that he bled.

Jesus and his companions went in a gate which they had agreed to enter in order to kill him, and there were thirteen with Jesus. When he was certain that they were coming in to him, he told to his companions the Apostles, who were twelve men, Peter, Jacob the son of Zebedee, John the brother of Jacob, Andrew, Philip, Bartholomew, Matthew, Thomas, Jacob the son of Hilkiah, Thaddaeus, Simon, and Judas Iscariot. According to what was mentioned about them, there was a man whose name was Sergius, whom the Christians deny, so they were thirteen other than Jesus. This is because he was the one who took the place of Jesus with the Jews. I do not know whether he was one of the twelve or if they were thirteen. But they denied him after Jesus was crucified, and they did not believe in what came to Muhammad, may the prayers and peace of God be upon him. If they were thirteen, then when they entered the hall, they were fourteen with Jesus, and if they were twelve when they entered the hall, they were thirteen. A man who had been a Christian and had become a Muslim reported that Jesus said when it came to him from God, I will raise you up to me. Said, O Company of Disciples, who of you wishes to be my companion in Paradise enough that he will represent himself to the crowd in my place so that they kill him in my stead? Sergius said, I, O Spirit of God. He said, Sit in my place. So he sat in it, and Jesus was raised up, may the prayers and peace of God be upon him. They entered, took him and crucified him, and Sergius was the one crucified. Their number when they entered with Jesus was known, for they had been seen and had been counted. When they entered to take him, they found Jesus, according to what it seemed, and his companions, and they missed a man from the number, and he is the one they disagree about. They did not know Jesus until they gave Judas Iscariot thirty dirhams so that he would guide them to him and make him known to them. So he said to them, When you come into him, I will kiss him, and he is the one I will kiss, so take him.

When they entered to him, Jesus was already raised up, and he saw Sergius in the form of Jesus, so he prostrated himself and kissed him, and he did not doubt that he was Jesus, and they took him and crucified him. Then Judas Iscariot repented about what he had done, and he hanged himself with a rope, committing suicide. He was cursed by the Christians, and he had been one of the ones counted on as a disciple. Some of the Christians assert that Judas Iscariot was the one who resembled Jesus and they crucified him while he was saying, I am not among your disciples; I am the one who led you to him. God knows which of that was true.

One who is not to be doubted reported on the authority of Wahb b. Munabbih the Yemenite: God took Jesus, the son of Mary, to Himself in the third hour of the day, but the Christians assert that it was the seventh hour. Then God resurrected him and said to him, Descend and go down to Mary Magdalene on her mountain, for no one cried as many tears over you as she, nor did anyone grieve as she. Then gather your disciplines to you and disperse them over the earth as missionaries for God, for you did not do that. So God sent him down to them.

The mountain flamed light when he went down. He gathered his disciples around him and sent them and commanded them to take to the people of the earth what God had commanded. Then God raised him to Him and garbed him in feathers and dressed him in light and cut off his desire for food and drink, so he flew among the angels, and he was with them around the throne. He was human and angelic, heavenly and earthly.

The disciples dispersed where he commanded them. The night in which he descended is the night in which Christians burn incense. Of those disciples and followers who went forth to Rome were Peter the Apostle, with whom was Paul, who was a follower and not of the disciples. Andrew and Matthew went to the land where its people eat men, and it is, according to our opinion, the land of the blacks. Thomas went to the land of Babylon in the east, and Philip to Kairouan and Cartagena, which is in Africa. John went to Ephesus, the village of the people of the cave. Jacob went to Jerusalem, which has the Holy Temple. Bartholomew went to Arabia, which is the land of the Hijaz. Simon went to the land of the Berber beyond Africa, but not one of the Apostles was sent to Europe, which had been the place assigned to Judas Iscariot before he did what he did.

ʿUmar b. ʿAbdullah b. ʿUrwah b. az-Zubayr reported from Ibn Sulaym al-Ansari, nee az-Zurqi, who said, One of our women was under a vow to climb to the top of al-Jamaʿ, a mountain near a canyon in the direction of Medina. So I climbed with her until we neared the top of the mountain where there was suddenly a huge grave on which were two great stones, a stone at the head and a stone at the foot, on which there was writing in a foreign script which I did not know. So I carried the two stones with me until a part of the mountain came down on me and I dropped one of them. I descended with the other and presented it to the Syrians to see if they knew its writing, but they did not know it. So I presented it to one who writes the psalms of the people of the Yemen and one who writes foreign scripts, but he did not know it. So when I did not find anyone who knew it, I threw it under a sarcophagus we had and it remained a few years. Then some people came to us of the people of Mah of Persia seeking pearls, and I said to them, Do you have any books? They said, Yes, so I brought out for them the stone, and behold, they could read it, for it was in their script: This is the grave of the Messenger of God, Jesus, the son of Mary, upon him be peace. To the people of this country . . . And they had been its people in that time, and he died among them, and they buried him on the top of the mountain.

Then they attacked the rest of the Apostles, exposing them to the sun, torturing them and walking them around. The king of Rome, who was an idolater, heard that, and they were under his authority. It was said to him that there was a man of the Children of Israel among these people under his control who was an enemy to him, and that they killed him. The king was told that he used to tell them that he was a messenger of God. He had shown them marvels and had resurrected dead for them and healed the sick and created birds for them of clay and breathed into them and they were birds by permission of God, and he told them of divine secrets.

He said, Woe to you. What prevented you from mentioning his and their affair? By God, if only I had known what had passed between them and him! Then he sent to the Apostles, snatched them out of their hands and asked them about the religion of Jesus and his affairs. So they told him his story, and he followed them in their religion. He took down Sergius and hid him, and he took the wood upon which he was crucified and honored it and preserved it so that it would not be harmed. He became an enemy of the Children of Israel and killed many of them. This was the start of Christianity in Rome.

Sources

at-Tabari, *Taʾrîkh* 712–713, 737–740

at-Tabari, *Tafsîr* 3:235, 3:238–239, 3:246, 3:264, 16:60, 16:61, 16:62, 16:68, 16:70, 16:75, 16:76, 16:77, 16:80, 16:82, 3:279, 3:275, 6:14–15, 6:15

ath-Thaʿlabî 207–208, 226

The Companions of the Cave

Chapter 18 of the Quran, usually called the Chapter of the Cave, presents a story that Western scholars identify as the story of the Seven Sleepers of Ephesus, a story that was redacted around the fifth Christian century in the Syriac martyriological tradition. For Muslims this story and the story of Dhu-l-Qarnayn in the same chapter of the Quran are revealed to Muhammad in response to a test posed by Arabian Jews.

The story of the Companions of the Cave in the *Kitâb al-Mubtad'a* continues the historical cycle of sin and disorder, which ultimately prompts divine intervention. In this case the followers of the Gospel—the term "Christian" is not used—have fallen away from correct worhip, have taken idols, and have become oppressed by kings. As can be observed throughout the *Kitâb al-Mubtad'a,* political oppression, like disease and famine, is a result of not worshipping God properly. This was one of the messages of Islam; the rise of the fortunes of the Arabs was a result of God's blessing. God's blessing was maintained and increased by Islam, the visible proof being the expansion of the Islamic empire. For the prince who read this story, it was also another reminder that only correct worship would ensure a lasting reign.

The theme of extranatural sleep/death and subsequent reawakening/resurrection is found in several places in the *Kitâb al-Mubtad'a*. Moses, after seeing God, died and was brought back to life. Jeremiah/Khidr sleeps or dies for a period of time and then is revived by God. The bones seen by Ezekiel are revived to praise God. The Companions of the Cave sleep and area wakened both to save them and as a proof of God's power over death. A fundamental belief in Islam is the promise of a life beyond this one and the power of God to fulfill that promise. These stories offer examples of God's fulfillment of the promise in the past. The same themes are also found in wider world literature. The folk theme of the magical sleeper is found in many cultures and is usually associated with some connection with the supernatural on the part of the sleeper. (For a brief treatment of this topic with references to world folk literature, see Schwarzbaum, *Biblical and Extra-Biblical Legends in Islamic Folk Literature.*)

Text

In the name of God, the Merciful and the Compassionate

The situation of the People of the Gospel dissolved into disorder. Sins became numerous among them, and kings became oppressive among them, until they worshiped idols and sacrificed to false gods. But among them was a remnant of the followers of Jesus, the son of Mary, adhering to the worship of God and His unity. Of those who acted badly was a king of Rome called Decius. He worshiped idols, sacrificed to false gods, and killed those who remained in the religion of Jesus, the son of Mary, who opposed him. He used to come down on the villages of Rome and kill everyone in the village who was of the religion of Jesus, the son of Mary, who would not worship idols and sacrifice to false gods. This continued until he came to the city of the youths of the Cave.

When Decius settled there, it became oppressive for the people of faith, and they feared him and fled in every direction. When he came there, Decius ordered that the faithful be followed. So the people gathered to him, and he took a group of unbelievers from the populace and had them follow the faithful to the places where they sought to hide, and they dragged them out to Decius. He would take them to an assembly area where he sacrificed to false gods and would give them the choice between being killed or worshiping idols and sacrificing to false gods. Of them were some who wished life and hated being killed and would apostatize, and among them were those who would deny worshiping other than God and would be killed. When stubborn people of the faithful saw that, they began to resign their souls to torture and being killed. And they were killed and cut up. Then he would tie up what he had cut up of their bodies and hang them on the walls of the city in every direction and on every door so that temptation of the faithful became great. Among them were those who disbelieved and left, and those who remained stubbornly in their religion, and they were killed.

When the youths who were the Companions of the Cave saw that, they grieved so greatly that they changed color, their bodies became emaciated, and they sought the help of God through prayer, fasting, charity, praising, glorification, exaltation, magnification, weeping, and beseeching. They were noble youths of the sons of the notables of Rome.

ʿAbdullah b. Abu Najih reported from Mujahid, who said, It was related to me that some of them were bright as new leaves. Ibn ʿAbbas said that they were that way because of their worship of God night and day, crying to God and seeking His help. They were eight: Maksilmina, who was the oldest of them, and he was the one who talked with the king about them, and Mahsimilinina, Yamlikha, Martus, Kusutunas, Dinamus, Batunus, and Qalus.

When Decius decided that he would gather the people of the city for the worship of idols and for sacrificing to false gods, they cried to God and besought Him and began saying, O God, Lord of the Heavens and the Earth, we will not call on any other than you. We have said it is enough, so take off this tribulation from your believing servants and remove the torment. Be kind to your servants who believe in you, for they are prevented form your worship except secretly, fearing to worship you openly.

While they were doing that, some of the city's polytheists who had ben assembled for the worship of idols and the sacrifice to false gods discovered them. They reported the believers' activity while they were withdrawn to a place of prayer they had in which they were worshiping God, beseeching Him, and dreading their being mentioned to Decius. So these polytheists came to their place of prayer and found them prostrating on their faces, imploring, weeping, and desiring that God save them from Decius and his trial.

When the chiefs of the polytheists saw them, they said to them, What causes you to stay away from the affairs of the king? Go to him. Then they left them and brought their matter up to Decius and said, You have gathered the people for sacrifice to your gods, and these youths are from the people of your house who sneer at you, laugh at you, disobey your commands and abandon your gods, going to a place of prayer they and the followers of Jesus, the son of Mary, have, to pray in it and beseech their God and the God of Jesus, the son of Mary, and the Companions of Jesus. You should not let them do this while they are with us under your control and sovereignty. They are eight persons, and their leader is Maksilmina. And they are the sons of the mighty of the city.

When they said that to Decius, he sent to them and brought them from the place of prayer they were in, their eyes flowing with tears, their faces soiled with tears. He said to them, What prevents you from witnessing the sacrifice to our gods who are worshiped in the land and doing like the people of your city? The people present with us will be rewarded. If you do not sacrifice to our gods as the people sacrifice, then I will kill you.

Maksilmina said, We have a God whom we worship who fills the heavens and the earth with His glory. We will never call on another god, and we will not confess to that which you invite us, ever! We worship God, our Lord, and to Him belong praise, magnification, and laudation, purely, forever. It is He whom we worship, and He whom we ask for help and salvation. As for the idols and their worship, we will never confess them out of fear of you or in terror of your servants, for we are not worshipers of the Satans, and our souls and our bodies are not made for the worship of them after God guided us rightly to Him. Do with us what you like. Then the companions of Maksilmina addressed Decius in a similar manner.

When they said that to him, he ordered their clothes of honor to be removed from them. Then he said to them, Since you have done what you have done, I will remove you from the people of my kingdom and folk of my country. I will be rid of you, and I will execute the punishment I promised you. The only thing that prevents me from proceeding with that is that I see that you are callow youth, and I do not want to destroy you immediately. I am going to give you a respite in which you can think back and your sense can return. Then he ordered the gold and silver ornaments removed and commanded them to be expelled from him.

After that, Decius went to a city like the city they were in, nearby, to do something he wished. When the youths saw that Decius had left their city, they were surprised by his departure and were afraid that when he returned to their city, he would remember them. So they agreed that each one of them would take adequate rations from his father's house. They gave it as alms and they provisioned themselves with the remainder. Then they departed to a cave near the city in a mountain called Pangloss. They remained there and worshiped God until Decius returned when they would go to him and stand before him and he would do with them what he wished. So when they said that to one another, each youth took provisions from his father's house, gave it as alms and departed with what remained. Their dog followed them until they came to that cave which was in that mountain. They remained in it, with no other occupation but prayer, fasting, praising God, glorifying Him and extolling Him, seeking the face of God and the everlasting life. They entrusted their means of support to a youth with them called Yamlikha. He was in charge of their food, buying their provisions from the city secretly from the people. That was because he was the most handsome and the staunchest of them, so Yamlikha used to do that. When he would enter the city, he would put away his good clothes and take clothes like those of the poor who beg for food. Then he would take his money and go to the city and buy food and drink for them and listen and spy out news for them, whether he and his companions were mentioned in any way among the crowds of the city. Then he would return to his companions with their food and drink and report to them about what he heard of the news of the people.

They remained this way for a time. Then Decius the tyrant came from the city he had left to his city, which was the city of Ephesus. He ordered the notables of the city to sacrifice to the idols, and the people of belief were afraid of that, and they hid in every hideout. Yamlikha was in the city buying food and drink for his comrades with some of their wealth, and when he returned to his companions, he was crying, and he had only a little food with him. He informed them that the tyrant Decius had entered the city and that they were remembered and missed and were sought among the notables of the people of the city so that they could sacrifice to the idols. When he told them that, they became very afraid and fell down prostrating on their faces, calling on God, imploring Him, and seeking His protection from the affliction. Then Yamlikha said to them, O brothers, raise your heads and eat of this food which I brought you and trust in your Lord. So they raised their heads, their eyes flowing with tears, on guard and fearing for themselves, and they ate of it, and that was at the setting of the sun. Then they sat down talking and studying and talking to each other about the grief, commiserating about the news their comrade had brought to them. While they were in that state, God closed their ears in the cave for a number of years with their dog spreading his forepaws at the entrance to the cave. So what happened to them happened, while they were believing, certain and trusting in the promise, and their money was still with them.

The following day, Decius looked for them, but he did not find them, so he said to the notables of the city, The condition of these youths who went away saddens me. They were thinking that I would be angry at them for what they did the first time out of their ignorance. I was not harsh with them for myself, and I would not blame one of them if only they would come back and worship my gods. If they do that, I will leave them alone, not restraining them, letting bygones be bygones.

The notables of the people of the city said to him, You are not right to be merciful to a people who engage in misconduct and are persistent in sin and rebellion. You gave them a respite from the punishment, and if they had wished, they could have returned during that delay. But they did not return and did not desist and did not repent what they had done. Since you left, they have been squandering money in the city, and when they learned of your arrival, they fled, and have not been seen afterward. If you wish them brought, send for their fathers and torture them and be harsh with them so they will lead you to them. They are hiding from you.

When they said that to Decius the tyrant, he became very angry and then sent for their fathers. They were brought to him, and he asked them about them. He said, Tell me about your rebellious sons who disobeyed my command and abandoned our gods. Bring them to me and tell me their place. Their fathers said to him, As for us, we are not rebellious to your command, and we do not leave you, for we have worshiped your gods and we have sacrificed to them, so do not kill us as a rebellious folk. They have left with our money, squandered it and destroyed it in the markets of the city. Then they left fleeing from you and climbed a mountain named Pangloss, and between it and the city is a wide land. When they said that, he let them go and began to take counsel about what he should do about the youths. So God put it in his heart that he should order the cave blocked over them as a miracle from God which He wished to bestow on them and on the bodies of the youths, having nothing go around them. He wished to resurrect them and make them as a sign to the community which would come after them and to make clear that the Hour would come in which there is no doubt that God sends forth him who is in the grave. So Decius ordered that the cave be blocked up over them. He said, Leave these rebellious youths alone who left my gods so they will die of hunger and thirst in the cave. The cave they have chosen for themselves will be a grave for them. So the Enemy of God did that to them. Aware of what he was doing, he thought they were awake. But God took their spirits, giving them a deathlike sleep, along with their dog whose forepaws were outstretched at the entrance to the cave. God enveloped the dog with what He enveloped them, turning them all to the right and to the left.

Then two men, named Bidrus and Runas, believers, who were in the house of the king, Decius, keeping their belief secret, decided that they would write about the youths of the cave, their origins, their names, the names of their fathers, and their story, on two tablets of lead. They made a coffin of brass for it and put the two tablets in it. Then, at the mouth of the cave, they wrote on it and sealed the coffin with their seals and said, Perhaps God will cause these youths to appear to believing people before the day of resurrection. The one who opens this up will know their story. Then they built a building over it.

Decius and his age lasted as long as God wished, and then He destroyed Decius and his age and many ages after him, and successor followed successor. Then a righteous man called Theodosius ruled the people of this country for sixty-eight years, during which time the people formed parties. Of them were those who believed in God and knew that the Hour was true, and of them were those that denied. This was distressing to the righteous king, Theodosius, and he wept to God and implored Him and grieved greatly when he saw the people of error increasing over the people of right, who were saying, There is no life but the life of this world, and the spirit and not the body is sent forth. And they forgot what was in the Scripture.

Theodosius began to send to those who he thought had good in them and were the leaders of the truth, but they began to deny the Hour until it was almost that the people were turned from the truth and the community of disciples. When the righteous king, Theodosius, saw that, he entered his house, locked it, wore a hair shirt, put ashes under him, sat on them, and spent the night and day imploring God and weeping to Him for what he saw among the people.

Then the Merciful and the Compassionate, who hates the destruction of His servants, wished that the youths of the cave appear to make their condition clear to the people, that He make them a sign and a proof to the people so that they would know without doubt that the Hour was coming, that He would answer His righteous servant, Theodosius, that He would perfect His grace on him and not remove his kingship from him nor the belief that He had given him, that he should worship God and not associate anything with Him and that He would gather in those believers who had been dispersed.

God put it in the soul of a man named Iuliyas, who was of the people of the country of the cave and the mountain Pangloss in which was the cave which belonged to that man, that he raze the building which was over the mouth of the cave and build a sheepfold there. So he hired two workmen, and they began to remove the stones and build a sheepfold with them until they removed what was at the mouth of the cave, opening the cave. God veiled the youths of the cave from the people with dread. They assert that the brave of those who wished to look on them would enter the door of the cave and then go until they would see their dog before them at the door of the cave, sleeping. When the two of them removed the stones and opened up the entrance of the cave, God, the Possessor of Power and Might, the Resurrector of the dead, gave permission to the youths that they sit in the cave, so they sat, happy, their faces glowing from clay. They greeted one another almost as if it were the hour they were supposed to have awakened in the morning after the night during which they slept. They got up for prayer and prayed as they used to, not being seen and not seeing on their faces or on their skin or in their color anything different from the way they were when they lay down, as it were, yesterday. They were thinking that the tyrant king, Decius, was after them and was searching for them.

When they had performed their prayers as they used to do, they said to Yamlikha, who was the one in charge of their wealth, had bought food and drink for them in the city and had brought news that Decius was searching for them and asking for them, O my brother, what did the people say last evening about us and that tyrant? They were thinking that they had been lying down as they used to, and it seemed to them that they slept only as long as they usually slept in a night, so they asked among themselves and said to one another, "How long have you tarried" [Q 18:20] sleeping? "They said, A day or part of a day; your Lord knows how long you have tarried" [Q 18:20]. And all of that went through their minds.

Yamlikha said, You are missed and sought in the city, and he wishes you to come to him today to sacrifice to the idols, or he will kill you, and what God wills is far from that. Maksilmina said to them, O brothers, know that you are decent. Do not apostatize when the Enemy of God calls you, and do not deny the life which does not end because of your belief in God and life after death. Then they said to Yamlikha, Go to the city and hear what is said about us today and whether we are mentioned by Decius. Be polite, and do not let anyone know about us, and buy some food and bring it to us, for it is now time for you to add to the food which you brought to us, for their is only a little, and we awoke hungry.

So Yamlikha did as he used to do. He put off his clothes, took the clothes in which he would not be recognized, and took a coin from their wealth which was struck with the imprint of Decius, the king. Yamlikha left, and when he passed by the door of the cave, he saw the stones removed from the door and was amazed. Then he went on, not worried, until he came to the city, fearing being stopped on the way, where he feared that someone of his family would see him, recognize him, and take him to Decius. The righteous servant did not know that Decius and the people of his time had been destroyed three hundred and nine years before that, or, as long as God wished, for the time between when they slept to their awakening was three hundred and nine years.

When Yamlikha looked at the gate to the city, he raised his eyes and saw a sign on the top of the gate, on the outside, which belonged to the people of belief. When he saw it, he was amazed and began looking at it, fearing. He looked to the left and to the right and was amazed. Then he left the gate and went around to another gate, looked and saw what surrounded the entire city. He saw something similar on every gate. It began to appear to him that this city was not the city which he knew. He saw many new people whom he had not seen before, so he began to walk, amazed, and it seemed to him that he was confused. Then he returned to the gate from which he had come and, astonished, said, I wish I knew what is going on. Last evening the Muslims feared this sign and concealed it, but today it is manifest. Perhaps I am dreaming.

Then he saw he was not asleep, so he took his covering, put it over his head, entered the city, began walking among the markets, and heard many people swearing in the name of Jesus, the son of Mary, and his fear was increased. He saw that he was perplexed, and he leaned his back against a wall of the city, saying to himself, By God, I do not know what this is. Last evening, there was not a person on earth who would mention Jesus, the son of Mary, except he be killed. But today I hear them, and every man mentions Jesus without fear. Then he said to himself, Maybe this is not the city which I know. I hear the speech of the people, but I do not know anyone of them. By God, I do not know a city which is near our city.

So he stood like one perplexed, not going in any direction. Then he met one of the city's youth and said to him, What is the name of this city, O youth, and by God, tell me the truth so that I can go out quickly before I am humiliated, or some evil happens to me and I am destroyed. This is what Yamlikha told his companions when he explained to them what happened. Then he got hold of himself and said, By God, I wish I could hasten my departure from the city before he becomes aware of me. He is shrewder than I. So he approached some food sellers and took out the coin which he had with him and gave it to a one of them and said, Sell me some food for this coin, O servant of God. The man took it, looked at the mint of the coin and its legend, and was amazed at it. Then he tossed it to another one of his companions, and he looked at it. Then they began to throw it around among them from man to man, marveling at it. Then they began to consult with one another, saying to one another that this man found a trove in the earth from a long time ago.

When he saw them conferring because of him, he feared greatly, began to tremble, and thought that they were aware of him and recognized him and that they wished to take him to their king, Decius, to present him to him. Other people began to come toward him and recognize him, so he said to them, greatly afraid of them, Be nice to me. You have taken my coin, so keep it, and as for your food, I have no need of it. They said to him, Who are you, O youth, and what is your situation? By God, you have found a trove of old treasure, and you want to hide it from us. Go with us, show it to us, and share it with us so that we can relieve you of what you have found. And if you do not do that, we will bring you to the ruler and give you to him and he will kill you.

When he heard their words, he was astonished and said, I have fallen into everything I guarded against. Then they said, O youth, by God, you are not able to conceal what you have found. Do not think to yourself that your difficulty will disappear. Yamlikha began not to know what to say to them and what to answer them, and he was so afraid that he could not answer. When they saw him not talking, they took his garment and wrapped it around his neck and began leading him through the lanes of the city by the collar until he heard someone say, A man who has a treasure has been taken. The people of the city gathered to him, great and small, and started to look at him and say, By God, this youth is not of this city. We have never seen him before. We do not know him.

Yamlikha did not know what to say to them in response to what he heard from them. So when the people of the city gathered around him, he grew afraid, became silent, and would not speak. If he said he was of the city, he would not be believed, yet he was certain that his father and his brothers were in the city and that he was reckoned among the most important people of the city, and that they would come to him when they heard. He had been certain last night that he had known many of the people, and today he knew no one.

While he was standing like a confused person looking to see when some of his people would come, his father or some of his brothers, they took him and went with him to the heads of the city and its two managers who governed its affairs. They were two righteous men. The name of one of them was Ariyus and the name of the other was Astiyus. When he was taken to them, he thought that he would be taken to Decius the tyrant, the king from whom he fled, and he began to turn from right to left. The people began to mock him like a madman is mocked, and Yamlikha began to cry. Then he raised his head to heaven and to God and said, O God, God of the Heavens and the Earth, give me a spirit from you today to support me with this tyrant, and he began weeping and saying to himself, I am separated from my brothers! Would that they knew what I have encountered. I am being taken to Decius the tyrant. If they knew, they would come and we would stand together before Decius, for we pledged to be together, not associating anything with God and not being ungrateful and not worshiping idols instead of God. Separated from them, they will not see me, and I will not ever see them. We are pledged not to be separated in life or death. Would that I knew what he will do with me, whether he will kill me or not. Thus Yamlikha said to himself, according to what he told his companions when he returned to them.

Then he came to the two righteous ones, Ariyus and Astiyus. When Yamlikha saw that he was not being taken to Decius, he got hold of himself and his weeping subsided. Ariyus and Astiyus took the coin, looked at it, and marveled at it. Then one of them said, Where is the trove which you found, O youth. This coin bears witness against you that you have found a trove. Yamlikha said to the two of them, I did not find a trove; this coin is a coin of my father's and the legend is of this city and its mint. But, by God, I do not know what state I am in, and I do not know what to say to you. One of them said to him, Where are you from? Yamlikha said to him, I do not know. I thought that I was from the people of this city. They said, Who is your father and who knows you? So he told them the name of his father, but no one was found who knew him, nor was his father found. So one of them said to him, You are a liar; you have not told us the truth.

Yamlikha did not know what to say to them except to drop his gaze to the ground. Some of the people around him said, This man is mad. Others said, He is not mad but pretends to be foolish to escape from you. One of them said to him, looking at him with a stern glance, Do you think that if you appear mad that we will send you away and believe you that this coin is of your father's property? The legend and the mint on this coin is more than three hundred years old, and you are a young man. Do you think you can lie to us just because you see we are graybeards, and around us are all chiefs of the city and the ones of its affairs? I think I will punish you with a harsh punishment, and then I will bind you until you make known the trove you have found.

When he said that, Yamlikha said, Tell me something I will ask you about, and if you do, I will tell you the truth about what is with me. Have you seen what Decius the king who was here in this city last evening did? A man said to him, There is no one on the face of the earth whose name is Decius. And there has not been except for a king who was destroyed a long time ago and after whom many ages perished.

Yamlikha said to him, By God, I am confused, and no one believes what I say. I know that we fled the tyrant Decius, and I saw him last evening when I entered the city of Ephesus, but I do not know whether this is the city of Ephesus or not. Go with me to the cave which is in the mountain of Pangloss, and I will show you my companion.

When Ariyus heard what Yamlikha was saying, he said, O people, perhaps this is one of God's signs which He has given you by the hands of this youth. So come with us and with him so that he can show you his companions as he said. Ariyus and Astiyus went out with him, and the people of the city, great and small, went with him toward the Companions of the Cave in order to look at them.

When the youths of the cave saw Yamlikha, whom they had put in charge of their food and drink, they thought that he had been taken and given to the king, Decius, from whom they had fled. While they were thinking that and being afraid, they heard voices. A clamor appeared around them, and they thought messengers from the tyrant Decius had been sent to them to bring them to him. When they heard that, they began to pray, wish each other peace, and commend the spirit to one another, saying, Go with us. We will come to our brother Yamlikha, for he is now in the hands of the tyrant Decius, waiting for us to come to him.

While they were sitting in the middle of the cave saying this, they did not see anyone but Ariyus and his companion stopped at the door of the cave. Yamlikha came in to them, crying. When they saw his crying, they cried with him. Then they asked him about his condition, and he told them the story and narrated the report, all of it, and they knew that they had been sleeping at God's command for all that time and were awakened to be signs to the people, a sign of the resurrection, and to inform them that the Hour was coming of which there is no doubt.

Then Ariyus entered, and while he stood at the door of the cave, he saw the coffin of brass sealed with a silver seal. He called the notables of the city and opened the coffin in their presence. They found in it two tablets of lead with writing on them, and he read: Maksilmina, Yamlikha, Martunus, Kustunus, Yuburus, Yakrunus, Yatbiyunus, and Qalush were youths who fled from king Decius the tyrant, fearing that he would cause them to apostatize. So they entered this cave. When he was told of its location, he ordered that the cave be closed with stone. We have written about their situation and story to inform him who comes after what happened.

When they read this, they marveled, and praised God who showed them the sign which He sent to them. They raised their voices in praise of God. Then they went in to the youths of the cave and found them sitting with resplendent faces, their clothes in ruins. Ariyus fell down, and his companions with him, prostrating and praising God, who showed them one of His signs. Then they talked with one another and told the youths whom they met who had fled from the king Decius the tyrant that Ariyus and his companion had sent a letter to the righteous king Theodosius that he should hurry: Perhaps you will see a sign which God has placed in your kingdom and made as a light for the world and a proof of the resurrection. So hurry to the youths whom God sent who have been dead for more than three hundred years.

When the report came to Theodosius, he got up from his couch. His mind was restored to him, grief left him, and he returned to God, the Mighty and the Powerful. He said, Praise be to you, O God, Lord of the Heavens and the Earth. I serve you and praise you and laud you. You have been patient with me and granted me mercy. The light which you gave to my ancestors and the righteous servant, Constantine, has not been extinguished. When he announced the event to the people of the city, they rode with him and traveled with him until they came to the city of Ephesus, and the people of the city met them and took them to the cave.

When the youths saw Theodosius, they were glad, and fell down prostrating on their faces. Theodosius raised them up to their feet and embraced them and wept, and they were standing before him on the ground, praising God and lauding Him, while he was saying, There is nothing like this since the disciples saw the Messiah. He said, God has comforted you, and it is as if you had been called forth from the grave. A youth said to Theodosius, We give you peace. Peace be upon you and the mercy of God. May God preserve you and preserve your kingdom in peace. We seek refuge for you in God from the evil of Jinn and men. May He grant you a life of love and deliverance from that which goes on in the hearts of men so that nothing will be known but grace.

While he was standing there, suddenly they returned to their beds and slept, and God took their souls by His command. The king stood with them and put his cloak on them and ordered that a coffin of gold be put for each man. When it was evening and he slept, they came to him in a dream and said, We were not created of gold and silver, but we were created of dust, and to dust we return. So leave us as we were in the cave on the dust so God can resurrect us from it. So the king ordered coffins of teak, and they put them in them. When they left them, God veiled them with dread, and no one was able to go in to them. The king ordered their cave to be a place of worship in which to pray, and set for them a great feast and ordered that every year it happen. This is the story of the Companions of the Cave.

Sources

at-Tabari, *Ta'rîkh* 776–778
at-Tabari, *Tafsîr* 15:199–204, 15:217–222
Al-Baghdadi 3:186, 3:188

Jonah

Jonah is a problematic prophet in the biblical tradition because of his reluctance to continue the office after the folk of Nineveh repent and because of his fleeing from God. In the *Kitâb al-Mubtada⁾*, Jonah is said to have vowed never to return to his people "as a liar," because he promised their destruction, which was averted by God's acceptance of their repentance. The proximate cause of Jonah's anger is said to be the Devil, but a larger issue is raised.

The Quran [Q 46:35 with Q 68:48] enjoins Muhammad to be stout of heart and steadfast, not like Jonah. Jonah is described as too narrow of frame to bear the burden of the prophethood, pictured as some kind of weighty mantle. He cast it off and ran fleeing from it. Ibn Ishaq has chosen once again to portray the very human nature of the prophets. We know from other stories that prophets are chosen before their birth and are guided by God throughout their lives. How, then, could a prophet go against the will of God? Muhammad himself committed several errors, or lapses, as when he recognized the three pre-Islamic goddesses as intercessors or when he promised Quranic inspiration without seeking God's permission. One gets a sense that Muhammad was sorely tried by the rejection of his message, and the humanity of Jonah is a reminder that God has chosen humans rather than angels to bear his message to mankind.

This story is placed in the section after Jesus because Jonah's father is thought by some Muslims to be Matthew (Mattai) rather than the biblical Amittai. Notwithstanding that, many of the details parallel Jewish sources; for example, Jonah's hearing the voices of the angels while in the belly of the fish, which is reflective of the heavenly court deciding Jonah's fate. (see *Midrash Jonah*).

Text
In the name of God, the Merciful and the Compassionate
Yazid b. Ziyyad reported on the authority of ꜥAbdullah b. Abu Salamah, who got it from Saꜥid b. Jubayr, that Ibn ꜥAbbas said, God, the Most High, sent Jonah to the people of his town, and they opposed what he brought to them and resisted him. When they did that, God revealed to him: I am going to send them a punishment on such-and-such a day, so go from their midst, and tell the townspeople what punishment God has promised them. They said, Keep him alive. If he goes out of your midst, then what He has promised you is so.

When it was the night before the promised punishment was to come, Jonah set out at nightfall with the people behind him keeping watch. He left the town, went to some open land, and kept away from every beast and its off-spring. Then the townspeople cried out to God and sought to speak with Him, and God spoke to them. Meanwhile Jonah was waiting for the report of the town and its people. A passerby came, and Jonah said, What did the people of the town do? He said, When their prophet left their midst, they knew that he had told them the truth about the punishment he had promised them, so they cried out to God and repented to Him, and He accepted it from them.

Jonah was angry at that and said, By God, I will not return to them as a liar, ever! I promised them a punishment on that day, and then it is turned from them. Anger passed over his face, and the Devil caused him to make a mistake.

Rabi'ah b. Abu 'Abd ar-Rahman reported that Wahb b. Munabbih the Ye-menite said, I heard that Jonah, the son of Amittai, was a righteous servant but was narrow of frame, so that when the weight of prophethood came on him, he could only bear it a little, breaking under it. So Jonah threw it in front of him and went fleeing from it. God said to His prophet, may the prayers and peace of God be upon him, "Have patience as the stout of heart of the mes-sengers had patience, and be patient for the judgment of your Lord, and do not be like one of the fish" [Q 46:35 with 68:48], that is, do not cast off my command as Jonah cast it off. This refers to God's words which said that Jonah went from his people angry at his Lord. This is a guide for those who turn their attention to the commentary on His words, "And he thought we had no power over him" [Q 21:87], meaning Jonah who went away from his peo-ple angry. It is asserted that Jonah's townsfolk did what they did unaware that a prophet of the Lord would be annoyed and would regard their actions as important. Jonah was angry at their chief and had gone away from his people angry, for they had done a serious thing which they had disavowed. That is the reason that those who say that Jonah went away angry from his Lord differ about the reason for his departure. Some of them say that he only did what he did because of an aversion to being among a people who had put him to the test. Others say that it was because of the discrepancy about what he had promised them and their being spared, and he did not know the reason that the trial was lifted from them. Some of those who said this said that there were those among his people who would kill anyone who tested by means of a lie, so perhaps they would kill him because of his promise of punishment and its not coming down on them as he had promised.

'Abdullah b. Rafi', a client of Umm Salamah, the wife of the Prophet, may the prayers and peace of God be upon him, said, I heard Abu Hurayrah say-ing, The Messenger of God, may the prayers and peace of God be upon him, asserted that when God wished to imprison Jonah in the belly of the fish, God inspired the fish to take him and not harm his flesh or break his bones. So it took him and sank down with him to his dwelling place in the sea. When he arrived at the bottom of the sea, Jonah heard a noise, and he said to himself, What is this? God inspired him while he was in the belly of the fish, and he heard angels praising Him. They said, O our Lord, we hear a weak voice in a faraway place. God said, that is my servant Jonah, who was rebellious to me, and I have imprisoned him in the belly of a fish in the sea. They said, Is that the righteous servant from whom there used to ascend good deeds to you every night and day? He said, Yes. So they intervened for him, and God ordered the fish to cast Jonah up on the shore, as He said. He was emaciated, and his emaciation was as God described: the fish cast him on the shore as a newborn child without flesh and with broken bones.

Sources

at-Tabari, *Ta'rîkh* 784–785, 788–789
at-Tabari, *Tafsîr* 17:76–77, 17:81, 23:102

The Three Messengers

This story glosses chapter 36 of the Quran with the story of a humble, pious believer named Habib. Because of the mention of a tyrant named Antiochus, the story seems to be set in the time of the Maccabees, but the historical details do not provide sufficient information to so ground it. Instead, the story seems almost allegorical. Indeed, some Muslim commentators on the Quran regard the chapter's title, "Ya Sin," as standing for "Ya Insan," "O Mankind." Habib's piety and martyrdom earn him the ultimate reward: being assumed into Paradise alive. Although this story is short, it has some of the important features of a well-developed martyrology. The reader's voyeuristic interests are met by the gruesome description of Habib's martyrdom, while the spiritual senses are rewarded with the triumph of good over evil.

Text
In the name of God, the Merciful and the Compassionate
Both Kaʿb al-Ahbar and Wahb b. Munabbih the Yemenite said that there was a man of Antioch whose name was Habib who worked with silk. He was a thin man who had leprosy. His house was at one of the gates of the city, far away. He was a believer, a person of righteousness, gathering his earnings when it was evening, according to that which they say, dividing them in half, feeding his household with half and giving half as alms. He was not grieved by his disease or his work or his weakness because of the purity of his heart and the upright nature of his disposition. The city he was in, Antioch, had a Pharaoh called Antiochus, the son of Antiochus, the son of Antiochus, who worshiped idols and was a polytheist. God sent three messengers to him: Sadiq, Saduq, and Shalum. God presented two of them to Antiochus and to the people of the city, who denied them. Then God sent them a third.

When the messengers invited and called Antiochus to the command of God and to comply with that to which he was ordained, he denounced their religion and what they were doing. He said to them, "We augur ill of you; if you do not cease, we will curse you and a dreadful punishment will overtake you. [The messengers] said, Your omens be with you; is it because you are reminded? No, you are a fractious people" [Q 36:18–19].

When he and his people had decided to kill the messengers, the news reached Habib at the farthest gate of the city, and he came running to them, invoking the name of God and calling them to follow the messengers. He said,

"O people . . . up to His words . . . and they are rightly guided" [Q 36:20–21]. That is, they do not ask you for any of your money for the guidance they have brought. They are advisers to you; so follow them and be rightly guided. Then he argued against their idol worship and revealed his religion and the worship of his Lord and told them that no other deities offered help or harm. He said, "Why should I not serve Him . . . up to His words . . . So hear me" [Q 36:22–25]. That is, I believe in your Lord whom you deny, so hear my voice.

When he said that to them, they jumped on him as one man. They killed him because of his weakened condition and his disease, and no one kept away from him. It was reported on the authority of some of the Companions that ʿAbdullah b. Masʿud used to say, They trampled him with their feet until his windpipe came out his anus. God said to him, "Enter Paradise" [Q 36:26], so he entered it alive, drawing sustenance there, God having removed his sickness and grief. When he arrived at the mercy of God, His Garden, and His honor, he said, "Would that my people . . . up to His words . . . one of the honored ones" [Q 36:26–27].

God became so angry at their treatment of him that He destroyed them completely, taking vengeance for what they had regarded as fair game. He said, "We did not send . . . up to His words . . . We never send down" [Q 36:28], saying, We did not inflict them with a group, that is, something easier than that for us. "It was but one shout and they were extinct" [Q 36:29]. God destroyed that king and the people of Antioch, and they became extinct on the face of the earth, and none remained of them.

Sources

at-Tabari, *Taʾrikh* 790–791, 791–793
at-Tabari, *Tafsîr* 22:156, 22:158, 22:159, 22:160, 22:161

Samson

Samson is not mentioned in the Quran, which raises an issue of why his story is included in the *Kitâb al-Mubtada*. It is clear that Ibn Ishaq generally knew the canon of biblical prophetic stories and that he had direct and indirect access to extrabiblical literature. Other prophets and biblical figures are not mentioned in the Quran, yet they do not appear in Ibn Ishaq's work. While the answer is not completely clear, it appears that the story of Samson offers a good measure of temptation, sin, repentance, and deliverance.

The story of Samson in the *Kitâb al-Mubtada* is very abstract. We have little sense of when and where Samson lived. But we do see his encounter with temptation in the form of "his woman." The woman in this story is unidentified, a kind of Everywoman, whose actions replicate the sins of Eve. Through repentance and calling on the strength of God, Samson is able to triumph over evil and destroy the enemy.

Some of the details of the story fit into an Arabian context, notably the change to a camel's jawbone. But the rabbis are familiar with the legend of the sweet water coming from the jawbone (*Numbers Rabba* 9.24). There are insufficient details, however, to definitely identify a specific parallel.

Text
In the name of God, the Merciful and the Compassionate

Among the people of the towns of Rome was one whom God had guided to His way while the rest of the inhabitants remained polytheists. Al-Mughirah b. Abu Labid reported that Wahb b. Munabbih the Yemenite said that Samson was a Muslim among them, and his mother made him consecrated to God. He dwelt with townsfolk who were plytheists and worshippers of idols, while his home was but a few miles away. He used to raid them alone and fight them in the name of God, causing them losses. They had things he needed, so he would kill, take prisoners, and attack their property. When he would attack them, he would attack with the jawbone of a camel. Then while they fought and he became thirsty and tired, sweet water would burst forth from a rock in the jawbone. He would drink from it until he was satisfied. He had been given strength, and he did not rely on iron weapons or anything like that. With all of that, he warred against them in the way of God, raided them, and got goods from them, and they were unable to do anything against him, so they said, You will not be able to go against him unless you get to his woman.

They went to his woman and made her a proposition. She said, Yes, I will bind him for you. So they gave her a stout rope and said, When he is asleep, bind his hand to his neck with that rope so that we can come to him and take him. When he slept, she tied his hand to his neck with the rope. When he started pulling it with his hand, it pulled from his neck. He said to her, Why did you do this? She said, I am testing your strength. I have never seen anyone like you. So she sent to them: I have tied him with the rope, and nothing avails. So they sent her a shackle of iron and said, When he sleeps, put it on his neck. So when he slept, she placed it on his neck and made it fast. When he tried to pull, it fell off his hand and neck. He said to her, Why have you done this? She said, I am testing your strength. I have never seen anyone like you in the world, O Samson. Is there anything in the world which will overcome you? He said, No, except one thing. She said, What is it? He said, I will not tell you. But she would not stop asking him about it.

Now Samson had a lot of hair. He said to her, Woe to you. My mother made me as a pledge to God, and nothing will overcome me and nothing will restrain me except my hair. So when he slept, she tied his hand to his neck with the hair of his head, and that bound him. She sent to the people, and they came, took him off, cut off his nose and his ears, put out his eyes, and threw him to the people in the midst of a tower. The tower had columns, and their king was on the uppermost part looking with the people at Samson and what was being done to him. Samson called on God to give him power over them because they had mutilated and fallen on him. So Samson was ordered to take two of the columns of the tower on which were the king and his people and pull them. He pulled them, and God returned his sight to him and restored his body. The tower fell with the king and those of the people on it, and they were destroyed in the wreckage.

Source

at-Tabari, *Ta'rīkh* 793–795

George

With the story of George we come to the last of the stories of prophets who came prior to Muhammad. We are brought relatively close to the time of the beginning of Islam, having started with creation. While George is not mentioned in the Quran, his story shows the virtues of patient endurance, strength of character, humanity, and anger, all of which characterize the prophets and messengers said to have been chosen by God.

The story of George is the story of the martyr St. George Megalomartyros, who opposed the Roman emperor Diocletian (245–313 C.E.). Many legends are associated with St. George, and the inclusion of this piece of martyrology indicates the popularity of the genre even outside its original Christian environment. In this form it was probably an important piece in the repertory of the storyteller preachers who would entertain the crowds with the lurid details of punishment and torture in a time before television made that a standard fare. Such descriptions were regarded as morally justified because they provided edification by example of the patient sufferer in the way of God (cf. the story of Job).

For Ibn Ishaq the story of George is the story of a messenger from God. George shares the experience of trial and torment with other messengers and prophets, and is aided by angels, as was Abraham. He is a prophet of destruction, like Noah, Hud, and Shuʿayb, who calls down God's anger after his people have rejected the clear proofs of God's power through his repeated resurrection. He bests the emperor's magicians, as did Moses, and, indeed, Diocletian is called a Pharaoh in the test.

Text
In the name of God, the Merciful and the Compassionate
According to what has been told, George was a righteous servant of God living in Palestine. He belonged to the remnant of the Companions of Jesus, the son of Mary. He was a trader, plying his trade to gain wealth and returning the surplus to the poor. Once he took goods to the king in Mosul. Wahb b. Munabbih and other scholars said that Diocletian was in Mosul. He was the king of all of Syria and was such a wild tyrant that only God could restrain him.

George was a righteous believer, keeping his belief secret along with others who also concealed their belief. They continued a tradition from the last of the

231

disciples and had heard them and learned from them. Sometimes George would have a great deal of money, would trade a lot, and would give much to charity. Then a turn of fate would come on him, and none of his money would remain, and he would become poor. Then fortune would strike, and he would get double what he had had. This was his luck with money. But he was always seeking money, prospering, acquiring it for charity, because the poor were dearer to him than wealth. And he would not trust the friendship of the polytheists, fearing that they would turn him away from his religion and cause him to apostatize.

George set out for the king of Mosul with some money he wished to give the king so that he would not give it to one of the other kings who had authority over him. So George came to the king of Mosul, appeared in his court, and found the notables of his people and their kings with him. The king had lit a fire and brought out various instruments of torture with which he would torture those who opposed him. The king called for an idol called Apollo, set it up, and the people would make a display before it. He who did not prostrate before it was thrown into the fire and tortured with instruments of punishment.

When George saw what the king was doing, he was disgusted by it. It was distressing to him, and he resolved to resist. God put loathing and belligerence in his soul. So he took the money which he had wished to give to the king and divided it among the people of his own religion until it was gone. He hated to use money and wished to resist by himself. He approached the king with the greatest anger and distress and said to him, Know that you are a slave, owned, and you do not own anything or anyone yourself, and that a Lord is above you who is the one who owns you and others. He is the one who created you and gave you food. He is the one who gives you life and death, harms and helps you. You have been turning to one of His creations. He said to it, Be, and it became dumb, not speaking or seeing or hearing or harming or helping, and it will not make you independent from God in any way. You decorate it with gold and silver in order to test the people. Then you worship it instead of God, tyrannize those who worship God, and you call on it as your lord. Thus George spoke to the king, magnifying God and praising Him and informing the king about the idol and that he would not be saved by its worship.

The king answered by asking him who he was and where he came from. George answered, I am a servant of God, the son of His servant, and the son of His community. I am humbled by His worship, and I am as poor as the dust from which I was created and to which I will return. George told him what brought him to him, his circumstance, and that he, George, called on the king to worship God and abandon the worship of idols. The king invited George to the worship of the idol which he worshiped. He said, If your Lord is as you assert, and if He is the King of Kings, as you say, then let His marks be seen on you as you see my signs on those kings of my people around me.

George answered him by glorifying God and exalting His authority. According to what was said, George said to the king, What about the case of Tranquilinus? What did he get from your association, even though he was one of the greatest of your people? And Elijah; what did Elijah get from the friendship of God? Elijah started out as a man, eating food and walking in the markets, and the honor of God did not come to him until he sprouted wings. God dressed him in light and he became part human, part angel, part heavenly, part earthly, flying among the angels. Tell me, what do you do with Magnentius? He got nothing from your association although he was a great man. And what of the Messiah, the son of Mary, and what did he get from the friendship of God? God preferred him over other men of the universe and made him and his mother signs for the discerning. Then George mentioned what honors God had given the Messiah. He also said, Tell me, what about the mother of this good spirit whom God chose for His Word, purified her for His spirit and made her preeminent over other mothers? What about her? What did Jezebel get from God and what from you? When she was one of your adherents and of your community, God exposed her among the great of her kingdom so that dogs jumped at her in her house, snapped at her flesh and lapped her blood, and the fox and the hyena pulled her limbs. What about Mary, the daughter of ʿImran, and what she got from her friendship with God?

The king said to him, You tell me about things of which I have no knowledge. Bring me the two men you mentioned so that I can look at them and consider them, for I deny that they are human.

George said to him, Denial only comes to you from heedlessness, by God. As for the two men, you will not see them, and they will not see you, unless you do as they did and occupy their place.

The king said to him, We forgive you. Explain your lie to us, because you have boasted of things that you are incapable of, and you have not brought proof. Then the king gave George the choice between punishment and prostration to Apollo so he could reward him. George said to him, If Apollo were the one who elevated heaven and enumerated all things like the power of God, you would have done right and given me good advice. But since that is not so, get away, O unclean accursed one!

When the king heard him revile him and his gods, he became very angry and called for a piece of wood. It was set up to be used for punishment, and George was attached to it. Combs of iron were brought, and his body was scraped with them so that his skin and flesh were lacerated, the fissures being moistened with vinegar and mustard. When the king saw that this did not kill him, he called for six pegs of iron, heated them until they were like fire, and ordered them driven into George's head until his brains flowed from him. When the king saw that that did not kill him, he ordered a basin of brass, heated it until it was like fire, put him in it, covered him up, and did not stop until it was cold. When the king saw that that did not kill him, he called to him, saying, Don't you find this punishment dreadful?

George said to him, Did I not tell you that you have a Lord who is closer to you than your soul? He said, Yes, you told me. He said, He is the one who removes your punishment from me and gives me the patience to remonstrate against you. When George said this, the king became certain of evil and feared for himself and his kingdom. He decided to put George in prison forever and said to his notables, If you treat him kindly, he will speak to the people and make them hostile to you. But let him be punished in prison, keeping him from talking with the people. Thus the king commanded, and George was thrown in prison on his face. His hands and feet were shackled with four shackles of iron in each corner. Then the king ordered a column of marble put on his back, the weight of which neither seven nor fourteen men could lift, but it took eighteen to pick it up. George lasted for a whole day shackled under the stone.

When night came, God sent George an angel, which was the first time he was supported by angels and was the first of his inspirations. The angel took away the stone, removed the shackles from his hands and feet, fed him, gave him drink, made him happy and consoled him. In the morning it took him out of prison and said to him, George, go up against your enemy and fight him; in God is the truth of His struggle. God says to you, Be joyful and persevering. I will try my enemy with you. These seven years will he torture you and kill you, and you will weaken four times. Each time I will return your soul to you. When the fourth time comes, I will accept your spirit and give you your reward, and those who remain will know nothing but that George is at their heads inviting them to God.

The king said to George, Are you George? He said, Yes. The king said, Who got you out of prison? George said, He took me out whose authority is above your authority. When George said that, the king was filled with ire, and he called for all of the kinds of instruments of torture, omitting none. When George saw them, apprehension filled his soul; then he addressed his soul, reproving it at the top of his voice while they were listening. When he finished reproving his soul, they put him between two boards, put a sword on the top of his head and sawed with it until it came out his legs, and he was in two pieces. Then they took the two pieces and cut them up. The king had seven savage lions in a pit, which were one kind of his instruments of torture. He threw George's body in to them. When it fell near them, God commanded the lions, and they bowed their heads and necks and stood on their claws, keeping him from harm. George passed the day like that, dead, and it was his first death. When night came, God gathered together his body piece by piece until it was whole. Then he returned his soul to him and sent an angel to him. It took him out of the bottom of the pit, fed him, gave him drink, made him happy and strengthened him.

When it was morning, the angel said to him, O George. George said, At your service. The angel said, Know that the power by which Adam was created from dust is that which brought you out from the bottom of the pit, so meet your enemy and fight him, for in God is the truth of His struggle. Die the death of the persevering.

The people did not know that George approached because they were busy with making festivities, rejoicing in George's death. When they saw George approaching, they said, What is this that resembles George? It is as though it is he. The king said, There is no doubt that it is not George since you saw him fall into oblivion.

George said, Nay, in truth I am he. You are evil people; you kill and torture; God has the truth and more mercy than you. He resurrected me and returned my spirit to me. Come forward to this great Lord who shows you what He shows you.

When George said that to them, they approached one another and said, This is a magician who has enchanted your hands and eyes. So they gathered the magicians of their country, and when the magicians came, the king said to the greatest of them, Show me your greatest magic which will dispel my anxiety. He said to him, Give me a bull. When it was brought to him, he blew in one of its ears, and it split in two. Then he blew in the other, and it became two bulls. Then he ordered a seed, and he plowed and sowed, and a plant grew and ripened, and he harvested it and then threshed, winnowed, ground, kneaded, made bread, and ate it in one hour while they watched. The king said to him, Are you able to transform George into an animal for me? The magician said, What sort of an animal shall I make him for you? He said, A dog. He said, Bring me a basin of water. When it was brought to him, he blew an incantation into it. Then he said to the king, Make him drink it. So George drank it to the last, and when he had finished with it, the magician said to him, How did you find it? George said, I found it good; I was thirsty. God was kind to me with this drink, and He strengthened me over you by it. When George said that to him, the magician approached the king and said to him, Know, O king, that you, if you were to stand up to a man like yourself, you would overcome him, but you are up against a giant of heaven. He is an angel who will not be moved.

A poor woman who heard about George and the marvels he did came to him while he was in the midst of his trials and said to him, O George, I am a poor woman without any money and no livelihood except a bull I plow with, and it died. I have come to you so that you will have mercy on me and ask God to make my bull come alive. George's eyes flowed with tears, and he called on God to make the bull come alive. He gave her a stick and said, Go to your bull and strike him with this stick and say to him, Live, with the permission of God. She said, O George, my bull died several days ago, the wild beasts devoured it, and it will take several days to return. He said, Even if you find only one tooth, strike it with the stick, and it will get up with the permission of God. So she took the stick and went to the place of the bull's death. The first thing that she found of her bull was one of its horns and a hair of its tail. So she gathered them together and struck them with the stick which George had given her, said as he had commanded her, and her bull came to life. She put it to work, and the report of that came to the people.

When the magician said to the king what he said, one of the king's companions who was the most powerful after the king said, O you people, hear what I tell you. They said, Yes, speak. he said, You have asked a magician about this man, and you asserted that he enchanted your hands and your eyes. He showed you that you tortured him, but your torture did not affect him, and he showed you that you killed him, but he did not die. Have you ever seen magic so powerful that it wards off death or revives the dead? Then he told them of George's actions and their actions with him and about what he did with the bull and its mistress, and he advanced all of that as an argument to them. They said to the companion, Your speech is the speech of a man who is inclined toward him. He said, I have not ceased being amazed by him since I saw what I saw of him. They said, Well, perhaps he has enchanted you. He said, No, I believe, and I testify to God that I am free of what you worship.

The king and his companions came to him with daggers, cut out his tongue, and it did not take long for him to die. They said, Plague struck him, and God took him quickly before he spoke. When the people heard of his death, it frightened them, and they kept it a secret. When George saw that they were keeping it a secret, he announced it aloud to the people, uncovered the matter for them, and told them his words. Four thousand followed the martyr's belief because of George's words. They said, He spoke truly, and what he said is pleasing. May God be merciful to him. Then the king made for them, bound them, and did not stop torturing and killing them until he annihilated them. When he finished with them, he turned to George and said to him, Why not call on your Lord so that He will resurrect these comrades of yours who were killed because of you? George said to him, He only let it happen to reward them.

One of the notables who was called Majlitis said, O George, you assert that your God is the one who started creation and then continues it. I will ask you something that, if your God does it, I will believe in you and testify that you are right and grant you these people of mine. Under us are fourteen seats as you see and a table between us on which are goblets and bowls, and all are made of dry wood from trees of different kinds. Call on your Lord to grow these vessels and these seats and this table as He created them the first time so that they return green, and we will know each wood by its color, its leaf, its flower, and its fruit.

George said to him, You have asked a difficult thing for me, but an easy thing for God. So he called on his Lord, and they had not left their places when the seats and the vessels turned green. The veins became soft, they put on bast, branched, sprouted leaves, flowers, and fruit until they knew each wood by its name, its color, its flower, and its fruit. WHen they looked at it, Majlitis, who had promised what he had promised, stood before the king and said, I will punish this magician for you with a punishment which will drive him from his plots. So he got some brass and fashioned it in the shape of a wide, hollow bull. Then he stuffed it with naphtha, lead, sulfur, and arsenic. Then he put George and the stuffing inside it and lit a fire under the image. It did not stop burning until the image was burned up, and everything in it was melted and mixed up, and George died in its inside.

When George died, God sent a raging wind which filled the heavens with black clouds in which were unceasing thunder, lightning, and thunderbolts. God sent cyclones which filled and land, raging and black, until what was between heaven and earth became black and dark. They remained for several days, confused in the darkness, not able to distinguish between night and day. God sent Michael, who bore up the image which contained George. He struck the earth one blow with it and frightened all the people of Syria, all of them hearing it at one time. They fell on their faces, dumbfounded from the strength of the terror. The image broke, and out of it came George alive. And when he stood speaking to them, the darkness was taken off and what was between heaven and earth glowed, and their souls returned to them.

A man called Tarqablina said to him, O George, we do not know whether you or your Lord does these marvels. If He is the one who does them, then call on Him to resurrect our dead. In these graves which you see are dead whom we know and those who died before our time. Call on Him to resurrect them so they return as they were, and we can talk with them and know whom we knew of them, and the ones we do not know can tell us their story.

George said, You know that God will not forgive you for this and will only show you these marvels to end this argument. You will be answerable for His anger. Then George ordered the graves dug up, which contained bones, mortal remains, and rotten corpses. Then he began to pray, and before they could move, they saw seventeen persons, nine men, five women, and three children, of which the oldest was ancient. George said to him, O you old man, what is your name? He said, My name is Yubil. George said, When did you die? He said, In such-and-such a time, and they calculated that he had died four hundred years before. When the king and his companions saw that, they said, The only torture left is to torture him with hunger and thirst. So they tortured him with that.

They went to the house of an old woman which was strongly fortified. She had a son who was blind, dumb, and lame. They imprisoned George in her house and would not allow any food or drink. When hunger reached him, he said to the old woman, Do you have any food or drink? She said, No, by Him who is sworn by, we have not known food or drink since such-and-such a time. I will go out and get you something. George said to her, Do you know God? She said to him, Yes. He said, Do you worship Him? She said, No. So he invited her to God; she believed in him and went out seeking something for him.

In her house was a pillar of dry wood holding up a beam of the house. George began to pray, and instantly the pillar turned green and sprouted all the kinds of edible fruit known or wished for. And a branch appeared on the pillar atop the house, shading it and what was around it. When the old woman approached, there was plenty to eat. And as she saw what happened in her house, she said, I believe in Him who feeds you in the house of hunger. Pray to this Lord to heal my son. George said, Bring him near me. So she brought him near. George spit in his eyes and he saw, and he blew in his ears and he heard. She said, Soften his tongue and his legs, may God be merciful to you. George said, Postpone that, for he has a great day coming.

The king went out walking in the city, and when he saw the tree, he said to his companions, I see a tree in a place I do not know one. They said, This tree sprouted for that magician whom you wished to punish with hunger. Whenever he wishes, he eats his fill of it, as does the poor woman, and he cured her son for her. So the king ordered that the house be razed and the tree cut. When they went to cut it, God dried it up as before, and they left it alone.

The king called for George, threw him on his face, made four pegs, called for a cart, loaded it with as many columns as it would bear, and put daggers and swords underneath the cart. Then he called for four oxen and hitched them to the cart with George under them, and George was cut into three pieces. Then the king ordered the pieces burned in a fire until, when ashes remained, he gave the ashes to men who scattered them in the sea. They had not moved when they heard a voice from heaven saying, O sea, God commands you to guard what is in you of this good body, for I wish to return it as it was. Then God sent winds which extracted George from the sea and brought him together until the ashes returned to a pile like they were before they were scattered, while those who scattered them were standing and not moving. Then they saw the ashes stirring up until George came out, dusty, shaking his head.

So they returned, and George returned with them. When they came to the king, they told the story of the voice which had resurrected George and the wind which had brought him together. The king said to him, O George, do you have someone better than me? If it were not for the fact that people would say that you conquered me and overcame me, I would follow you and believe in you. But if you make one prostration to Apollo or sacrifice a sheep to him, then I will do what will make you happy.

When George heard this, he resolved to destroy the idol when he went to it, hoping that when his idol was destroyed, the king would despair of it and believe in him. So George misled him and said, Yes, if you wish, take me to your idol, and I will prostrate to it and sacrifice to it. The king was happy at his words, got up, kissed his hand and feet and head, and said, I swear to you that this day will not darken nor will you pass the night except in my house, on my bed and with my family, so that you can relax and the discomforts of the torture will go from you, and the people will see your nobility with me. So the king let George go to his house and took out those who were in it, and George remained therein until, when he saw it was night, he got up praying and reciting the psalms. He had the most beautiful voice, and when the wife of the king heard him, she paid attention to him. George did not perceive her there until she was behind him, crying with him. George invited her to belief, and she believed, and he commanded her, and she kept her belief a secret.

In the morning George went out with the king to the house of the idols to prostrate to them. The old woman in whose house George had been imprisoned was told, Do you know that George is seduced, inclines toward the things of this world, and the king has encouraged him so that he has gone to the house of the idols to prostrate them? So the old woman went out reluctantly, carrying her son on her shoulder, scolding George while the people were harassing her.

When George entered the house of the idols along with the people, he saw the old woman with her son on her shoulder, nearest of the people to him. He called the son of the old woman by his name, and he answered, although he had never talked before that. Then he jumped down from the shoulder of his mother, walking on his legs, the two of them whole, and he had not set foot on the ground before that, ever. When he stopped in front of George, George said, Go and call these idols for me. They are now on a raised platform of gold, seventy-one idols which they worship along with the sun and the moon. The youth said, What do I say to the idols? George said, You say to them that George asks you and adjures you by that which created you that you come to him. When the youth said that, they approached, rolling down to George. When they stopped in front of him, he hit the earth with his foot, and they sank into it along with their seats. Iblis came out of the middle of an idol, fleeing the sinking, and when he passed George, George took hold of him by his forelock so that he bowed his head and his neck to him. George spoke to him, saying, Get away from me, O you unclean spirit and cursed creature. What is it that compels you to destroy yourself and the people with you? You know that you and your host will go to Hell. Iblis said to him, If I were given the choice between what the sun looks down on and what the night darkens and the destruction of the Children of Adam and their being led in error, even one of them, instantly I would choose the latter. The same passions and pleasures were not given to me as they were to all the rest of creation. Do you not know, O George, that God caused all the angels to prostrate to your father, Adam, so Gabriel, Michael, Israfil, and all the angels prostrated along with all the people of heaven? But I refused to prostrate, and I said, I will not bow down to this creature. I am better than he. When he said this, George let him go, and Iblis has not entered an idol since that day, fearing the sinking, and will not enter them ever, according to what they say.

The king said, O George, you misled and duped me, and you destroyed my idols. George said to him, I only did it to show and teach you that, if they were gods as you say, they would have prevented me. Where is your confidence? Woe to your gods who were not able to keep themselves from me while I am only a weak creature who does not own anything except what my Lord gives me. When George said this, the wife of the king spoke to them, and this was when she disclosed her faith to them and explained her religion to them and enumerated George's deeds for them and the lessons he had shown them. She said to them, Do not expect from this person anything but prayer. He will cause you to sink into the earth, and you will be destroyed as your idols were destroyed.

The king said to her, Woe to you, Alexandra. How quickly this magician led you in error, in one night, and I endured him for seven years, and he got nothing from me. She said to him, Do you not see God, how He gives him victory over you and gives him power over you? Salvation will be his, and the proof goes against you in every place. So he ordered that she be put on George's piece of wood on which he was suspended, and she hung there. The same comb which was applied to George was put on her, and when the pain of the torment was terrible, she said, Call on your Lord, George, to make it easier for me, for I am tormented. He said, Look above you. And when she looked above, she laughed. The king said, What are you laughing at? She said, I see two angels above me with a crown of jewels of Paradise waiting for my soul to come out. When it came out, she was adorned with that crown. Then they took her up to Paradise.

When God accepted her spirit, George began to pray, saying, O God, you are the one who honored me with this trial to give me the graces of martyrdom. O God, this is the last of my days on earth which you give me for tribulation. O God, I ask that you not accept my soul and not take me from my place until an assault and an attack comes down on this haughty people which they have not had, and that you not heal my breast and ease me while they are punishing me and torturing me. God, I ask that no one pray after me in tribulation or beseech you in my name but that you release them from it and be merciful to them and allow me to intercede for them.

George

241

When he had finished with that prayer, God rained fire on them. When they burned, they made for George, striking him with swords, angry at the strength of the burning, in order that God, the Most High, give His fourth killing as He had promised it.

When the city and all in it was burned and had become ashes, God bore it from the face of the earth. Then He put its topmost on the bottom and it remained for a long time with smoke coming from under it. No one could smell it without becoming very ill. The total of those who believed in George and were killed with him was thirty-four thousand, along with the wife of the king, may God be merciful to her.

Source

at-Tabari, *Taʾrīkh* 795–812.

Bibliography

Abbott, Nabia. *Aisha the Beloved of Muhammad*. Chicago: University of Chicago Press, 1942.

——. *Studies in Arabic Literary Papyri*, vol. 1, *Historical Texts*. University of Chicago Oriental institute Publications, 75. University of Chicago Press, 1957.

——. *Studies in Arabic Literary Papyri*, vol. 2, *Qurʾanic Commentary and Tradition*. University of Chicago Oriental Institute Publications, 76. University of Chicago Press, 1967.

Ahmad, B. *Muhammad and the Jews*. New Delhi: Vikas Press, 1979.

Amamd, Mirza Bashir. *Sources of the Sirat*. Qadian, India: Nazir Dawat-o-Tabligh, n.d.

al-ʿAsqalani, Ibn, Hajar. *Tahdhîb at-Tahdhîb*. Heyderabad, 1325–27.

Al-Azraqi, Abu-l-Walid Muhammad b. ʿAbdullah. *Kitâb ʾAkhbâr Makka*, ed. F. Wuestenfeld. Beirut: Khayyat Reprint, 1964.

Al-Baghdadi, Abu Bakr Ahmad b. ʿAli. *Taʾrîkh Baghdâd*. 14 vols. Cairo, 1931.

Al-Baghdadi, ʿAla ad-Din ʿAli b. Muhammad b. Ibrahim al-Khazan. *Lubâb at-Taʾwîl fî Maʿânî at-Tanzîl*. 4 vols. Cairo, 1955.

Al-Baladhuri, Ahmad b. Yahya. *Futûh al-Buldân*, ed. M. J. de Goeje. Leiden: Brill, 1866.

Al-Bukhari, Abu ʿAbdullah Muhammad b. Ismaʾîl. *Kitâb at-Taʾrîkh al-Kabîr*. Heyderabad: 1361–1377.

——. *Sahîh*. 9 vols. Cairo: Bulaq, 1311–13.

Al-Kisaʾ î, Muhammad b. ʿAbdullah. *Vita Prophetarum*, ed. Isaac Eisenberg. Leiden: Brill, 1922–23.

Al-Maqdisi, Abu Nasr al-Mutahhar b. Tahir. *Kitâb al-Badʾ wa-t-Taʾrîkh*, ed. Cl. Huart. Paris, 1899.

Al-Masʿudi, Abu al-Hasan ʿAli b. al-Husayn b. ʿAli. *Murûj adh-Dhahab*. 4 vols. Cairo: Dar al-Rijaʾ, 1384.

Al-Sijistani, Abu Hatim. *Kitâb al-Muʿ ammarîn*. . . . Cairo, 1961.

Al-Waqidi, Abu ʿAbdullah Muhammad b. ʿUmar. *Kitâb al-Maghâzî*, ed. M. Jones. 3 vols. London: Oxford University Press, 1966.

Andrae, T. *Mohammed: The Man and His Faith*, trans. T. Menzel. New York: Harper, 1960.

——. *Der Ursprung des Islams und das Christentum*. Uppsala and Stockholm: Almquist and Wilksells, 1926.

Arberry, A. J. "The *Sîra* in Verse." *Arabic and Islamic Studies in honor of H. A. R. Gibb*. Cambridge, MA: Harvard University Press, 1965.

At-Tabari, Abu Jaʿfar Muhammad b. Jarir. *Taʾrîkh al-Rusul wa-l-Mulûk*. M. J. de Goeje et al. 16 vols. Leiden: Brill, 1879–98.

————. *Jâmi͑ al-Bayân fi Tafsîr al-Qurʾân*. 30 vols. Cairo: Mustafa al-Halabi and Sons, 1954.

ath-Thaʿlabi, Ibn Ishaq Ahmad b. Muhammad. *Qisas al-Anbiyâʾ*. Cairo 1950.

az-Zamakhshari, Muhammad b. ʿUmar. *Tafsîr al-Kashshâf*. 4 vols. Cairo: Halabi and Sons, 1966.

Atiya, A. S. *A History of Eastern Christianity*. Notre Dame, IN.: University of Notre Dame Press, 1968.

Babylonian Talmud, The. Trans. with notes and glossary by R. I. Epstein, et al. London: Soncino Press, 1948.

Baumstark, A. "Das Problem eines vorislamischen Christlichkirchlichen Schrifttums in arabischer Sprache." *Islamica* 4 (1931): 562–75.

————. "Eine altarabische Evangelienuebersetzung aus dem Christlich-Palaestinenseben." *Zeitschrift für Semitistik* 7 (1923): 201–09.

Becker, C. H. "Christliche Polemik und islamische Dogmenbildung." *Zeitschrift für Assyriologie* 26 (1912): 175–95.

————. *Islamstudien, vom Werden und Wesen der islamischen Welt*. 2 vols. Leipzig: Quelle and Meyer, 1924–32.

————. "Prinzipielles zu Lammens' Sîrastudien." *Der Islam* 4 (1913): 263–69.

Bell, R. *Introduction to the Qurʾân*. Edinburgh: Edinburgh University Press, 1963.

————. *The Origin of Islam in Its Christian Environment*. London: Cass, 1926.

————. "Muhammad and Previous Messengers." *Muslim World* 24 (1934): 330–40.

————. "Muhammad's Pilgrimmage Proclamation." *Journal of the Royal Asiatic Society* (1937): 232–44.

Birkeland, H. *The Legend of the Opening of Muhammad's Breast*. Avhandlinger utgitt av det Norske Videnskaps-Akademi i Oslo, 2 (Hist.-filos. Klasse) 1955, no. 3.

————. *Old Muslim Opposition against Interpretation of the Koran*. Avhandlinger utgitt av det Norske Videnskaps-Akademi i Oslo, 2 (Hist.-filos. Klasse) 1955, no. 1.

Blachere, R. *Le probleme de Mahomet, essai de biographie critique du fondateur de l'Islam*. Paris: Presses Universitaires de France, 1952.

————. "Regards sur la litterature en Arabe au Ier siecle de l-Hegire." *Semitica* 6 (1956).

Bravmann, M. M. *The Spiritual Background of Early Islam*. Leiden: Brill, 1972.

Brinner, W. M. *The History of al-Tabarî*, vol. 2, *Prophets and Patriarchs*. Albany: State University of New York Press, 1987.

Brockelmann, C. *Geschichte der arabischen Literatur*, 2d ed., 2 vols. Leiden: Brill, 1943, 1949.

————. *ibid., Supplement*. 3 vols. Leiden: Brill, 1937–42.

Broennle, P. *Die Commentatoren des Ibn Ishâq und ihre Scholien*. Inaugural Dissertation, Halle, 1895.

Buhl, F. "Ein paar Beiträge zur Kritik der Geschichte Muhammeds." *Orientalische Studien Th. Noeldeke gewidmet*, 1 (1906): 7–72.

Bulliet, R. W. *Conversion to Islam in the Medieval Period*. Cambridge, MA: Harvard University Press, 1979.

Burton, J. *The Collection of the Qurʾân*. Cambridge: Cambridge University Press, 1977.

Bibliography

Caetani, L. *Annali dell'Islam*. 10 vols. Milan: University of Hoepli, 1905–26.

———. "La Biographia di Maometto." *Studi di Storia Orientale, 3*. Milan: University of Hoepli, 1914.

Carlyle, T. *The Hero as Prophet—Mahomet*. New York: Maynard Merrill and Co., 1902.

Charlesworth, J. *The Old Testament Pseudepigrapha*. Garden City, NY: Doubleday, 1983.

Cheikho, L. "Quelque legendes musulmanes anteislamique." *Actes du XVe Congres International des Orientalistes*. Copenhagen, 1908.

Cook, M. *Muhammad*. Oxford: Oxford University Press, 1983.

Coulson, N. J. *A History of Islamic Law*. Islamic Surveys 2. Edinburgh: Edinburgh University Press, 1964.

Crone, P., and M. Cook. *Hagarism*. Cambridge: Cambridge University Press, 1977.

Crone, P., and M. Hinds. *God's Caliph*. Cambridge: Cambridge University Press, 1986.

Finkel, J. "An Arabic Story of Abraham." *Hebrew Union College Annual* 12–13 (1938): 387–409.

Fischer, A. *Biographien von Gewährsmännern des Ibn Ishâq, hauptsaechlich aus adh-Dhahabî*. Leiden: Brill, 1890.

Fraenkel, S. "Der Sâmirî." *Zeitschrift der deutschen morganländischen Gesellschaft* 56 (1902): 73ff.

Friedlander, I. "Muhammedanische Geschichtskonstruktionen." *Beiträge zur Kentniss des Orients* 9 (1911): 17–34.

———. "Alexanders Zug nach dem Lebensquell und die Chadirlegende." *Archiv für Religionswissenschaft* 13 (1910): 161ff.

———. *Die Chadirlegende und der Alexanderroman*. Leipzig, 1913.

Fueck, J. W. "Ibn Sa'd." *Encyclopedia of Islam* 8:922–23.

———. *Muhammad ibn Ishâq: literarhistorische Untersuchungen*. Frankfurt a. Main, 1924.

———. "Muhammad-Persoenlichkeit und Religionsstiftung." *Saeculum* 3 (1952): 70–93.

Geiger, A. *Was hat Mohammed aus dem Judenthume aufgenommen?* New York: KTAV, rpt. 1970.

Gibb, H. A. R. "Pre-Islamic Monotheism in Arabia." *Harvard Theological Review* 55 (1962): 269–80.

Gibson, J. C. L. "John the Baptist in Muslim Writings." *Muslim World* 45 (1955): 334–45.

Ginzberg, L. *The Legends of the Jews*. 7 vols. Philadelphia: Jewish Publication Society, 1968.

Goitein, S. D. "Muhammad's Inspiration by Judaism." *Journal of Jewish Studies* 9 (1958): 149–62.

Goldziher, I. *Abhandlungen zur arabischen Philologie*. 2 vols. Leiden: Brill, 1896–99.

Bibliography

————. "Lâ Misâsa." *Revue Africaine* 268 (1908): 23ff.

————. *Muhammedanische Studien.* 2 vols. Halle, 1889. Trans. by C. R. Barber and S. M. Stern as *Muslim Studies.* 2 vols. Chicago: Aldine, 1968, 1971.

Graham, W. *Divine Word and Prophetic Word in Early Islam.* The Hague: Mouton, 1977.

Gregoire, H. "Mahomet et le Monophysisme." *Melange Charles Diehl* 1 (1930): 107–19.

Grimme, H. *Koran.* Paderborn: F. Schöningh, 1923.

Gruenbaum, M. *Neue Beitraege zur semitischen Sagenkunde.* Leiden: Brill, 1893.

Guillaume, A. "The Biography of the Prophet in Recent Research." *Islamic Quarterly* 1 (1954): 5–11.

————. *The Life of Muhammad.* Lahore: Oxford University Press, 1967.

————. "The Pictorial Background of the Qurʾân." *Annual of Leeds University Oriental Society* (1961–62): 39–59.

————. "The Version of the Gospel used in Medina circa 700 A.D." *Al-Andalus* 15 (1950): 289–96.

Hamadeh, Muhammad Maher. Muhammad the Prophet: A Selected Bibliography, University of Michigan Dissertation, 1965.

Hamidullah, M. "The Christian Monk Abu ʾAmir of Medina of the Time of the Holy Prophet." *Journal of the Pakistan Oriental Society, 7 (1958): 231–40.*

————."Two Christians of pre-Islamic Mecca, ʾUthman ibn al-Huwairith and Waraqa ibn Naufal." *Journal of the Pakistan Oriental Society,* 6 (1959): 97–103.

Heller, B. "La legende biblique dans l'Islam." *Revue des études juives* 98 (1934): 1–18.

————. "Mûsâ." *Encyclopedia of Islam* 3: 738–39.

Hirschfeld, H. *Beitraege zur Erklaerung des Koran.* Leipzig: O. Schulze, 1866.

————. *Juedische Elemente im Koran: Ein Beitrag zur Koranforschung.* Berlin, 1878.

————. *New Researches into the Composition and Exegesis of the Qoran.* London: Luzac & Co., 1902.

Hodgson, M. G. S. *The Venture of Islam.* 3 vols. Chicago: University of Chicago Press, 1974.

Horovitz, J. "Biblische Nachwirkungen in der Sira." *Der Islam* 12 (1922): 184–89.

————. "The Earliest Biographies of the Prophet and Their Authors." *Islamic Culture* 1 (1927): 535–39; 2 (1928): 22–50, 164–82, 495–526.

————. "The Growth of the Mohammed Legend," Muslim World, 10 (1920): 49–58.

————. *Jewish Proper Names and Derivatives in the Koran.* Cincinnati: Hebrew Union College, 1925.

————. *Koranische Untersuchungen.* Berlin: W. de Gruyter, 1926.

————. "Zur Muhammad-Legende." *Der Islam* 5 (1914): 41–53.

————. "Die Poetischen Einlagen der Sîra." *Islamica* 2 (1926): 308–12.

————. "Der Ursprung des Islams und das Christentum." *Orientalische Literaturzeitung* 29 (1926), col. 841–45.

Horst, H. "Israelitische Propheten im Koran." *Zeitschrift für Religions—und Geistes* 16 (1964): 42–57.

Ibn Abu Hatim, ʿAbd ar-Rahman ar-Razi. *al-Jarh wa-t-Taʿdîl.* 4 vols. Hyderabad: Dâr al-Maʿarif, 1952–53.

Ibn ʿAsakir, ʿAli b. al-Hasan. *at-Taʾrîkh al-Kabîr.* 7 vols. Damascus, 1911–12.

Ibn Chabib, R. Jacob. *ʾAgadah ʿEn Yaʿqob (En Jacob),* ed. adn trans. S. H. Glick. New York: Hebrew Publishing Co. 1921.

Ibn Hajar al-ʿAsqalani. *Tahdhîb at-Tahdhîb.* 12 vols. Hyderabad: Nizâmiyyah, 1907–09.

Ibn Hisham, Muhammad B. ʿAbd al-Malik. *Kitâb at-Tajân.* Hyderabad: Dâr al-Maʿârif, 1347.

———. *Das Leben Muhammeds,* ed. F. Wuestenfeld, 3 vols. Goettingen: Dieterich, 1860.

Ibn Ishâq, Muhammad. *Sîrat Rasûl Allâh.* 4 vols. Cairo: Al-Halabi adn Sons, 1955.

Ibn al-Kalbi, Hisham. *Kitâb al-Asnâm: The Book of Idols,* trans N. A. Faris. Princeton: Princeton University Press, 1952.

Ibn an-Nadim. *Kitâb al-Fihrist,* ed. G. Fluegel. 2 vols. Halle, 1872.

Ibn Saʿd, Muhammad. *Kitâb at-Tabaqât al-Kabîr,* ed. Sachau et al. Leiden: Brill, 1940.

Idris, H. R. "Reflexions sur Ibn Ishâq." *Studia Islamica* 17 (1962): 23–35.

Jastrow, M. *A Dictionary of the Targumim. The Talmud.* 2 vols. New York: Pardes, 1950.

Jeffery, A. *The Foreign vocabulary of the Qurʾân.* Baroda: Oriental Institute, 1938.

———. *Materials for the History of the Text of the Qurʾân.* Leiden: Brill, 1937.

———. "The Quest of the Historical Muhammad." *Muslim World* (1926): 327–48.

Jensen, P. "Das Leben Muhammeds und die David-Sage." *Islam* 12 (1922): 84–97.

Jones, J. M. B. "Ibn Ishâk." *Encyclopedia of Islam* 2d ed. 3:810–11.

Keyes, C. F. "Charisma: From Social Life to Sacred Biography." *Charisma and Sacred Biography,* ed. M. A. Williams. Journal of the American Academy of Religion Thematic Studies 48/3, 4 (1982).

Khoury, R. G. *Wahb b. Munabbih.* Wiesbaden: O. Harrasowitz, 1972.

Khoury, Th. "Die Christologie des Korans." *Zeitschrift für Missionwissenschaft und Religionswissnschaft.* (1968): 49–63.

Kister, M. J. "Haddithû ʿan banî isrâʾîla." *Israel Oriental Studies,* 2 (1972).

———. "The Massacre of the Banû Qurayza: A Re-examination of a Tradition." *Jerusalem Studies in Arabic and Islam* 8 (1986): 61–96.

———. "The Sîrah Literature." *Arabic Literature to the End of the Umayyad Period,* ed. A. F. L. Beeston et al. Cambridge: Cambridge University Press, 1983.

Levi della Vida, G. "Siʿa." *Encyclopedia of Islam* 4:472–76.

———. "Pre-Islamic Arabia." *The Arab Heritage,* ed. N. A. Faris. Princeton: Princeton University Press, 1944.

Lidzbarski, M. *De Propheticis, Quae Dicuntur, Legendis Arabicis.* Leipzig: G. Drugulini, 1893.

———. "Wer is Chadhir?" *Zeitschrift für Assyriology* 7 (1892): 104–6.

Littman, E. *Thamûd und Safâ.* Leipzig, 1940.

Bibliography

247

Louka, N. "Judaisme, Christianisme et Islam d'apres un chretien copte d'Egypte." *Orient* 15 (1960): 145–60.

Margoliouth, D. S. "The Use of the Apocrypha by Moslem Writers." *Muslim World* 5 (1915): 404–8.

Midrash Rabbah, The, ed. R. H. Freedman et al. 5 vols. London: Soncino Press, 1977.

Moubarac, Y. *Abraham dans le Coran*. Paris: J. Vrinn, 1958.

———. *Moise dans le Coran*. Paris: J. Vrinn, 1954.

Newby, G. D. "Abraha and Sennacherib: A Talmudic Parallel to the Tafsir on Surat al-Fil." *Journal of the American Oriental Society* 94 (1974): 431–37.

———. "Arabian Jewish History in the Sîrah." *Jerusalem Studies in Arabic and Islam* 7 (1968): 124–31.

———. "The Drowned Son: Midrash and Midrash Making in the Qur'an and Tafsir." *Studies in Islamic and Judaic Traditions: Papers presented at the Institute for Islamic-Judaic Studies*, University of Denver. Atlanta: Scholars Press, 1986.

———. "An Example of Coptic Literary Influence on the *Sîrah* of Ibn Ishâq." *Journal of Near Eastern Studies* 31 (1972): 22–28.

———. *A History of the Jews of Arabia*. Columbia: University of South Carolina Press, 1988.

———. "Observations About an Early Judaeo-Arabic." *Jewish Quarterly Review* (1971): 212–21.

———. "The *Sîrah* as a Source for Early Arabian Jewish History." Jerusalem Studies in Arabic and Islam 7 (1986): 121–38.

———. "*Sûrat al-'Ikhlâs*: A Reconsideration." *Orient and Occident* (1973): 127–30.

———. "*Tafsir Isra'iliyat*: The Development of Qur'an Commentary in Early Islam." *Journal of the American Academy of Religion* 47 (1979): 685–97.

Newby, G. D., and David Halperin. "Two Castrated Bulls: A Study in the Haggadah of Ka'b al-Ahbâr." *Journal of the American Oriental Society* 102, (1982).

Noeldeke, T. *Geschichte des Qorans*. Rpt. Hiblesheim: G. Olms, 2 vols., 1970.

———. *Das Leben Muhammads nach den Quellen Populaerdargestellt*. Hanover: Carl Rümpler, 1863.

———. "Die Tradition ueber das Leben Mohammeds." *Der Islam* 5 (1914): 160–70.

Ong, W. *Orality and Literacy*. New York: Methuen, 1982.

Paret, R. "At-Tabarî." *The Shorter Encyclopedia of Islam*. Leiden: Brill, 1961.

———. "Das Geschichtsbild Mohammeds." *Welt als Geschichte* (1951): 214–24.

———. *Die legendäre Maghazi Literatur*. Tübingen: Mohr, 1930.

———. "Recent European Research on the Life and Work of the Prophet Muhammad." *Journal of the Pakistan Historical Society* 6 (1958): 81–96.

Parrinder, G. *Jesus in the Qur'ân*. New York: Barnes and Noble, 1965.

Pines, S. "Al-'Îsâwiyya." *Encyclopedia of Islam* 2d ed. 4: 96.

Reynolds F. E., and D. Capps, eds. *The Biographical Process*. The Hague: Mouton, 1976.

Rippin A. "Literary Analysis of *Qurʾân, Tafsîr, and Sîra:* The Methodologies of John Wansbrough." *Approaches to Islam in Religious Studies,* ed. R. C. Martin. Tucson: University of Arizona Press, 1985.

Robson, J. "Ibn Ishâq's Use of the Isnâd." *Bulletin of the John Rylands Library* 38 (1955–56): 449–65.

Rodinson, M. *Mohammed,* trans. A. Carter. New York: Pantheon, 1971.

Rosenthal, F. "The Influence of Biblical Tradition on Muslim Historiography." *Historians of the Middle East,* ed. B. Lewis and P. M. Holt. Oxford: Oxford University Press, 1964.

Rudolph, W. *Die Abhaengigkeit des Qorans von Judentum and Christentum.* Stuttgart: W. Kohlhammer, 1922.

Schacht, J. "Une citation de l'Evangile de St. Jean dans la Sîra d'Ibn Ishâq." *Al-Andalus* 16 (1951): 489–90.

———. *The Origins of Muhammadan Jurisprudence.* Oxford: The Clarendon Press, 1950.

Schapiro, I. *Die Haggadischen Elemente im erzaehlenden Teil des Korans.* Leipzig: H. Itzkowski, 1907.

Schwarzbaum, H. *Biblical and Extra-Biblical Legends in Islamic Folk Literature.* Walldorf-Hessen: Verlag für Orientkunde Dr. H. Vorndran, 1982.

Sellheim, R. "Prophet, Chalif und Geschichte, die Muhammad-Biographie des Ibn Ishâq." *Oriens* 18–19 (1967): 33–91.

Serjeant, R. B. "Professor A. Guillaume's Translation of the Sîrah." *Bulletin of the School of Oriental and African Studies* 21 (1958): 1–14.

Sezgin, F. *Geschichte des arabischen Schrifttums,* vol. 1. Leiden: Brill, 1967.

Shahid, Irfan. "A Contribution to Koranic Exegesis." *Arabic and Islamic Studies in Honor of H. A. R. Gibb,* ed. G. Makdisi. Cambridge, MA: Harvard University Press, 1965.

———. "Pre-Islamic Arabic." *Cambridge History of Islam,* 1: 3–29.

Sidersky, D. *Legendes musulmanes.* Paris, 1933.

Silver, D. J. *Images of Moses.* New York: Basic Books, 1982.

Smith, B. H. "Narrative Versions, Narrative Theories." *On Narrative,* ed. W. J. T. Mitchell. Chicago: University of Chicago Press, 1981.

Speyer, H. *Die biblischen Erzaehlungen im Qoran.* Rpt. Hildescheim: Georg Olms, 1961.

Stewart, D. J. "Mythomorphism in Greco-Roman Historiography: The Case of the Royal *Gamos.*"*Bucknell Review* 22 (1976): 188–89.

Thackston, W. M. *The Tales of the Prophets of al-Kisaʾi.* Boston: Twayne, 1978.

Waldman, M. "Primitive Mind/Modern Mind: New Approaches to an Old Problem Applied to Islam." *Approaches to Islam in Religious Studies,* ed. R. C. Martin. Tucson: University of Arizona Press, 1985.

———. *Toward a Theory of Historical Narrative, a Cast Study in Perso-Islamicate Historiography.* Columbus: Ohio State University Pres, 1980.

Wansbrough, J. *Quranic Studies: Sources and Methods of Scriptural Interpretation.* Oxford: Oxford University Press, 1977.

———. *The Sectarian Milieu: Content and Composition of Islamic Salvation History.* Oxford: Oxford University Press, 1978.

Wasserstrom, S. Species of Misbelief: A History of Muslim Heresiography of the Jews. Ph.D. Dissertation, University of Toronto, 1985.

Watt, W. M. "The Early Development of the Muslim Attitude to the Bible." *Trans. of the Glasgow Or. Soc.* xvi, pp. 50–62.

———. Muhammad at Mecca. Oxford: Oxford University Press, 1953.

———. Muhammad at Medina. Oxford: Oxford University Press, 1956.

Waugh, E. H. "Following the Beloved: Muhammad as Model in the Sûfî Tradition." *The Biographical Process,* ed. F. E. Reynolds and D. Capps. The Hague: Mouton, 1976.

———. "The Popular Muhammad: Models in the Interpretation of an Islamic Paradigm." *Approaches to Islam in Religious Studies,* ed. R. C. Martin. Tucson: University of Arizona Press, 1985.

Wensinck, A. J. "Mohammed und das Judentum." *Der Islam* 2 (1911): 286–91.

———. "Mohammed und die Propheten." *Acta Orientalia* 2 (1924): 168–98.

Yaqut ar-Rumi, Ibn ʿAbdullah. *Kitâb Irshâd al-Arîb* . . . , ed. D. S. Margoliouth. Leiden: Brill, 1907–1927.

———. *Muʿjâm al-Buldân,* ed. F. Wuestenfeld. Leipzig: F. A. Brockhaus, 6 vols., 1866–1873.

Zwettler, M. *The Oral Tradition of Classical Arabic Poetry.* Columbus: Ohio State University Press, 1978.

Index

Index

Index

261

Index

262

Index of Quranic Citations